A HISTORY

THE *Woman's Athletic Club* OF *Chicago*

1898–1998

by Celia Hilliard

table of *Contents*

Message from the
Centennial Presidents

AS IMMEDIATE PAST PRESIDENT, I AM honored to present the Woman's Athletic Club centennial book.

Celia Hilliard, WAC historian, is the author and she has captured the heart and soul of the club with incredible and loving skill. We will be eternally grateful to her for her untiring devotion to the innumerable anecdotes of fact, humor, and tenderness expressed throughout these pages. Throughout her search, love truly prevailed.

We rest secure in the celebration of our centennial, which acknowledges many rich traditions, and we embrace the next hundred years with new ideas, monumental technology changes, and admiration for this venerable club.

Our precious members have devoted hours of dedicated work in their administrative efforts for success while at the same time tending to the club's continued strong programs in health, dance, poetry, music, literature, food, journalism, and comedy. We've had one grand time these past hundred years!

Over the years, the members of the WAC have been ambassadors of graciousness, dignity, integrity, and love. These qualities, and our beautiful building, reflect our standards, sense of the past, and elegance.

In retrospect, it is difficult to realize the years of perseverance in the establishment of women's rights that paved the way for the birth of a "woman's club" 100 years ago. Failure never entered into the hearts of past WAC women. Their ambition and determination to establish such a club was realized through hard work, creative ideas, strength, moral courage, stamina, and sheer joy of accomplishment. That is freedom!!

We sparkle with pride. To paraphrase Mark Twain: "In Boston they ask, "How much does he know?" In New York, "How much is he worth?" In Philadelphia, "Who were his parents?" In Chicago, "Does she belong to the WAC?"

May the spirit of warmth and camaraderie expressed in these pages prevail throughout the next century.

Lovingly,

HELEN DILLEN MILLER
President, 1996–98

AS THE FIRST WOMEN'S ATHLETIC CLUB in the United States, the WAC has a unique and rich history. An integral part of Chicago society, the WAC has always been identified with graciousness and elegance – an oasis in the heart of the city for its members. We are proud that the club has maintained its traditions over ten decades while embracing the great changes in our society – especially the changing role of women.

It was a monumental undertaking to capture one hundred years of WAC history. Celia Hilliard, the club's longtime historian, accepted this challenge and has compiled and written this wonderful book as a tribute to our founders, members, and employees. The book also chronicles the history of our venerable landmark building and its precious furnishings. In the pages that follow, you will read of the great determination and courage of the WAC members who persevered to secure a permanent location for the WAC. You will also read of the wonderful generosity of the members who have given many fine treasures to the club.

Our building and its furnishings embody the spirit of the club, but the soul of the club is represented by the hearts of thousands of women over one hundred years who have come together under the WAC roof. They have gathered for weddings, children's swim lessons, Duck Dinner Dances, and simple luncheons with friends. These are women who have always been broadly interested and actively engaged in the critical events of the day – demonstrated by the quality, timeliness, and scope of the programs they have planned and enjoyed.

As we stand poised on the eve of the new millennium, there is much to contemplate. How will the role of women in our society continue to evolve? What will the needs of WAC members be in the future? With more choices than ever, how can we ensure that the WAC retains its position as the preeminent women's club in the region? Today's board of directors is committed to ensuring a vibrant future for the WAC, embracing positive change while preserving the traditions and customs that are essential to the WAC's unique identity.

Because of the efforts, talents, and dedication of so many members, the WAC has a solid foundation on which to approach its second century. It is, indeed, an honor to serve as president during the centennial year – a year in which we celebrate and honor those who came before us – and a year in which we focus our energies on the WAC members of the future.

Sincerely,

MARY BURRUS BABSON
President, 1998–

Author's note

I STILL REMEMBER THAT SPRING LUNCHEON over fifteen years ago when Barbara Lawson asked me to serve as WAC historian. Seated before a platter of my favorite seafood crepes, I accepted with pleasure. There would be a few nostalgic afternoons pouring over the scrapbooks, and then I would take another month or so to organize the ledgers and loose papers stashed in closets and corners around the building. How green I was.

The centennial history that follows is the result of many years' search in a multitude of sources. Aside from the WAC's own records, remnants of the club's past reside in the collections of the Chicago Historical Society, Newberry Library, Art Institute of Chicago, University of Chicago, and other local institutions. Tidbits of news and gossip were hidden in the back issues of newspapers which once covered goings-on in the city's clubhouses as a matter of course. Most satisfying by far were the stories and memories shared by many longtime members, including daughters and granddaughters of the club's founding families. An oral history program conducted several years ago by myself and fellow WAC devotees recorded some of those precious voices on tape.

Nevertheless, this history could not have reached publication without the ongoing encouragement of the club's two centennial presidents, Helen Miller and Mary Babson, as well as the seasoned judgment of centennial co-chairs Fran Beatty and Joan Gifford. My thanks forever to the entire board of directors, which voted to provide crucial support when it was evident that more time and resources were needed to bring off the project as planned. Plus many kudos to the good ladies of the Publications Advisory Committee whose fresh ideas, insight, candid advice, and careful reading of the manuscript produced a more accurate and sturdy picture of the club's activities than I could have managed alone. They include Mary Babson, Mary Beth Beal, Fran Beatty, Jane Conlan, Clarice Dykema, Joan Gifford, Jane Hunt, Barbara Lawson, Helen

Miller, Michal Miller, Linda Salisbury, Mary Ellen Swenson, Faith Vilas, and Caryl Wright. In addition, several members of the staff provided many hours of assistance, even when they had almost no moment to spare. My abiding gratitude to our manager Jan Ahern and the ever able and enthusiastic Claudia Pernal.

We are particularly delighted with our publication's elegant appearance. Though this owes something to the devastating good looks of many past and present members, we were also fortunate in our photographers and draw special note to recently commissioned work by John Alderson, Alan De Rolf, Michal D. Miller, Stuart-Rodgers Photography, Jessica Tampas, and Michael Tropea. A grateful salute to Holly Madigan, whose kind efforts made it possible to reprint vintage pictures from the files of the *Chicago Tribune*. All of these illustrations and our text have been woven into a graceful and stylish whole by Studio Blue, exceptional designers who understood the sense of our story from the first and brought it to full flower. And finally, a volley of trumpets for Kim Coventry, our talented producer, whose imagination, taste, and wide-ranging expertise kept this project moving forward and infallibly on track.

The story of the Woman's Athletic Club is a glorious saga and a notable chapter in the larger tale of Chicago. Except for a few flush seasons, there were no "easy" years. The WAC's 100th birthday marks a century of struggle by women of drive and purpose to carry on the traditions of a warm and gracious sisterhood through constantly changing times. The landmark clubhouse on North Michigan Avenue is a visible testament to their signal victory, a triumph that belongs to all the club's members but especially to its long line of wise and distinguished presidents, to whom this book is respectfully dedicated.

CELIA HILLIARD
November 1998

THE CLUBHOUSE IN 1929
on Chicago's elegant new Michigan Boulevard.

MRS. PHILIP D. ARMOUR
founding president of the Woman's
Athletic Club of Chicago.

1

A new kind of club for Women

THE PROVIDENTIAL YEARS following the World's Columbian Exposition saw an extraordinary cultural flowering in Chicago. Beautiful and brilliant women played an important role, often through the clubs and societies they formed to foster this dramatic civic expansion. By the year 1896 the *Blue Book* listed 66 women's groups in the city, earnestly devoted to issues ranging from clean streets to prison reform to the proper understanding of Tolstoy. While their ideals and strenuous good deeds enhanced the public welfare, many projects begun as fresh and novel experiments rapidly devolved into frantic obligations. A visitor to the city observed that Chicago women "have to be always 'up and doing'. They are swept along, as if blown into town on the edge of a cyclone, all showing visible signs of a wreck."

One discerning lady, Mrs. Paulina Harriette Lyon, noted that although there were several private clubs where men could retreat to exercise and enjoy a relaxed meal with friends, there was no such haven for women in Chicago or, in fact, anywhere else in the country. One quiet afternoon she sat down in her study with paper and pen, and when she emerged several hours later she had drawn up a plan to create the Woman's Athletic Club of Chicago.

Paulina Lyon came from a family that "did things." Her uncle, Dr. John C. Burroughs, had been president of the first University of Chicago at 35th and Cottage Grove, and another one of her ancestors was a founder of Dartmouth College. Energetic and resourceful, with a wide circle of acquaintance and great gifts of persuasion, she took her plan for a new kind of club to various wealthy women who were in a position to back her ambitious idea. The first women she approached were enthusiastic but backed off when they understood just how much this experiment might cost.

Then came the legendary little dinner at the Prairie Avenue mansion of Philip D. Armour, meatpacking king of Chicago. Mrs. Lyon was a guest that evening, and when some of the women present complained of fatigue after yet another week of committee meetings, she once again described her vision of a club that would minister to the needs of the whole woman, a retreat where health, grace, and vigor could be restored. On this evening she was finally fortunate in her listeners.

Belle Ogden Armour was not an athlete herself. As her daughter-in-law recalled many years later, "Mother Armour never walked more than a block. The exercise she took was walking around Marshall Field & Company's store." She was a quiet high-bred woman whose gentle poise was a marked contrast to her husband's back-slapping bonhomie. (Philip Armour always said, "My culture is mostly in my wife's name.") She was widely traveled with cosmopolitan tastes yet had no trace of affectation. A note following her address in the *Bon Ton Directory* said simply, "Friends always welcome." Though she was seldom seen at large balls and liked to entertain modestly at home (serving a choice roast, of course, and one of her husband's favorite hot mince pies), a large number of prominent society people were genuinely devoted to her. In addition, both the Armours were supremely philanthropic and never turned down an idea they thought could benefit Chicago. So in spite of the doubts expressed that night by the men at the table, when Mrs. Philip D. Armour declared that this new kind of club could be a very important move for the women of the city, Paulina Lyon knew she had found her sponsor. A short time later Belle Armour pledged $50,000 to put the project in motion.

Encouraged by this powerful benefactor, Mrs. Lyon sent invitations to a thousand leading women of Chicago to attend a meeting at the Auditorium Theater and hear plans for a handsome new club where women could nurture their physical and mental well being. As she recounted years later, "The day came, but not the women; at least, only an apathetic and unlucky thirteen of them." Moreover, these thirteen didn't arrive to show support. Their attitude was "Give it up."

Undaunted, Mrs. Lyon and Mrs. Armour next secured the support of three prominent women, all of them members of pioneer Chicago families. One was Mrs. William Hale (Medora) Thompson, a widow with extensive downtown real estate holdings. Her father, Stephen Gale, was one of the 38 incorporators of the town of Chicago in 1833. Another was Mrs. C. K. G. (Blanche) Billings, married to the head of the People's Gas Light and Coke Company. Her husband, a sportsman known all over this country and Europe as "America's Horse King," had just inherited $20 million. The third woman was Mrs. William R. (Nellie) Linn, a cordial southsider widely applauded for her charitable activities. She liked to bet friends she would wear the same little beret all winter if they would make a substantial contribution to her favorite charity. They often took her up on it, sure she would buy a new hat after the first heavy snow. She never did, and several local institutions were much the richer for it.

Following the legal petition of these five founders, the Woman's Athletic Club of Chicago was officially incorporated on September 13, 1898. They immediately began meeting as often as every few days in rooms at the Columbus Memorial Safe

MRS. PAULINA H. LYON, who first proposed a temple of physical culture for the women of Chicago.

MRS. WILLIAM HALE THOMPSON, SR. Her son was later known as "Big Bill," Chicago's last Republican mayor. She deplored his flamboyant habits and urged him to carry on the family real estate business, which included ownership of several lots near the corner of State and Madison.

THE PHILIP D. ARMOUR RESIDENCE at 2115 Prairie Avenue. During a dinner party here Mrs. Armour agreed to start a woman's athletic club, though the men at the table dismissed the project as an excellent joke.

MISS FLORENCE HIGINBOTHAM
(later Mrs. Richard T. Crane), whose father was president of the World's Columbian Exposition. Junior memberships were created for such young single ladies. As soon as she married, a Junior moved to full Resident status, no matter what her age.

THE COLUMBUS MEMORIAL BUILDING
at the corner of State and Washington. The first board of directors met in the safe deposit rooms here to organize the club's affairs.

MRS. C. K. G. BILLINGS dressed for a charity pageant as Gainsborough's Lady Sheffield. Her father, Andrew MacLeish, established Carson Pirie Scott & Co.'s State Street store. Her brother Archibald was later Librarian of Congress.

Deposit Vaults building at the southeast corner of State and Washington. The club's affairs progressed rapidly. With the founders serving as the first board of directors, Mrs. Lyon drafted a set of bylaws and Mrs. Armour was unanimously elected president. In an unusual arrangement, Mrs. Lyon served as both secretary of the board and salaried manager. She received about $130 a month and was also paid an initial fee of $2,500 to organize, promote, and secure financial support for the club. In October the board was expanded to include six more women – Mrs. Samuel E. Gross, Mrs. William J. Chalmers, Mrs. Theodore Perry Shonts, Dr. Sarah Hackett Stevenson, Mrs. Jeannette I. Leeds, and Mrs. Thomas A. Griffin.

This impressive roster was chosen for its appeal to different social and civic factions in the city. After some thrashing about, six classes of membership were established, by invitation only, to women deemed "proper persons." Resident Members, not to exceed 500 in number, would pay an initiation fee of $100 and $40 annual dues. Non-Resident Members, those living farther than 50 miles from the city, would pay only $50 initiation and $20 dues. There could be 100 Non-Residents. In order to cover the costs of remodeling and furnishing a clubhouse, the board also issued 100 bonds in the amount of $500 each, paying 6% interest, and women who purchased at least one of these bonds (thus being creditors of the club or guarantors of its obligations) were eligible for Corporate Membership, which was limited to 25 persons.

In an additional effort to raise seed money, the board created the category of Life Membership. One hundred of these were available, for a flat onetime payment of $500 each. A woman was then exempt forever from dues and assessments of every kind. Upon her death this membership could be passed once to a female heir with a $100 transfer fee, or it could be sold outright to some unrelated party. In retrospect, these Life Memberships turned out to be the bargain of the century and a thorny economic problem for later administrations. It must be remembered, however, that in 1898, even for affluent women, $500 was a large capital outlay. This new enterprise was a big gamble, and more than one husband was heard grumbling that the punching bags in this ladies' establishment must be made of solid gold.

In an afterthought, the board decided to add a class of Junior Members, as a favor to the unmarried daughters of the Corporation Members. This privilege cost their mothers $10 a year. "The matrons and the maidens," they were called. This "maiden class" was shortly expanded to include the daughters of the first 200 Resident Members, as another enticement for their mothers to join.

In a spectacular public relations gesture, which was almost certainly the idea of Mrs. Lyon, the board invited Mrs. William McKinley, wife of the President of the United States, to become the club's first Honorary Member, a distinction she accepted graciously. The following May three more Honorary Members were elected. They were the suffragist Susan B. Anthony, often called "the Napoleon of the women's rights movement"; Julia Ward Howe, author of the great Civil War anthem, "Battle Hymn of the Republic"; and Mrs. Clinton Locke, the popular and charming wife of the pastor of Grace Episcopal Church. With this solid structure in place, the board worked hard to persuade prominent women to join. Mrs. Lyon told everyone who would listen, "This club is a necessity and not a fad."

As soon as the House Rules were drawn up, there were squabbles about liquor and card playing. Some of the young marrieds insisted the club rooms would be gloomy without cocktails. "There are so many young girls," countered Mrs. Lyon, "that I think the example that would be set would be perfectly deathly." With her strict Baptist background and both the Armours being teetotalers, there was never any real possibility of serving alcohol, but dissatisfied women spread it about that the club might be like a Sunday school or a Y.W.C.A. The additional announcement that there would be no card playing brought so many letters of complaint that eventually it was decided to permit such games as whist and euchre (but absolutely no gambling).

After a few months of scattered applications 63 Resident Members were elected in December 1898, many of them applying for Corporate status and subscribing for one or more bonds. After that the membership rolls grew every month and eventually included a large part of the city's commercial elite, their family names including Allerton, Blair, Caton, Clow, Crane, Cudahy, Donnelley, Drake, Henrotin, Hutchinson, Laflin, Lowden, McCormick, McNally, Noyes, Palmer, Pullman, Pike, Ryerson, Selfridge, Smith, and Swift.

Meanwhile, quarters had been rented from Ezra J. Warner at 150 Michigan Avenue, a six-story building on the west side of the street just a few doors north of Adams. Its wide bow windows looked across to the Art Institute and the lakefront park. It was one of a row of formerly elegant townhouses, one of them the girlhood home of Mrs. Potter Palmer. This fashionable stretch had gradually been enveloped by the downtown business district after the Chicago Fire of 1871. Many of the houses had since been torn down. Others, like the one in which the WAC rented the first, second, and basement floors, had been converted to commercial uses. At the time the club signed its new lease, a livery stable occupied the lot next door.

Space in the house at 150 Michigan was leased for a period of ten years at an average annual cost of about $6,500, with Mrs. Billings and Mrs. Linn personally guaranteeing the rent. A young architect, David E. Postle, was engaged to gut portions of the building and remodel it into sumptuous quarters suitable for every kind of physical culture. Work began in January 1899, and in spite of five labor strikes in as many months, the old rooms were slowly transformed into handsome parlors, library, cafe, gymnasium, swimming tank, bowling alley, and space for hairdressing, manicures, and Turkish baths. The budget for this project was around $60,000, but by the time Postle installed Flemish oak paneling, imported fireplaces, and a pure white marble pool, the cost came closer to $100,000.

All along the enterprise was dogged with unrelenting masculine ridicule. Scrappy reporters ran stories predicting the women would shortly "plant pond lilies in the swimming pool, turn the gymnasium into a continuous pink tea reception, and

MRS. WILLIAM R. LINN, the daughter of Oliver Morris Butler who established the first paper firm in the midwest.

use up all the club stationery for curl papers." A few men suggested that instructing women in the expert use of Indian clubs and dumb bells could be a menace to society. Most of the new members' husbands seemed to take the whole idea as a good joke, and even the kindest of them liked to call Mrs. Armour aside and whisper that she should expect the club to last no longer than six months at the outside.

A grand housewarming party was organized for Wednesday, May 24, 1899. Invitations were sent to 1,500 people. It was the largest social affair of the week in the city, and by this time even the society set in New York ("where everything is *supposed* to start," as Mrs. Lyon liked to say) was watching. Labor troubles had not yet been settled, and a large billboard was still planted in front of the entrance the day before the party. The plaster inside was hardly dry, the hardwood floors were bare, and marble workers stayed on strike, refusing to finish laying the pool or hang the mirrors around it. Mrs. Armour toured the premises and declared the opening would take place as scheduled. In the space of 24 hours Oriental carpets were laid, carpenters hammered the paneling into place, and a crew of scrubwomen polished every surface to a high shine.

At two o'clock on Wednesday afternoon, the five directors waited together in the first-floor reception room as carriages pulled to the curb on Michigan Avenue. A boy in a suit with brass buttons opened the great oak doors, carved with the club's new monogram, and the first guests stepped inside. They wandered through the large bright entrance hall, across the mosaic floors, past a broad staircase and a wooden stand where a leather visitors' book awaited their signature. They took a look in the cozy manager's office. Farther down the hall they stepped into the parlor, finished in mahogany and decorated in shades of light green and warm crimson. Little cornice bulbs spread a soft light over the whole room, which was filled with magnolias and daffodils. Mrs. Armour and her receiving line smiled expectantly. To their immense pleasure and relief, the praise never stopped flowing till the party ended at eleven o'clock that evening.

THE FIRST CLUBHOUSE at 150 Michigan Avenue (third from right), ca. 1908. The WAC occupied the bottom half of this six-story building in the block between Monroe and Adams. Note the horse and carriage waiting at the front entrance.

All day a crush of people poured through the corridors and rooms of the new club. The pride of the place was the brilliant "natatorium," where the new white marble pool glowed with an almost oriental splendor. In the fabulous double-story gymnasium, two new instructors staged exhibitions of rhythmic exercises and fancy dancing. The party spilled down the stairs to the hardwood bowling alley in the basement, where the women and men examined the pins and large balls under green-shaded lights.

On the second floor was a parlor even more luxurious than the one below and a big library with alluring deep-cushioned sofas and long tables stacked with recent issues of *Scribner's* and *Ladies Pictorial*. Small writing desks with the club's monogrammed stationery were particularly attractive. After a tour of the hairdressing parlor, manicure tables, and retiring rooms at the rear of this floor, guests walked through an immense arched doorway into the tea room, set with a sea of small tables covered in white cloths. Vases of daffodils were scattered artfully around the room. During the afternoon a group of young matrons, including Mrs. Armour's two daughters-in-law, poured tea and served little cakes on delicate china with silver forks bearing the club's monogram. At eight in the evening Mrs. Armour's caterers laid out an elaborate supper, and an informal dance was given in the gymnasium. An orchestra seated behind a bank of tropical palms played waltz tunes and patriotic songs.

The party-goers left that night deeply impressed by the glories of the new clubhouse. The carved oak, rich fabrics and silk lampshades, the long vistas across to Lake Michigan — these were immediately appealing. Yet the whole notion of strenuous sport for women was still quite foreign. Its wholesome physical benefits and its possibilities as an expression of new feminine freedoms were just catching on. Maybe a handful of the ladies at the opening reception played golf on a regular basis, rode bicycles, or swam at the seashore during summer holidays. Even most of these were utterly baffled by the rope ladders, pulleys, and boxing gloves they saw in the gymnasium, and it is safe to say that few of them had ever held a bowling ball or a fencing foil before. Amazing as it may seem to later generations, almost none had ever been swimming in an indoor pool.

For years Mrs. Lyon liked to recount a little episode that took place the night of the grand opening. It gives an idea of just how uncharted this new athletic territory really was. Though all the clubrooms were opened for the party, on account of the labor strikes some parts were still under construction, including the pool, where all the marble had not yet been laid. Accordingly, it was empty.

"The pool being unfinished," she said, "a number of oriental rugs had been placed on the bottom to conceal its incompleteness. Two ladies stood looking at this great marble bathtub, studying it.

"Suddenly one said, 'Why are those rugs there?'

"To which the other replied, 'Oh, the marble would be so cold to our feet. We *must* have them.' "

MRS. LAVERNE W. NOYES,
an early, much admired member
of the club.

2

In the Pink

THE WOMAN'S ATHLETIC CLUB quickly gained a strong following. At the turn of the century there was simply nowhere else in the city where a woman could spend the day in complete freedom and privacy in an atmosphere of such quiet refinement. Members grew used to dropping in for the morning or even a whole day to exercise, read, write letters, catch a nap, or make calls on the club's "long distance" telephone. Shoppers who didn't have time for luncheon came by for a bracing cup of tea or a snack of salted almonds. The reputation of this splendid retreat spread far beyond Chicago, and Mrs. Lyon declared, "So often has the word unique been applied to our organization that we think the Librarian of Congress ought to grant us the copyright of that word."

Buoyed by her second wind, Mrs. Lyon brought off another dramatic coup. In the fall of 1899 President William McKinley came to Chicago to lay the cornerstone of the new Federal Building at Dearborn and Jackson. When it was hinted that Mrs. McKinley might accompany him on this trip (which was unusual as she suffered recurrent bouts of epilepsy and was still in mourning for her brother, who had been murdered the previous year), Mrs. Lyon took the train to Washington and personally delivered an invitation for both of them to be guests of honor at the club. To the immense delight of all, the invitation was accepted.

On the morning of October 10, following dedication ceremonies at the new building site, the presidential party galloped down Michigan Avenue to the club. Despite an hour's delay after a fractious horse broke loose and bolted with the President's carriage, crowds were waiting to cheer them as they arrived at the great front doors of the clubhouse. Inside a large assemblage of prominent citizens lined up to greet the couple in the gymnasium, which had been gorgeously decorated. Garlands of Southern smilax were hanging from the balcony rails, and the ceiling had been transformed into a web of wild asparagus ferns with orchids clustered in the center, each flower shading a tiny electric lamp. While the Harrisons and the Dawes and other members of Chicago's political and social elite waited to shake hands with the President, Ida McKinley was seated in a chair draped with American

PRESIDENT WILLIAM MCKINLEY'S
entourage parading along the Chicago
lakefront.

Beauty roses, her favorite flower. Her private physician close at hand, she looked frail but charming in a gray satin gown with a brocaded wrap pulled over her shoulders.

Escorted down the hall to the white marble pool, the distinguished guests were seated in the visitors' gallery, where they watched a fabulous swimming and diving exhibition by the club's instructor, Madame Marion Liljenstolpe, and her star pupils, little Misses Margaret Nixon and Miss Marie Huhn. Many of those present, in particular the husbands who had last seen the pool in its unfinished state at the opening reception, were now able to gauge the full glory of this showplace. Four great opalescent globes hung from the ceiling, throwing soft emerald, turquoise, and pink shadows on the water below. One wall of the room was mirrored straight down into the water, in effect doubling the whole enchanting scene. The show closed with Madame Liljenstolpe swimming across the pool, triumphantly holding aloft the American flag, which she then presented to President McKinley.

A sumptuous breakfast was laid out afterwards, including hothouse grapes, rolled breast of partridge, terrapin, stuffed chops, and fancy cakes and ice creams with German strawberries. Edith Rockefeller McCormick brought in a gold cup which had once belonged to Napoleon, from which the President drank his champagne. After the meal Mrs. McKinley was taken for a quiet drive through Lincoln Park, and on returning to her hotel she received a great floral bouquet five feet high made entirely of spun sugar, a farewell tribute from the club.

Any man present at this grand event who had been lukewarm about his wife's association with the new Woman's Athletic Club was now a raving enthusiast. Having achieved a firm place in the social and cultural firmament of the city, the membership rolls continued to grow.

The women took to their new athletic life in earnest, with the real devotees arriving by nine o'clock in the morning. Going into the little dressing rooms, they would struggle out of their silk petticoats and corsets, each one saying to herself (as one of them told a news reporter), "I look a sight! But thank heavens, everybody else does too!"

Members starting out in the gymnasium donned the club's regulation navy bloomers with a blue and scarlet blouse, a costume which looked as good on the gray-haired as it did on the young. First off was the physical culture class. A pianist played soft rhythmic tunes while the ladies rotated arms and torsos and lay on the floor with feet in the air. The idea was to take off weight, build up the chest, and reduce waist, hips, and abdomen. The course schedule expanded into aesthetic dancing of all kinds, including the clog, the skirt dance, and even the military drill, which was thought to develop "a graceful and self-possessed carriage." They would shuffle about, whirl, and kick up their feet, a routine which members like Mrs. James Channon and Mrs. Darius Miller claimed was every bit as effective as plain old exercising. It was all, they said, "a matter of mind, spirit, and discipline."

As the morning progressed, much of the equipment would come into use. Ladies were striking at punching bags, lifting pulley weights, climbing the poles, and running around the track, which was situated halfway between the ceiling and the floor. Every so often some stately matron would unexpectedly descend on a rope. A small coterie took fencing lessons, and Mrs. Albert H. Farnum organized a group of ardent bowlers into a club-within-a-club. There were six fiercely competitive bowling teams. During the winter they conducted their own tournaments and engaged an official scorekeeper to keep the count straight on a blackboard. Mrs. Armour loved to watch these games in the basement and offered gold medals every year to the winners. Following her lead, Mrs. Gross, another board member, offered a trophy to the winning basketball team, also a club sport.

In 1900 indoor swimming, even in that pure white marble pool, was still a bit exotic, and club members who could dive backwards, swim underwater, and swing by their ankles on the trapeze were minor celebrities. For most of the women just being able to float was an "aquatic feat." They relied on poles and safety wings and were shy about getting into the natty but revealing bathing suits recommended by the instructor. Those who did without skirts and leggings in the pool still wore stage tights that came all the way up under their trunks and tied around the waist. Even some of the crack swimmers were self-conscious about being seen in public in bathing clothes.

"Why aren't you swimming in the contest?" someone once asked Mrs. Frederick Tyler, one of the club's champion athletes.

"Oh, I wouldn't do it for anything," she said. "I think it's perfectly awful to take off your stockings before all of these women."

When Madame Liljenstolpe left, her place was taken by Miss Stella Amick, an old-fashioned swimming instructor who stayed with the club until her death in 1921. She watched over the beginners carefully, and her greatest joy was helping

DR. JOHN B. MURPHY with his wife (right) and their daughter Mildred. Dr. Murphy was one of the physicians invited every year to judge the healthful benefits of the WAC's athletic program. Mildred's daughter Jeannette (Mrs. Don Reuben) was later among the many third-generation members of the club.

TWO EXPERTS matching swords in a fencing demonstration.

FANCY DANCING CLASS in the gymnasium.

the timid ones find a stroke they could master and encouraging them to venture into the nine-foot deep end.

After a swim the members would typically snatch up a towel, slip into sandals, and go dripping to the Turkish baths, where they sat first in a tiled hot room to induce heavy perspiration. This was followed by a shower and a massage with various ointments to soothe overstrained muscles. After this they could nap in one of the cozy blue and white sound-proofed resting rooms, where a large "Silence!" warning was posted on the wall. Sometimes they went directly to the hairdressing department, where they would be shampooed at a marble basin "by a coiffeuse," as one of them remembered years later, "who used only her fingertips and never got so much as a soap bubble on her white cuffs."

To Mrs. Lyon the results of this systematic physical culture were perfectly apparent in the firm muscles, ruddy cheeks, and flowing tresses of the members, to say nothing of their sunny dispositions and the disappearance of nervous headaches. Starting in 1901 the club held regular "Physicians Nights," when as many as 150 prominent doctors and their wives were invited to the club to observe firsthand the practical facilities and the bounding good health of the members. In fact, Dr. Sarah Hackett Stevenson, a noted doctor and the first woman on the staff of Cook County Hospital, was one of the club's earliest board members and a great promoter of its therapeutic benefits.

Apparently the club members themselves were pleased with their newfound youth and good looks and especially relieved that they did not appear "mannish," which some critics had warned would be the result of all these muscle-building projects. To keep tabs on their daily progress, the clubrooms were well stocked with looking glasses. One male visitor could not get over the number of mirrors in the club. "A mirror for the back of one," he noticed, "and a mirror for the side of one, with of course a composite triple affair for the full length front, side, and back, are a necessary household equipment. We had not thought, however, of a mirror for when you swim and another for when you dance. They are there, though." Nevertheless, even he agreed that the ladies were enchantingly "in the pink."

While food service was always essential to the club's atmosphere of relaxed hospitality, it started as a very simple operation. The first tea room was described as "quaint," and the menu did not go much beyond bouillon, salads, sandwiches, chocolate, and fruit. Members quickly discovered, however, that it could be quite pleasant and much easier to host friends at the club than at home. Some subscription dances and holiday suppers were held from time to time, but most of this entertaining took place in the daytime — birthday parties, matinee teas, receptions for out-of-town visitors. Small favors and decorations were the rule at even the most intimate get-togethers. If the guest of honor was about to set off on a tour of Europe, say, the menu cards might be in the shape of an ocean liner or a steamer trunk. On the first day of spring, several tables would be covered with May baskets. Mrs. LaVerne W. Noyes, an amateur photographer, loved to snap "kodaks" of her friends and make small keepsake scrapbooks. Mothers and daughters often dined together in the same luncheon party, and the twin daughters of Mrs. Charles Kohl, shy little girls who were always dressed alike in Mosier suits, lunched under the constantly watchful eye of their governess, Mrs. Faville.

As time went on other women's organizations — The Friday Card Club, The Twentieth Century Club, the Club Francais — met at the WAC regularly. It became a popular place to hold benefits, usually musicales or little bazaars. One of the most delightful was an Easter party in 1903 for the Armour Institute's School of Domestic Arts and Sciences. Candy was sold in silken bags, and one of the instructors from the school taught the young matrons how to "manufacture" cheese souffles and fig cups over the flame of a chafing dish.

As the club became a fashionable center for social affairs, it was not surprising to see a University of Chicago professor, a Polish violinist, or a curator from some European museum in the dining room on the same day. Sir Herbert Beerbohm Tree, the famous English actor-manager, came one day for lunch. Mrs. Charles P. Taft and Alice Roosevelt Longworth (who arrived in one of her famous "Alice blue" hats) attended a large reception at the club in 1908 for the Daughters of the American Revolution.

The members themselves were very smart looking. Marshall Field's sister Laura (Mrs. Henry Dibblee) had a different hat for every dress, almost all of them trimmed

IN

THE SWIM

TO MRS. HAMMER,
at Woman's Athletic Club, following the Swimming
Contest, June 9, 1908.

Although each club guest of today	But hearts of all are rightly placed
Is wondrous neat and trim,	And no one's head's awhirl;
It cannot truthfully be said	Each one a friend indeed – a good
That all are "in the swim."	Old-fashioned "summer girl."
And if directoire costumes slim	Dear Mrs. Hammer hits the heads
Are "au fait" as they state,	With shafts of brilliant wit,
Not one of our athletic guests	And wins all hearts so mightily
Is strictly "up to date."	That we know she is "it."

From a book of verse by Ida E. S. Noyes, published by her husband
LaVerne after her death in 1912. He gave funds in her
memory to build Ida Noyes Hall, a social and athletic center for women
students on the campus of the University of Chicago.

MRS. PHILIP D. ARMOUR, JR.
"You can imagine how hard it was to start an athletic club in 1898," she said. "The husbands thought we were crazy." (Widowed in 1900, she married Patrick A. Valentine two years later.)

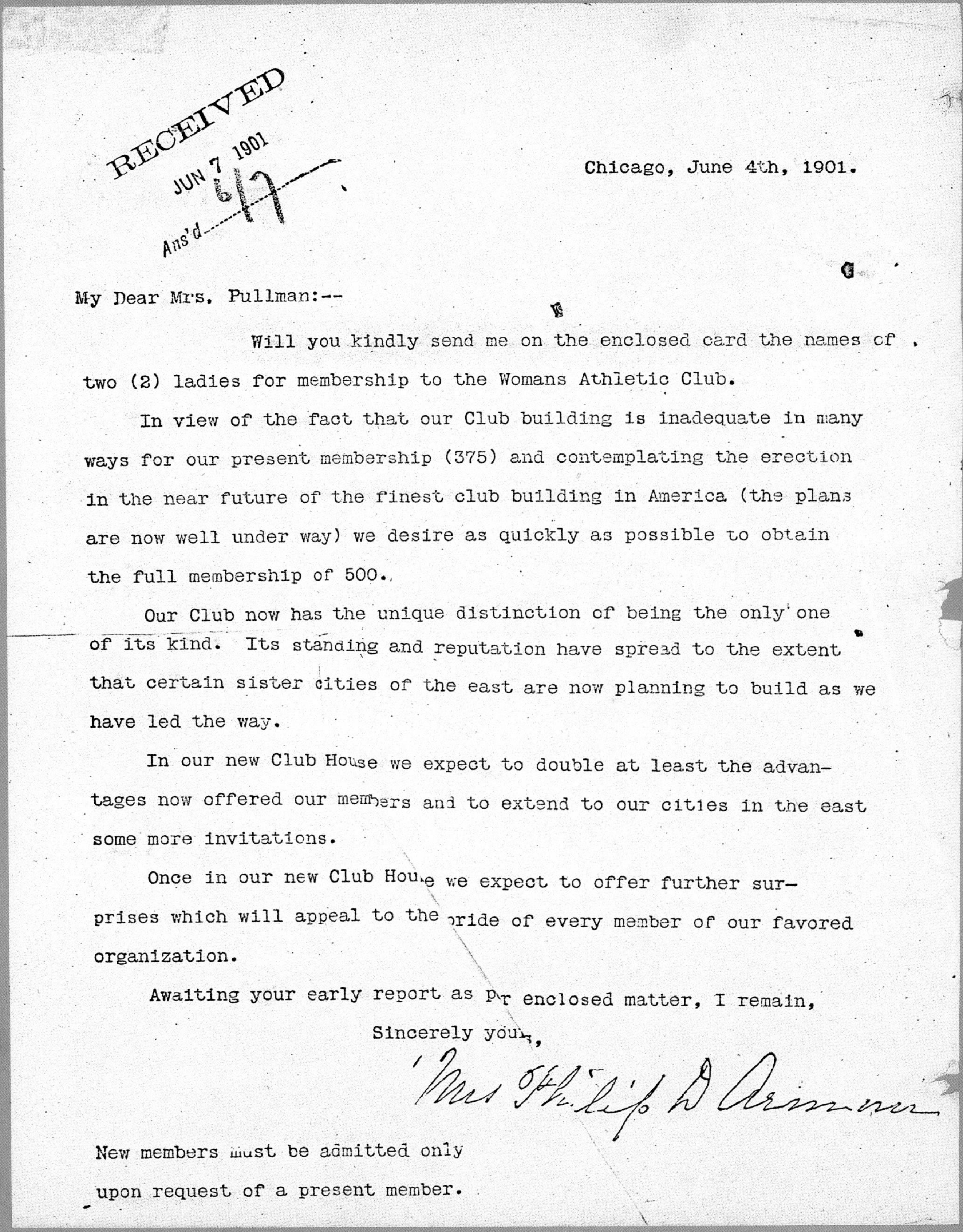

Chicago, June 4th, 1901.

My Dear Mrs. Pullman:--

Will you kindly send me on the enclosed card the names of two (2) ladies for membership to the Womans Athletic Club.

In view of the fact that our Club building is inadequate in many ways for our present membership (375) and contemplating the erection in the near future of the finest club building in America (the plans are now well under way) we desire as quickly as possible to obtain the full membership of 500.

Our Club now has the unique distinction of being the only one of its kind. Its standing and reputation have spread to the extent that certain sister cities of the east are now planning to build as we have led the way.

In our new Club House we expect to double at least the advantages now offered our members and to extend to our cities in the east some more invitations.

Once in our new Club House we expect to offer further surprises which will appeal to the pride of every member of our favored organization.

Awaiting your early report as per enclosed matter, I remain,

Sincerely yours,

Mrs Philip D Armour

New members must be admitted only upon request of a present member.

A LETTER FROM MRS. PHILIP D. ARMOUR
to her friend, Mrs. George Pullman. Mrs. Armour worked ceaselessly to promote the fortunes of the club.

in ostrich plumes. Mrs. J. Ogden Armour was usually attired in a perfectly tailored navy blue suit, dark blue, she said, being the only really correct color for morning. Mrs. John J. Mitchell, on the other hand, dressed up and wore her beautiful pearl dog collar even at tea. Tall tightly-corseted Princess Engalitscheff, a Chicago girl who married a Russian prince, was just as exotic as some of the guests. She kept a monkey for a pet, which was a frequent topic of conversation (though the animal was never allowed in the clubhouse).

Maybe the most unusual among the early members was Mrs. Edward A. Leicht, whose mother had been Miss Blatz of Milwaukee. Angelina Leicht was considered an almost professional beauty, with so many minutes in each day reserved for dressing hair, applying hand lotion, and so on. Reputed to have the most expensive wardrobe in Chicago, her gold-braided gowns and velvet coats were often considered too colorful and flashy for local taste. (A negligee she wore of silver metal cloth was particularly grating to some of the more conservative members.) She ate very sparingly. She would come to a party, sip a little something, and leave early. She was driven about town in a spectacular limousine with round windows like the portholes of a ship. She spent many summers in the chateaus and villas of Europe, and it was her idea in 1908 to grant WAC membership privileges to the wives of army and navy officers and the diplomatic corps stationed in Chicago, thus

THE INTREPID MRS. J. OGDEN ARMOUR (far left). She thwarted a burglar one night when she grabbed the barrel of a pistol aimed right at her head. Said one witness, "Coolest woman I ever saw."

MRS. EDWARD A. LEICHT, an elegant member of Chicago's German set whose stone mansion at Lakeview and Fullerton was furnished in the style of the Hapsburg nobility.

initiating the club's Consular Membership program. Though Mrs. Leicht was sometimes criticized as too swank or even bizarre, she supported the club unfailingly with hard cash when it was badly needed, and years later, when her family suffered financial reverses during the Depression, she was one of the charter members who were offered honorary status without hesitation.

By 1903 the social side of the club had grown enormously, and food service accounted for a large portion of its revenues. An additional floor was rented for a spacious new dining room, which was fitted up with oak paneling, handsome fireplace, and Tiffany lamps on the tables. Small rooms to the side were used for private luncheons and bridge games. Men were now encouraged to dine here at noon on their own, and an elevator was installed so they could go straight to the third floor without invading any feminine sanctuary. The press reported that a new menu offered 350 items, including *pate de foie gras*, ham, truffles, and various flavored bonbons. People were already starting to laugh about the club's supposed "athletic" purposes. It was whispered that the members were now eating too much and too often, some of them actually growing, yes, stout. Several specialties were indeed boosting the club's culinary reputation, including French mushrooms on toast, lobster salad, and a wonderful coconut cake made every day with freshly grated coconuts.

Not surprisingly, the issue of serving alcohol was continually revisited. Mrs. Lyon tried to hold the line at slightly laced punches for evening parties, probably in deference to masculine tastes. The menu cards contained nothing stronger than apollinaris water and ginger ale, but a determined faction at the club finally won an exception to this no-liquor ruling. If fortified by a prescription from a doctor, a member could imbibe something "medicinal" in the seclusion of a private dining room. These private dining rooms became very popular and were always praised for their "cheerful atmosphere."

THE
CLUB PIN

THIS ART NOUVEAU PIN was designed for the club in 1900 by W. T. Meyer of Juergens & Andersen, a distinguished State Street jewelry firm. It was made of burnished green gold and featured the classic face of Diana beside the artistic WAC monogram. On request, the round notch above her forehead could be fitted with a tiny diamond.

Paulina Lyon otherwise held an iron grip on the club's management all through these years. She had a male private secretary, Mr. Fitch, and did all the hiring, firing, choosing, and deciding. Written complaints were delivered straight to her. Verbal complaints were not allowed. After the first year or so the board abandoned the idea of committees altogether and simply let her run the ship.

Mrs. Lyon's ambitions for the club were enormous. She saw it as a social trust which should push its work across the country and out into the whole world. Some day there would be a chain of such clubs, she said, with women having reciprocal privileges at every sister institution. This mission would get off the ground when the WAC had built a magnificent clubhouse of its own, with hotel rooms to accommodate many guests. In 1901 she asked the architects Pond & Pond to draw plans for a six-story clubhouse. She herself suggested its new swimming pool might be built into a grotto and fed from a central fountain. It would be, she said, "a sort of "jeweled rendezvous patterned after the baths of ancient Rome." Later on she imagined a 12-story structure, with the club renting out several commercial floors to the members' husbands and occupying the top floors itself. A swimming pool of marble and mosaic would be installed under an arched glass roof open to the sky.

Such expensive ideas could not be funded with initiation fees and dues. The project dragged, and Mrs. Lyon became discouraged until she hit upon another flamboyant scheme. She insured her life in the club's favor for $300,000, on the condition that 60 members would annually contribute a dollar a day (about $22,000 a year in aggregate) towards the erection of a truly worthy athletic palace.

This insurance maneuver did create a local sensation. The bylaws were amended to admit 200 Corporate Members, and many of them (including Mrs. Leicht) agreed once more to buy another bond issue in support of Mrs. Lyons' grand-scale dreams. To most of the women, however, it was all overblown and intimidating. The whole matter drew energy away from the everyday business of the club and seemed to set off a slowly escalating series of underground quarrels. A number of members resigned, and some of those who stayed let their house accounts go long overdue. In order to maintain services, new women were invited into the club at reduced initiation fees or none at all. Some who agreed to become Life Members were charged up to $750 for the privilege, only to find out later the board had never authorized any increase in the price. In fact, for long periods the board simply stopped meeting. Mrs. Armour stepped down as president in 1905, and no one else would accept the office. With mounting debts, the club began to skip interest payments on all those bonds, and then word got out that it was borrowing to meet running expenses. Mrs. Lyon moaned there was "so much talk about the clubhouse collapsing that the members were afraid to come into it."

Matters came to a head in May of 1907 when the club, six months in arrears on the rent, received a near-eviction notice from the landlord. Mrs. Armour refused to get involved, though she reminded the board what her interest had been for the

ENTRANCE AND RECEPTION ROOM

THE PARLOR

Mrs Philip D Armour

THE LIBRARY

THE DINING ROOM

THE RESTING ROOM

THE GYMNASIUM

Mrs Paulina H Lyon

THE BOWLING ALLEY

THE POOL

THE WOMAN'S ATHLETIC CLUB OF CHICAGO
REPRODUCTIONS OF PHOTOGRAPHS BY J. W. TAYLOR

club. "I would never have given what I did," she wrote, "only for the loyalty and hard work Mrs. Lyon has put in the last ten years. The Board has left her to do it all."

Mrs. Lyon, meanwhile, handed in her resignation. After 11 years of constant work without a single vacation, she said, "This club seems to me almost a child which has had the best hours and the best thoughts of my life." She then announced she was going to remarry, joking that she had met a man "who wants an athletic manager." She denied that her efforts to clamp down on the "doctor's prescriptions" in the private dining rooms had anything to do with her leaving, though she admitted it was always a sore spot. The following September she did marry Mr. Albert R. Pritchard and moved to Rochester, New York, where her wealthy new husband was president of the Pritchard Stamping Company.

There were tears and protests, but it was now unavoidably clear that the club had to reorganize or disband. A temporary managing committee was appointed to hold the situation together while an auditor made a thorough review of the books and a lawyer assessed the club's legal position. In July 1907 Mrs. Lyman A. Walton was "declared" president. A bit later Mrs. Ida Cronk, who had supervised the dining room for a year or so, was given the post of manager, though not with the far-reaching authority Mrs. Lyon has exercised. Intense efforts were made to bring resigned members back into the fold.

Committees were formed again. A House Commitee selected new tablecloths and bath towels. Plumbing was repaired. Someone donated a pair of silver candlesticks for the buffet. After a long period when only private affairs were given, a new Dance Committee put on a series of international evenings, decorating rooms as a street in Venice or an Egyptian banquet hall, with foods of corresponding flavor. One night the dining room was decked out to represent an apple orchard full of blossoms in the light of a new moon. A morning program about Dolly Madison brought 200 women into the club for luncheon again. Remembering the crush at the swimming exhibition for Ida McKinley, they organized a one-day athletic meet, and the club's own junior members put on a spectacular show of fencing, gymnastics, and fancy dancing. The day ended with the girls in a dazzling chorus line, sidestroking across the pool in unison under a sea of pink Japanese umbrellas.

A year after Mrs. Lyon's departure revenues were again exceeding expenses. Acknowledging that without Mrs. Armour's support the club could never have survived to its tenth anniversary, the board made a new pledge to carry on. It was their hope, they wrote, that "some day she may see a Club which will do credit to her and she will look with pride on the first Woman's Athletic Club ever started in America." A year later Mrs. Philip D. Armour was elected Honorary President for life.

(LEFT) A GLIMPSE INSIDE
the rooms of the first clubhouse.

33

THE MAIN DINING ROOM
in the club's new quarters.

3

Coming of Age

THE FIRST BIG TEST of the club's newfound health and harmony came sooner than anyone would have wanted. On September 1, 1908, the board received a letter informing them that their clubhouse had been sold to the Peoples Gas Light and Coke Company. A few days later they read in the real estate pages of the Chicago Tribune that the company planned to tear it down, clearing all the land south to Adams to make way for a new 20-story corporate headquarters building.

A hue and cry went out among the members. Just as their clubhouse had truly become a "downtown home," it was going to be wrecked. They worried that members might get out of the club habit altogether if there was a long disruption in services. "And lose all the fittings of the old building!" they moaned. The idea of seeing all that costly marble and Flemish oak woodwork hacked to bits seemed to disturb them more than anything else.

The board moved quickly to find quarters elsewhere and within a matter of weeks negotiated with Harold McCormick to take space in the brand new International Harvester building at the corner of Michigan and Harrison. There was some concern that this spot was so close to the Auditorium Annex Hotel that members would be tempted to go in there for lunch instead of eating at the club. The location on the first and second floors of a building on Michigan Avenue, however, was so much more desirable than being buried somewhere in the business heart of the Loop that the board decided to take a chance on it. (It's interesting to note that the Harvester company had recently moved out of their original home at the northwest corner of Michigan and Monroe, a property which they then leased to the University Club, which built a 14-story clubhouse on that site in 1909.)

After years of floundering financially between grandiose dreams and casual bookkeeping, the board was now fully aroused to the necessity of strict budgeting. Wangling a bonus from the Peoples Gas Company to get out of "150" before their lease was up, they found a sympathetic contractor who agreed to painstakingly extricate all those expensive fittings (even down to the electric light fixtures) from the old clubhouse and move them to the new space. The marble swimming tank was taken apart piece by piece and reinstalled in the basement of the Harvester building, where it was bordered by lockers, steam and slab rooms, and a shower bath. Other than the club's offices, which were situated in a corner of the main lobby, the rest of the Woman's Athletic Club rooms were located on the second floor.

The quarters at "150" had featured a web of parlors, reading rooms, and intimate private resting rooms. Indeed, after a few remodelings, the layout was so confusing that one of the young members, a Miss Hutchinson, was able to successfully evade two bailiffs who came to the club to serve her with papers for back rent on her apartment. Declaring that no woman need permit officers of the law to interfere with her social program, Miss Hutchinson persuaded Mrs. Cronk to warn her if and when they arrived at the front door. By the time the bailiffs had pushed their way up the stairs, into the baths, and through a maze of dressing rooms, females shrieking loudly all the way, Miss Hutchinson had had time to throw on her clothes, board the freight elevator, and escape out the rear door. (Some time later the law did catch up with our Miss Hutchinson.)

The new rooms in the Harvester building were much more open and designed with an eye to simplicity and comfort. A large living room 50 feet square was furnished with charming wicker chairs and settees, all of them upholstered with high plump cushions. Soothing rose-colored draperies framed the broad windows overlooking the park. The fragile *escritoires* from the old club were replaced by a few writing desks of ample proportions, and guests were welcome to plunk out a tune

THE INTERNATIONAL HARVESTER BUILDING (below left) at the southwest corner of Michigan and Harrison, ca. 1908, the year it was completed.

THE CLUB'S INFORMAL NEW LIVING ROOM (right) was fifty feet square and furnished in silvered wicker.

on a piano in the corner in the room. Mrs. Darius Miller brought in two live canaries in a brass cage, which seemed to round out the "homelike" atmosphere.

The doors to this living room were easily thrown open to connect with a long dining room along Harrison Street, creating an expansive space for personal entertaining and large society events. Farther west were the gymnasium and a number of rooms for hairdressing, manicures, massage, and resting. A pleasant sun parlor was fitted up where ladies could wait in comfort for the next appointment. The kitchens at the rear of the floor were, of necessity, much more elaborate than the old ones, with every modern convenience, supersize sinks, plate-warming rack, meat block, a refrigerator just for salads and ice, and a special cupboard for storing pastries.

By the time of their official housewarming in these new quarters on January 16, 1909, the club's calendar was already filled with a long list of luncheon and card party dates. One of the pessimists who had predicted the club's sure collapse after the Peoples Gas announcement was heard at the party saying (as she collected her second cup of punch), "Wasn't it the luckiest thing that could have happened to us?"

The move did prove to be a tonic, but the fact that it came off so well was due in large part to astute leadership. Mrs. Lyman A. Walton succeeded to the presidency at a low point in the club's fortunes, when board members typically stared down at their knitting when the nominating committee called for candidates. Abigail Walton was later remembered as a woman who "combined social authority with intellectual keenness." In her own drawing room on Woodlawn Avenue she presided over a kind of Hyde Park literary salon, and one of her daughters married Ernst Freund, a professor who played a major role in the founding of the University of Chicago Law School.

Mrs. Walton was especially interested in the stage (and later served as president of the Chicago Drama League). As a way of strengthening the general WAC membership and pulling a large group of young women into the club at the same time, she conceived the idea of organizing the junior members into a theatrical troupe. For this task she enlisted the brilliant assistance of Alice Gerstenberg, recently home from Bryn Mawr, a budding playwright who was pleased to assemble her exuberant girlfriends to put on shows for their delighted mothers. Miss Gerstenberg later published more than 50 one-act plays, one of them a classic called *Overtones* which Eugene O'Neill acknowledged as the model for some of his own stage techniques.

Back in 1908 Alice Gerstenberg was writing "girl plays," which were perfect vehicles for the WAC juniors. They first put on clever charades and sunny musical numbers, and the cast included Edna and Elsie Dixon, Marguerite Henneberry, Josephine Lydston, Helen Marsh, and Margaret Theurer. Their jokes brought down the house, and over 200 ladies stayed to lunch besides. Anticipating continued large luncheon revenues, the board allowed the girls $40 for their next show (a performance of Miss Gerstenberg's farce *The Class Play*), which went to pay a painter from the Art Institute to design some fancy scenery. This show was an even bigger hit. These productions bound the girls together in lifelong friendships, and they also seemed to enhance mother-daughter relations (as Mrs. Walton had intended all along). After a couple of years the ranks of the juniors had swelled to about 140 members.

Mrs. Walton was followed in office by one of the most gifted civic leaders Chicago has ever known, Mrs. Frederic W. Upham. Helen Hall Upham went on to found the Chicago Symphony Orchestra Women's Association, the Civic Music Association, and the Welfare Council of Metropolitan Chicago. She chaired the first White Elephant Sale at Children's Memorial Hospital and was head of women's defense activities in Illinois during the Second World War. In 1909, when she was elected president of the WAC, Mrs. Upham was just 33 years old. She had come to the city from Iowa to continue voice lessons and married Fred Upham instead, president of the Consumers Coal Company, a man often called the financial genius of the Republican Party. Possessing strong organizing and diplomatic skills herself, she abandoned her singing career and quickly established herself as a full partner in her husband's civic endeavors. Bracing and magnetic, she was one of those people who take hold of a situation quickly and act with dispatch.

After an era when ladylike dithering about money had brought the WAC near financial ruin, Mrs. Upham worked to make every member aware of means and ends. She had the courage to raise annual dues to $60. Many of the original bond-holders were persuaded to turn those documents over to the club, effectively converting their investments into contributions (though Mrs. Armour's large note was eventually paid off in full). A new employee Christmas Fund was organized and brought in so much money some of the waitresses and scrubwomen received as much as two months' extra salary, creating a large store of staff loyalty and good will. The surplus was set aside for a Benevolent Fund to help employees with doctor bills and personal emergencies.

The board had expanded from 11 to 15 members in 1908. Advancing a spirit of openness, Mrs. Upham cautioned the Corporate Members against forming cliques that excluded regular members from news and decisions. Many women who had left the fold during stormier times returned to the club, and Mrs. Upham labored tirelessly to bring in attractive recruits. She established "Guest Day," one Tuesday a month when prospective members were invited to explore even the most private nooks and crannies in the clubhouse. She went out and persuaded Non-Resident members to sign up a favorite neighbor in their own hometowns.

Perhaps her most longlasting contribution was to establish a calendar of morning programs which would draw members into the club on a regular basis. Not surprisingly, her taste and social connections were mostly musical. She began by organizing a variety of classical and popular recitals. One morning there would be

a soprano. Another day someone might talk on "Sunny Spain" and dancers would perform. Miss Kitty Cheatham, who could sing and reminisce for two hours in an intimate "musical *conversazione*," was enormously popular. When the Chicago Grand Opera Company was organized at the Auditorium Theater, Miss Anne Shaw Faulkner and her accompanist Max Oberndorfer came to preview the season's offerings. These opera lectures required tickets in addition to the price of lunch. Another crowd-pleaser was Jessie Braman Daggett, who gave eccentric interpretations of bird songs. During Lent, when no programs were scheduled, a pianist would play during the luncheon hour on Wednesdays. Among the frequent diners was Mrs. Theodore Thomas, widow of the late Chicago Symphony conductor, who was now an Honorary Member.

At the end of Helen Upham's tenure as president income exceeded expenses by an astonishing $9,000. For the first time in the club's history the Resident Membership stood full at 500, with some rather influential ladies parked on a waiting list that grew longer every month. All the future successes of the club were built upon this now sturdy rock of financial security and stable membership. Mrs. Upham always deflected credit, saying she had "come in the top of a wave of

MRS. VOJTA F. MASHEK cinched into a Gibson Girl shirtwaist.

INVOICE issued in 1912 to Mrs. Mashek, a new member.

THE AMERICAN EAGLE

THE WOODCHOPPER

SKETCHES OF MISS SAIDA BRUNK, the gym instructor, demonstrating aesthetic dance steps to achieve a willowy figure.

prosperity," but on the morning of the annual meeting, when the gavel was handed to her successor, the members rose to give her a standing ovation.

During those transitional years the idea of an athletic sisterhood was still alive at the club, but the members were increasingly preoccupied with the aesthetic aspects of sport. Not two years after the move to the Harvester building it was decided to remodel the pool area to resemble a lake in the hills of Italy. Under the charge of Mrs. J. B. McFatrich a local artist painted a cycloramic wall mural of tall trees, splashing fountains, and distant castles. White marble benches were placed around the tank. Cement columns were treated to resemble ancient ruins, and two ornamental entrance gates were added, flanked by great vases of flowers. As it turned out, it made a lovely scene for a party.

The devotees still came for a swim every week, and in 1913, after Rose Chatfield-Taylor nearly drowned in a strong undertow off a Florida beach, there was a year of serious life-saving classes supervised by a young man from Australia. As time went on, however, in spite of the enchanting backdrop and skillful instructors, the pool was more and more the site of children's swimming lessons. Young people were originally restricted to certain set hours in the water. By 1914 all girls and the boys under 7 who came with their sisters could use the pool any day of the week. (Older boys still had to abide by rigid rules.)

The aristocratic sport of fencing enjoyed a brief vogue. Arthur J. Eddy, who may have been the city's closest approximation of an international man of wealth and leisure, brought a couple of saber champions to the club one day and lectured on fencing as "ideal exercise for the high-strung." His reputation as connoisseur of Cubist pictures, friend of Whistler, art critic, and globe trotter drew an eager audience. Explaining that fencing required calm, concentration, and complete control of the body, he described his own bouts with the swordsmen of Paris. "Chicago women have a great chance to win honors in this sport," he assured them, and after watching a demonstration, several ladies did purchase outfits and foils and sign up for lessons. (There was some disappointment, though, when it turned out that Mr. Eddy would not be teaching the class himself.)

Many more women joined the aesthetic gymnastic and dancing classes given by Miss Saida Brunk. She developed a series of specially tailored motions designed to straighten the back, expand the chest, clear up wrinkles, and smooth out the neck and arms. This was so important, she would explain, to women whose social lives called for the frequent wearing of decollete gowns. Miss Brunk made these sometimes odd-looking exercises fun by giving them little names. "Chopping wood" and "striking anvil" were two of her favorites. She encouraged her pupils to spend quiet evenings by the fire "tree swaying." The youngsters were included too. A peek into the gymnasium on a Friday afternoon would reveal Miss Brunk

DR. EMILY NOBLE, who lectured members on the benefits of rhythmic breathing.

enthusiastically leading a dozen small girls in braids and pigtails through the Highland Fling and the Mountain March. Sometimes a small supper was served afterwards. By the time their mothers came to collect them after attending the weekly concert at Orchestra Hall, the children were almost ready for bed.

Then there was the tango craze. After the legendary Vernon and Irene Castle conquered the dance-mad public of Europe, everyone wanted to learn the new steps. The club initiated a series of "tango teas" and invited the Castles to perform. Mrs. Deming, who had come into the club as an exercise instructor, was sent to the East Coast and Europe with instructions to bring back all the latest dances. Ballroom classes were organized in 1913, though husbands agreed to attend only on the condition that nothing be said about it. The women understood. Men of high stature in the business and professional communities could not be embarrassed in the act of learning. So the men would arrive late in the afternoon. There would be a little dinner and libations to help limber up. Then Monsieur Maurice and Miss Florence would demonstrate such numbers as the Castle polka, the Ta-Tao, the la Russe, or a really new one called the Foxtrot. Later on it was Mr. Carlos and Miss Beatrice swooping and twirling. The classes continued till the summer of 1914, when the guns of war called a halt to most official events and parties at the club.

While the dance frenzy lasted, no debutante was more excited about the tango than Mrs. William J. Chalmers, then in her late 50s. Joan Chalmers was the daughter of Allan Pinkerton, chief of President Lincoln's secret service and founder of America's most famous detective agency. An imperious high-tempered dowager accustomed to her own way, she liked to fix people with her piercing blue eyes and declare she meant to "die young." This meant she wanted things smart and new.

Everyone agreed she was a fabulous dancer. A Chicago man recalled, "I saw her dance the cake-walk in my mother's living room when she was crowding eighty." Mrs. Chalmers hosted private tango classes at the club for her friends, perhaps to insure a supply of skillful partners in her own rarefied social circle. (She tried to decline the WAC vice-presidency in 1914, saying no board should be burdened with "dead wood." They protested she was "very live wood!" She was elected unanimously.)

All through the 'teen years the club kept inventing new and broader offerings. Programs ranged far beyond the original light concerts. There were lectures and theatrical performances. Ruth Draper, who appeared at the club long before she became known all over America, gave her remarkable monologues. Faxton Ferguson came from Magdalen College at Oxford to talk about ancient English legends. Mrs. Joseph Bowen discussed the presidential candidates. Some of the most controversial speakers brought in the biggest crowds. Jane Addams talked about suffrage. Minnie Madern Fiske, best known as a vaudeville actress, was a fierce crusader for animal rights. After a short and light-hearted theatrical sketch, she spent the rest of her time at the podium begging the roomful of elegantly dressed members not to wear fur coats.

The Program Committee showed real courage in 1915 when they invited Mrs. Havelock Ellis to speak on her famous husband's sex research. At that time his publications were available only to the medical profession. The Chicago Superintendent of Public Health was appalled, declaring that these "free love lectures" filled with "insinuations that are not good for the young," would have dreadful consequences. Nevertheless, several hundred WAC members and their daughters packed the parlors and also the gymnasium, which had to be opened up to accommodate the overflow. No men were allowed to be present. Mrs. Ellis urged "ripe education" and predicted the time was coming when "the prude would be regarded as abnormal." The papers reported next day that the ladies found Mrs. Ellis "full of soul love" and were warmly appreciative of her point of view.

Along with its popular programs, the club's culinary reputation continued to grow. Its lobster salad was known on both coasts, and members insisted that the club's signature coconut cake be on the menu every day. During dull times, when the maids weren't hemming aprons or marking towels, they were putting up thousands of jars of assorted jellies, pickles, and preserves for use in the dining room and also for carry-out customers. By the end of the decade the club was selling over a thousand cakes a year for home consumption, and at holiday time a small fortune was realized from the sales of such fare as plum pudding and mincemeat pie.

Another source of extra income was the large amount of cosmetic lotions and oils bottled under the club's own label. Along with the usual assortment of hat pins, orange sticks, and wooden clogs for the pool, the Personal Service Department also sold other exclusive products like Madame Grace's Skin Food and Faker's Nail Polish. Services were continually modernized. Pompadours were washed and dressed every day, but the operators were trained to do water waves when these became fashionable. There was an interesting service on the ticket called "Emergency Facial." For members who did not want to spend time doing Miss Brunk's chopping exercises, there was an electric blanket treatment, which was advertised to cure rheumatism and take off pounds while it covered you. An old-fashioned boot black booth did a surprisingly good business.

Women were spilling out of the place. Under Mrs. Reuben H. Donnelley, a warm and expansive social leader who followed Mrs. Upham as president, the dining room was taxed to capacity. It became *the* place to hold engagement parties, birthday celebrations, vacation reunions. The board organized a children's Christmas party, with the *Tribune*'s "story lady," Georgene Faulkner, in German costume, reading tales of Hansel and Gretel and leading the group in carols. The party was so successful it became an annual event. When Mrs. Harry Gordon Selfridge returned home for a visit, her husband still busy setting up his London department store, an elaborate luncheon was given in her honor at the WAC. This event was, sadly, a goodbye as well, for a few years later the sweet Rose Selfridge contracted a fatal case of pneumonia nursing wounded soldiers at their home, Highcliff Castle, during the war.

The club was open from eight in the morning till eight at night every day but Sunday. The place was so busy they began to charge members 25 cents to reserve the Silence Room, and they had to make rules about governesses and personal maids using the pool. It was necessary to install piano stools in the telephone booths for members who wanted to make all their calls at the club. The cab station at the front door was mobbed, and the Atlas Taxicab Company agreed to pay the salary of a third doorman to handle the extra business. Guest cards for out-of-town friends were much in demand (though a temporary Censorship Committee was organized when some of the older members complained about seeing "too many actresses using the club so freely"). The affairs of the club received so much publicity, in fact, that finally a Press Committee was formed to monitor the amount of information available even to society reporters. Deciding the only value of mention in the papers was to remind the members at their breakfast tables of the day's events, the committee henceforth limited news of the WAC to short notices. Unhappily for posterity, it also ruled that no photos could be released to the papers or even taken in the clubhouse without its express permission.

In 1916, under the bold direction of Mrs. Thomas K. Lyon, the board voted to rent an additional floor in the Harvester building and enlarge the Resident membership to 650. Since by this time it was possible to join the club only when someone died or resigned, there was already a waiting list of at least 150 women ready to come in right away. Nevertheless, this expansion was accomplished gradually, over a full

MRS. THOMAS R. LYON. After war broke out in Europe, President Lyon called for contributions of cash and goods, which were then sent abroad and distributed through the British Red Cross.

MRS. REUBEN H. DONNELLEY. All departments of the club prospered during her presidency, especially the dining room, where new appetizers and ala carte items were added to the daily menu.

year's time, to keep the regular members comfortable during renovations. Actually, it was not even decided upon "without quakes and shakes," as the board later confessed, since the expansion required more staff and a substantially larger supply of such goods as tablecloths, forks, tea kettles, and bath sheets. At this time the club was greatly helped, as it had been all along, by members who generously donated furnishings like clocks, mirrors, candle shades, rugs, paintings, and chairs from their own homes. Tulips and roses seen around the club often were sent down from summer estates in Lake Geneva, and almost all the books and magazines in the library were gifts, including a book from the Lakeside Press received every year at holiday time, compliments of Miss Naomi Donnelley. The board could turn a profit from accumulated junk as well. One day Mrs. Will Lyford collected a raft of unwanted articles plus every item in the Lost and Found closet and organized a sale. An excellent auctioneer, she sold all the sundry hatboxes, umbrellas, and gloves left at the club. Someone was able to buy a beautiful man's wool overcoat for just five dollars.

With all their hardships and tragedies, the years of the First World War drew the club members into an even closer bond, especially after the poignant death of Mrs. Charles Plamondon, who drowned with her husband when German torpedoes sank the *Lusitania*. When the United States declared war in 1917, the WAC immediately mobilized for service. Mrs. Philip D. Armour declared, "Every woman who is not working to support herself should be giving the whole of her time to war work. It is a time when every woman in the nation has to prove herself as true and loyal as the men."

So as husbands and sons were drafted and sent overseas, WAC members jumped in with the same spirit on the home front. During Registration Week at the club about 280 of them signed up to work for the Woman's Council of National Defense. Notices were sent out urging every member not yet enrolled in the American Red Cross to join and take classes in First Aid or Home Nursing. The women wrapped bandages and knitted scarves, wrote to soldiers they'd never met, and shipped all the club's unused books and magazines abroad. Bundled in mufflers and heavy boots, they marched in the parades on Michigan Avenue and poured coffee in the canteens. As the holidays approached, 845 Christmas bags were mailed to the boys at the front and thousands of dollars collected for the orphaned children of Europe.

In 1918 Mrs. Homer Dixon hosted in her home at 40 E. Erie what must surely have been one of the most amazing meetings of the Woman's Athletic Club ever held. Mrs. Armour was there, Mrs. Pullman, Mrs. Borden, and Mrs. McCormick. Over a hundred women stood in several rooms of that grand house while Billy Sunday, the Bible-thumping fire-breathing evangelist, railed against the kaiser. He thundered about the prophecies of Jeremiah. "If you are for Uncle Sam and are helping him beat that hog-jowled, yellow-livered pusilanimous cutthroat of Germany," he cried, "you are walking in the light!" Peals of applause rang out. At the end of the service all joined in singing a chorus of "Brighten the Corner." Pledges were

later signed for large quantities of Liberty Bonds. In 1919 Mrs. Herbert Perkins, speaking for the club's Victory Loan Committee, reported that over the course of the war WAC members had purchased over $640,000 worth of Liberty Bonds, for which they were awarded a commemorative flag.

During the war the club also flew a service flag with a star upon it in honor of Mrs. Charles H. Thorne, who left husband, children, and a comfortable apartment on Lake Shore Drive to serve in a French hospital where, as she wrote back, she was allowed only a little hot water once a week. Several other members also served abroad, and the ones who remained at home put themselves to considerable trouble and expense to raise money for relief and ease the daily lives of servicemen yet to sail.

In fact, the war brought people from all parts of the city into the club. Members who worked downtown at the Red Cross invited their colleagues to dine, and the business and social meetings of so many other patriotic groups were held there that club rules had to be loosened to allow guests to pay cash for their own lunches and dinners. Every day at noon the dining room was crowded with handsome well-known women, most of them decked in the white ravelings of service insignia.

Starting in November 1917 the club was thrown open every Saturday evening for soldiers and sailors, and over the next year more than 2,000 troops were entertained. These "jackie parties" were wildly popular with the servicemen and also the members and their husbands and daughters, who were always on hand to welcome them.

The club put on an enormous holiday dinner shortly before Christmas, and other nights the parties included music, moving pictures, and dancing. A few of the mothers (and some of their daughters too) were apparently cautious about all this social mixing. A story from those days tells of a young lady who declined to dance with a good-looking private, explaining to her next partner that she never danced with any man under the rank of second lieutenant. He informed her that she had missed a turn with one of the finest men in the world. "I ought to know," he told her. "I was his chauffeur for three years."

Petty snobberies aside, concern about the presence of many strangers in the club was not always misplaced. Late one day for an appointment with her hairdresser, Mrs. William Kenly left her diamond rings on a sink in the washroom and came back minutes later to find them gone. After police pressure on certain suspects brought no results, Mrs. Kenly insisted on bringing her own Pinkerton detectives into the clubhouse. The board of directors objected strenuously until a small black silk purse with another expensive ring in it also disappeared. Several months later a Waukegan man, formerly a trainer of horses for the kaiser, confessed to the crimes. The missing jewelry was indeed found in his apartment, along with some papers belonging to officers at the naval training station, which led WAC members to conclude the man must have been a spy. The police discovered, however, that he had also pilfered several trunkfuls of women's silk underwear, casting some doubt on the spy theory.

All of the wining and dining and ceaseless patriotic endeavors were accomplished in spite of strict wartime rationing of food and fuel and the skyrocketing cost of just about every kind of household materials. With great foresight Mrs. George W. Dixon bought up supplies of staples like soap, flour, oils, and ammonia before these became almost impossible to obtain. Beginning in October 1917 the federal government declared every Tuesday a meatless day in public eating places in America. Every Wednesday was wheatless and every single day as nearly sugarless as appetites would allow. Ladies in the WAC dining room made do with many more egg and vegetable dishes and one lump of sugar instead of two in a cup of coffee or tea. Employees were served chicken instead of turkey for their annual Thanksgiving Dinner. About half as many pints of jellies and jams were put up over the summer, and the struggle to keep coconut cake on the menu every day was finally abandoned. (Mrs. A. B. MacCaughey triumphed over this difficulty by inventing a wheatless cake that some members said they liked even better.) The club's troubles were complicated by staff demands for salary increases almost every month. One day, when the board refused to raise the pay of the waitresses one more time, they all walked out at two o'clock in the afternoon, necessitating the procurement of an entire new work force before the club opened the following morning.

Long after the Armistice on November 11, 1918, programs at the club continued to center around wartime concerns and the new world order. Captain Reed Landis, one of the country's leading aces, told stories of his battle exploits in the air. A French prisoner of war talked about life in a Bavarian fortress, and as famous a politician as Jan Masaryk gave a speech at the club about the just-formed state of Czechoslovakia, the new country of which he would later be president. One of the most touching appeals came from one of the club's own members, Grace Gassette, a sculptor who had lived part-time in Paris for many years. During the war she designed a set of splints to help wounded soldiers recover the use of paralyzed arms, wrists, and ankles. These appliances effected such amazing cures they became standard equipment in military hospitals. Though she received the Legion of Honor from the French government for her inventions, Gassette still depended on American contributions to keep up the atelier where she and her workmen made the splints. The club gave her a third of all the money still in the coffers for the jackie parties and awarded her an Honorary Membership as a way of recognizing her distinguished contributions to the Allied victory.

Society in Chicago was forever changed by the excitements and dislocations of the war years, and this was true for the WAC as well. In the founding days all energies were focused on carving a comfortable and useful niche in the personal lives of the city's prominent women. The necessities of wartime moved the club into a wider community. Striding, marching, and dancing into the 1920s, women were a stronger and more independent breed, and the Woman's Athletic Club was now called on to meet a whole new set of aspirations.

CAPTAIN REED LANDIS with his parents, Mr. and Mrs. Kennesaw Mountain Landis. Captain Landis was one of several veterans who addressed the club, soliciting funds for devastated French villages.

MISS MILDRED WETTEN
(later Mrs. T. Lloyd Kelly,
then Mrs. Edward H. McDermott).
She joined the club in
1916 and is currently its longest-
standing member.

4
Roaring On:
the dazzling twenties

THE TWENTIES BLOSSOMED in America as a time of high spirits, big money, and delightful nonsense. The Woman's Athletic Club shared in that wave of prosperity and optimism, riding high throughout the decade with a full membership and ever increasing revenues. The clubhouse was dizzy with debutante parties, wedding receptions, Junior League rehearsals, celebrity luncheons, and tea dances for girls home on vacation from Miss Porter's and Westover.

Members flocked to hear lectures on James Joyce, contemporary art, and Indian mystics. Mah-Jongg lessons were offered. Children had a new-fangled "Marine Monster" toy to play with in the swimming pool. The club was so mobbed during the 1920 Republican Convention in Chicago that special bonuses had to be paid to maids, kitchen help, and waitresses to work double shifts. Close to a thousand luncheons were served the weekend of the Army-Navy game. Members who ten years before had cautiously lurched up to the curb outside in little electric runabouts now insisted on clogging the club's narrow "carriage entrance" with sleek fast-looking automobiles. (At one point the board of directors tried to influence City Hall to have Harrison Street extended into Grant Park so that members could have a place to park.) Inside the elevators were so overloaded around the noon hour they broke down on the average of once a week.

Youthful high jinks reigned. Some time during this period the club received a letter from a gentleman in search of a vigorous lady. "I am a young man," he wrote, "of good physique and appearance that would like to correspond with any member interested in wrestling, bowling or weight-lifting—especially wrestling." He signed his full name and address. This letter was read aloud with much amusement at more than one annual corporation meeting.

The club held to its gracious traditions throughout, with fresh lobster salad and that supreme confection, coconut cake, on the menu every day. In fact, the club was baking almost 1200 cakes a year. Most of them were coconut, but there were other favorites too like chocolate marshmallow, angel, orange, and a popular new version of the Lady Baltimore. In 1923 the club held a Silver Anniversary Tea, and members chipped in for a handsome silver service to commemorate the milestone. Many women who were young brides when the club first opened were present to reminisce over the teacups. Dainty pastries were served and a harpist played. A purse of $250 in gold was presented to Miss Larson, the able and much beloved bookkeeper who had been with the club since the founding.

Yet even as these lovely ceremonies continued, generational tensions were developing between the older more traditional members who still considered themselves the backbone of the club and a younger contingent responding to the changing look, habits, and interests of the modern American woman. The young English novelist Rebecca West crossed the United States on a lecture tour in 1923 and wrote this letter to a friend after speaking at the club:

I find it very difficult to foresee my audiences from their titles. The Woman's Athletic Club of Chicago I had imagined to be a collection of husky young women in sweaters. They turned out to be a collection of elderly ladies who certainly weighed 250 lbs. apiece and wore all the Crown jewels. They explained their title by saying that they had a swimming tank in the basement. I could hardly refrain from asking what on earth happened if two of them got in it at once.

This unflattering appraisal suggests just what the young flappers were worried about. They thought the place was getting too stodgy, too sedate. The establishment, on the other hand, declared its firm opposition to any "bolshevist movement."

There was very little for the young upstarts to criticize in the club's programming, which was refreshingly up to date. The great battle of suffrage had been won, women were in all branches of public life, and for several years running Mrs. Anthony French Merrill's Wednesday morning lectures on politics and current affairs were among the club's best-attended programs. When Madame Curie came to the U.S. in 1921 to raise $100,000 for the gram of radium she needed to continue her experiments, the WAC hosted a city-wide meeting to prepare for her reception in Chicago. Contributions from WAC members accounted for one-sixth of the entire sum she collected here. The board voted to endorse Dr. Frank Billings' antivivisection movement. Princess Cantacuzene, a niece of Mrs. Potter Palmer who had married a Russian prince, gave a frank talk about her experiences in Siberia, where she had been with the White Russian Army. Life Member Ruth Hanna McCormick, who was pictured on the cover of *Time* in 1928 as the first woman in America elected to a national statewide office, lectured on the "Year of Women in Politics."

The really contentious issues seemed to center more on the image and atmosphere of the club. The younger members wore short skirts, flesh-colored stockings, and high-heeled slippers, which the older women deemed foolish. To their horror even the nice girls were using lipstick and an outlandish brown face powder and "beading" their eyes. Nevertheless, some gradual accommodations were made. The club was persuaded to list a "Marcel" alongside "Pompadours, Washed and Dressed" in the beauty parlor offerings, and later one of the operators was given permission to bring a permanent waving machine into the club. In 1924 the board sent out a notice that a woman had been hired who would bob hair.

The younger members wanted to replace the painted wicker furniture in the living room. They did not want to eat creamed chicken and sweetbreads every day and pressed for a menu of simple sandwiches. They deplored the absence of the new "cocktail" (a question which had been firmly settled by Prohibition laws), and above all, they resented having to toss their cigarettes away before coming into the clubhouse. Back in 1916, Mrs. Thomas R. Lyon, the club's president, declared, "Women never have smoked at the Athletic Club. It is absolutely against the rules, and I certainly do not approve of it." During the war, when people from all over the city were regular guests at luncheon meetings in the dining room, an effort was made to modify the rules. The old guard nevertheless moved that "women should not be permitted to smoke in the Club anywhere, at any time." The motion lost. Thereafter smoking was permitted first in a small private room, later in the back dining room, and then in the assembly hall upstairs. In 1924 all restrictions were dropped and cigarettes went on sale in the Personal Service Department.

The pressure to modernize was complicated by growing competition from other city clubs. The new Casino, situated in a pink plaster building on Chestnut Street, had captured a strong segment of the well-heeled ladies' luncheon and party business. The Arts Club was offering avant-garde exhibitions and tea with luminaries like Igor Stravinsky and Robert Frost. The Fortnightly announced plans to move its

LIFE MEMBER RUTH HANNA MCCORMICK campaigning for the U.S. Senate.

MENU

SOUPS

CONSOMME WITH RICE 30
OYSTER STEW 50

SANDWICHES

HOT SWISS CHEESE SANDWICH 65
TOASTED CHICKEN SALAD AND TOMATO SANDWICH 65
TOASTED RYE BREAD 25
TOASTED CASTLE BREAD 15

COLD DISHES

INDIVIDUAL CHICKEN ASPIC WITH TOMATO AND MAYONNAISE . 1.25
CHICKEN SALAD . . . . . 1.25   LOBSTER SALAD 1.35

HOT SPECIALS

BROILED WHITEFISH WITH CUCUMBERS 1.00
CREAMED CHICKEN IN PASTRY SHELLS 85
CORNED BEEF HASH WITH RELISH 70
BROILED SQUAB ON TOAST 1.25
BROILED LAMB CHOPS WITH PEAS 1.00

VEGETABLES

NEW FRESH PEAS 35
FRESH SPINACH 35
HASHED BROWNED POTATOES 30

SALADS

ALLIGATOR PEAR 65
FRENCH ENDIVE AND GRAPE FRUIT 65

SWEETS

CHOCOLATE CREAM CAKE 35
COCOANUT CAKE 35
CARAMEL CAKE 35
PUMPKIN PIE 30

ICES AND ICE CREAM

ICE CREAM SURPRISE WITH CARAMEL SAUCE 65
ORANGE ICE 40
VANILLA ICE CREAM 40   RASPBERRY ICE 45

FRUIT-JELLY-CHEESE

SHREDDED PINEAPPLE 65   BAR-LE-DUC AND CHEESE . .40
ORANGE MARMALADE 40   GUAVA JELLY 40

BEVERAGES

MAILLARD'S CHOCOLATE OR COCOA 30
HOT TEA OR COFFEE 25   BULGARIAN MILK . . .25
ICED CHOCOLATE OR COCOA 35   ICED TEA OR COFFEE 30

FOOD SERVED IN DEPARTMENTS 25 CENTS EXTRA
SERVICE CHARGE OF 5 CENTS PER PERSON

Club Luncheon

$2.00 Per Plate

CONSOMME WITH RICE

BRAISED SWEETBREADS ON TOAST, BROWN SAUCE

FRENCH PEAS

ROLLS   COFFEE

COLD SLAW SALAD WITH PINEAPPLE

VANILLA ICE CREAM WITH HOT CHOCOLATE OR
HOT CARAMEL SAUCE
OR
PUMPKIN PIE WITH CHEESE

A TYPICAL LUNCHEON MENU
of the Twenties.

GYMNASIUM

Corrective Gymnastics . . . . $ 1.00
Use of Gymnasium Equipment for Season . 5.00
Gymnasium Class Work Free

DANCING

Single Lesson (One Hour) 3.50
Six Lessons (Half Hour) 10.00
Twelve Lessons (Half Hour) 20.00
Twenty-four Lessons (Half Hour) . . . 40.00

NATATORIUM

One Lesson (Swimming) 1.00
One Year Course (25 Lessons) 20.00
Use of Swimming Pool (Single Ticket) . . .25
Use of Swimming Pool (25 Tickets) . . . 5.00

LOCKERS

Locker, Large, per Year 8.00
Locker, Small, per Year 5.00

BATHS

Turkish Bath 1.00
Turkish Bath (Ticket for 6 Baths) . . . 5.00
Russian Bath 1.00
Electric Tub, Cabinet, or Electric Blanket . 1.50
Alcohol Rub 25
Alcohol Rub with Bath 25
Oil Rub 1.00
Salt Glow 50
Body Massage 1.50
Silence Room (except in connection with Baths) .25

HAIRDRESSING AND MANICURING

Shampoo . . . . $ .75
Dry Shampoo 50
Scalp Treatment (Single Treatment) . . .75
Scalp Treatment (Ticket for 8 Treatments) . 5.00
Hot Oil Treatment 1.00
Brushing 50
Singeing or Clipping 50
Hairdressing (Water Wave) 1.00
Hairdressing (Marcel Wave) 75
Hairdressing (Plain) 50
Pompadours, Washed and Dressed 50
Transformations, Washed and Dressed . . .50
Hair Dyeing (Price according to work)
Depilatory (Hands and Arms) 1.50
Depilatory (Under Arms) 1.00
Manicure 50

FACIAL MASSAGE

Facial Massage (Single Treatment) . 1.00–2.00
Facial Massage (Ticket for 6 Treatments) . 10.00
Facial and Neck Massage (Single Treatment) 3.00
Facial and Neck Massage (Ticket for 6 Treatments) 15.00
Hand Massage (Single Treatment) . . . 1.00
Hand Massage (Ticket for 6 Treatments) . 5.00

CHIROPODY

Chiropody (Price according to work) .
Pedicure 75

MISCELLANEOUS

Umbrella 1.00
(Money refunded if returned within one week.)

PAGES FROM AN OLD PRICE LIST
of club services.

handsome tapestries, furniture, and historic artifacts into the fabulous old Lathrop house on Bellevue Place. Even the venerable Chicago Woman's Club, an old-line group of earnest reformers, had hired architects to design glamorous new headquarters on property they purchased off Michigan Avenue at 11th Street. At the same time the men's clubs were dressing up their facilities for women. The brand new Racquet Club went so far as to hire the aristocratic Rue Carpenter to decorate sumptuous quarters for women, with lovely chintz, old wallpapers, and dainty dressing rooms to lure female guests.

The most direct threat to the WAC's standing came from a new organization bold enough to call itself the "Chicago Woman's Athletic Club." The name was later adjusted, following pressure from the WAC's lawyers, to the "Illinois Woman's Athletic Club." This group, which was born in the ferment of the suffrage movement and bolstered by the financial support of such society leaders as Mrs. Waller Borden and Mrs. Robert McCormick, mounted a fierce membership drive and signed up close to 1,700 women. They bought a choice lot on Tower Court from the Prentice estate and put up a Venetian Gothic skyscraper with pool, tennis courts, billiard rooms, ballroom, and a running track like the one the WAC had had once upon a time. They even set aside a waiting room for husbands. Most pointedly, they had a great number of bedroom suites and were beautifully equipped to furnish lodging and meals to suburban and non-resident members for a short stay in town. (The IWAC did not survive the Depression, and its clubhouse is today part of Loyola University's near north side campus.)

Eventually all the WAC's pressing dilemmas over social change and the club's proper place in the Chicago firmament seemed to coalesce around the issue of moving. Their lease in the Harvester Building would expire in 1926. Should they leave? If so, where should they go? Most terrifying, how much was it going to cost?

As far back as 1913 a Site and Building Committee chaired by Mrs. Upham had been organized to keep in touch with real estate conditions. They had hopes of building but, realistically, looked first for a more desirable rental. In every instance the space offered was either too costly, too small, too large, or too high up. (They would not consider moving into quarters above the fourth or fifth story.) Their rooms at the Harvester were increasingly cramped, with locker space so short some members had to store their street clothes in boxes. The boy swimmers had no dressing room at all. With war and severe austerity measures on the horizon, however, the club had made the sensible decision to stay put and renew their lease.

After the Armistice was signed in 1918, members had expected conditions would shortly return to normal. But even with conscientious management the treasury did not stabilize again for several years, and the search for new quarters was put off. Payroll costs, which had escalated dramatically during the war, kept going right on up. Every month at least a dozen employees asked for a raise. One by one the pastry cook, the Turkish bath girls, then the cake packer and the door boy would request an extra two or three dollars a week. Next month it would be the switchboard operator, the manicurist, cook's extra helper, and the night cleaners. The board tried to hold the line on salaries, but after attending the Hotel Men's Conference in 1920 and grasping just how much the employment picture had changed, the president, Mrs. A. B. MacCaughey, returned to the clubhouse and promptly granted a raise to every member of the staff, whether it had been requested or not.

These increases, together with the high cost of all commodities, meant a deficit in every department, the only profits coming from sales of candy, cosmetic lotions, and coconut cake. After the enforced economies of the war years, much restocking of dishes and linens was also necessary, adding to the financial burden, and there were expensive emergencies out of the board's control. Freezing and bursting pipes sometimes flooded the kitchen on the busiest winter Mondays, and there were always trying times like the day the sewer backed up and not a dish was washed for 24 hours. During the year 1920 the club's expenses increased by almost $50,000.

The board worked mightily to resteady the budget and build a reserve. Accordingly, dues were raised to $100 a year and then again in 1924 to $125. There was a concerted effort to buy up Life Memberships as they became available and then charge double to the next applicant. The price of meals and services went up. Swimmers were allotted just two towels each and billed for the use of bathrobes. The price of a body massage was lifted to $2.50, for instance, and a rubdown to 75 cents. If a member was not satisfied with the Bath Department's Bay-Rum or Witch Hazel, she was asked to bring her own alcohol from home. A less expensive stationery, stamped not engraved, was ordered for the writing desks. Instead of repainting the gymnasium walls, they were carefully washed. Not a hairpin was unaccounted for. It helped that members were generous with donations from their own homes, enabling the club to have on hand exquisite silver urns, brass finger bowls, fancy cake baskets, and the like, which were otherwise completely beyond its means.

Several members also made regular gifts to the staff, which tended to sweeten the atmosphere after the wage battles. Mrs. H. Newton Hudson furnished everyone with a turkey at Christmas time. Mrs. Thomas R. Lyon donated many gallons of homemade ice cream every summer to the employee dining room and paid for punch on New Year's. Mrs. Charles Kohl, wife of the famous theater owner, presented everyone with tickets to see a Shakespeare play. Along with many boxes of candy and topped by cash bonuses from the annual Christmas Fund which sometimes amounted to more than a month's pay, the staff was contented again.

This turn-around was also enhanced by the able and untiring Mrs. Draper, who came to the club as manager in 1920. With the help of Miss Larson (this longtime bookkeeper was a veritable bureau of information about the WAC and by now the institutional memory of the place), Mrs. Draper got a strong hold on the tiller. She came from an old hotel family in Oconomowoc, Wisconsin, and understood the whole business of personnel and budgets and commodity management very well. "Many little puffs that threatened to become a storm," the House Chairman reported, "were blown away by her calm and sensible manner of reasoning." The year that Mrs. Draper came on board the club was able to buy a $5,000 Liberty Bond, which was set aside in anticipation of the move. By 1925 the ladies had amassed a war chest of $250,000 and were ready to make a substantial investment.

Word got around town that the club was now looking in earnest. "The WAC talks again of building," noted a local gossip sheet. "Rumors have brought down upon the officers the cards of architects and a swarm of real estate men with cigars in their mouths to rival the crowd in Mike Faherty's office in City Hall." Mrs. George Dixon, who was re-elected to the presidency in 1923, took on this project as the central cause of her term in office. A woman of considerable business talent herself, she enlisted the help of a Men's Committee, husbands of board members, to bring some added expertise and clout to the rough and tumble of the Chicago real estate market. Colonel William N. Pelouze, a wealthy well-connected enterpreneur who was brother-in-law to the Mayor, headed this committee.

A citywide building boom was underway. There was much new construction in the Loop, but the big story was the creation of the double-decker Wacker Drive along the river and the development of the glorious new North Michigan Avenue. Originally a narrow residential road called Pine Street, this stretch was widened in 1918, demolishing many fine old houses and their lawns and gardens. After the Michigan Avenue Bridge was completed in 1920, the street was gradually

MRS. GEORGE W. DIXON
(far left), moving force behind
the club's search for a new site.

MRS. JAMES SIMPSON
with her husband, the president of
Marshall Field & Company.
During Mrs. Simpson's tenure on
the board, the club's furnishings were appraised free of charge
by store officials whenever
necessary.

THE NORTHWEST CORNER OF MICHIGAN AND ONTARIO in 1920. The entire block was once occupied by the house and gardens of Walter Newberry. His rambling brick mansion burned to the ground in the Chicago Fire of 1871.

MRS. ALLAN M. CLEMENT, a prominent member of the Search Committee. She later gave the club much exquisite tableware, including a collection of Capodimonte china. Here she holds her granddaughter and namesake Grace, a future WAC president (Mrs. Philip L. Cochran).

COLONEL AND MRS. WILLIAM N. PELOUZE (below right). The Colonel was head of the Men's Committee, which advised the club on real estate matters. Helen Pelouze was president during the three crucial years of 1928 through 1930.

transformed into a cosmopolitan Parisian-style boulevard, lined with smart shops, hotels, and offices. Enterprises like auto showrooms, poolrooms, laundries, garages, and bars were banned. The Drake Hotel anchored the north end of the street and the Wrigley Building the south, with the Tribune Tower finished a short time later. Structures like the Allerton Hotel and the Lake Shore Trust and Savings Bank appeared in between. Both on and off the avenue the old-fashioned houses still standing were remodeled into artistic studios for the army of architects, decorators, antique dealers, modistes, and advertising firms who served this burgeoning new neighborhood. Filling in the interstices were tiny kitchenette apartments with just a kettle over the gas and a crop of small cafes, typically painted in bright blue or yellow with names like the Wind Blew Inn and Bright Shawl. The whole district blossomed as a fresh sophisticated mix of modern business and bohemian charm, and few areas in the city could match its appeal. Naturally, it was priced accordingly, and the prize lots and leases went to buyers with the deepest pockets.

Mrs. Dixon and her committee chased all over, visiting rooms here, an empty lot there, brokers' offices where blueprints were rolled out on tables. William Wrigley offered a large space in his new north tower (where the Arts Club did move), but the rent was too high. Mrs. Dixon tried hard to secure rooms in the new London Guarantee building just south of the bridge. Nothing suitable was available. A scheme to lease land at the southwest corner of Michigan and South Water Street went quite far, to the point of having an architect draw plans. In the end the broker was unable to finance the deal as promised. The club then negotiated to build at the southwest corner of Michigan and Lake. Next they considered the southeast corner across the street. They looked at a lot at Lake and Wabash and another one on South Water Street. The triangular-shaped lot where the Christian Science headquarters was built many years later was thought to have unusually good light, air, and a spectacular river view. The ladies were also encouraged to buy property at the northwest corner of Rush and Ontario, then at the southeast corner of Michigan and Erie. This last site had an asking price of $1,125,000, a sum utterly beyond their reach.

The search seemed to yield one disappointment after another. Discouragement turned to grief when Mrs. Dixon died in the winter of 1926. Doubt spread that the club could really bring off such a project, especially after the women were forced to sign another short-term lease in the Harvester building. A snide news column recalled "the effective political hands" of the founding members and suggested the club's glory years were largely behind it. "We will believe in a Woman's Athletic Club building," the reporter concluded, "when we see the same."

Early in 1927 a proposal appeared which finally met the approval of all the board members. John Root of Holabird and Roche was designing the long-anticipated tower at the southeast corner of the bridge, to be called "333 North Michigan." A group of WAC ladies working under the leadership of Mrs. Allan M. Clement negotiated a 20-year lease there for all of the fourth and fifth floors, the entire south half of the sixth, and all of the ground level below the boulevard, where a magnificent swimming pool and bath department would be installed. The club was to have its own entrance onto the bridge plaza at the northeast corner of the building and two private elevators inside. Though Colonel Pelouze expressed doubts that the club could really afford the $77,060 yearly rental when it was added to the cost of completely new furnishings, the premises would clearly be beautiful and pristine and situated in a very stylish building. The women voted to sign at "333." Digging for the foundations was started on June 1.

Two weeks later a letter arrived at the club from real estate broker Frederick M. Bowes, addressed to "My dear Colonel." Bowes reported that a choice piece of land at the northwest corner of Michigan and Ontario had just become available. Its owner, John V. Farwell, did not want to pay the enormous taxes he would face on a sale but would be willing to make the club a 99-year ground lease. Farwell had asked Philip Maher, an architect who had just finished a building for his brother up the street, to provide sketches for a multi-story clubhouse. Farwell specified a basement pool, sidewalk-canopy entrance on Ontario, and Michigan Avenue frontage for six high-grade shops which could bring in as much as $40,000 a year in rent, income which could reduce a club's overhead tremendously. It was a very attractive opportunity.

Suddenly there was a horse race, the "333" team competing with backers of the new Farwell scheme. The president, Mrs. William Sherman Hay, who was said to have "that rare faculty of seeing a question from all sides and giving decisions with justice to all," presided over an exciting meeting where the pros and cons of each choice were debated. Mrs. Samuel Slade presented the case for the Farwell lot. In a building of its own, the club would have more square footage. They could get any ceiling heights they wanted. They would have their own permanent canopy, whereas their entrance at "333" would be a simple unmarked door. Ontario Street had easy motor access and (amazingly, to future generations) "unlimited parking." On a cost-per-year basis the project came out to less money than the rental quarters at "333." At the end of 20 years all the expensive fixtures at Ontario Street would still belong to the club for another 79 years, while at "333" the club would forfeit their whole investment. There were considerable smoke and cinders from river and street traffic at "333" but practically none farther north. About the only advantage of "333" that seemed to stick was that it was perceived as being "more centrally located," but opponents pointed out that the cost of a taxi from the Loop to the Farwell site was trivial.

JOHN V. FARWELL, owner of
the northwest corner of Michigan
and Ontario. He purchased
the site in 1912 from Frederick
W. Bowes.

PHILIP B. MAHER'S 1927 presentation drawing. He later boasted that his original conception was not altered one iota, but note the classic maidens standing in the niches at the seventh floor. Why and how two winged griffins appeared in their stead remains a mystery.

MRS. WILLIAM SHERMAN HAY, a Wellesley graduate who taught school in Puerto Rico after the Spanish-American War. She brought the same intellectual vigor and spirit of service to her two terms as WAC president.

Remembering this historic debate, Mrs. William F. Petersen recalled a small but telling point. The club's old address was 606 South Michigan. The new address would be 626 North Michigan. To many of the women it seemed like an overwhelming coincidence, as if a giant finger were pointing to the right choice. "They were all so pleased with themselves," she recalled. "I think they bought the place just because it was in the 600 block."

In truth, once the whole membership had fully contemplated the prospect of at last having a home of their own, on the glamorous new Michigan Boulevard, in the magnificent French Empire clubhouse Philip Maher was sketching out for them, an unquenchable momentum built for the Farwell site. When John Farwell threw in an offer to loan the club $375,000 to help finance a building, the matter was sealed. Gingerly, they pulled out of the agreement at "333," explaining simply, "The trend is uptown."

During the Depression, when the club struggled to meet its rent payments while faced with unpaid dues and delinquent shop rentals, there was criticism of the cozy way this real estate deal had come about. There is no doubt that Messrs. Pelouze, Bowes, Farwell, and Maher were involved in many interrelated business projects. Fifty years later Maher was still gloating about the turn of events that took the WAC away from "333" and into the clubhouse of his design. "Heh, heh, Holabird and Roche lost their client.... We told Mrs. Pelouze we could arrange to have her own the building rather than rent from someone else. In years' time that was to be an enormous advantage. She told the Colonel and that seemed all right to him. He was in real estate, you understand. We turned up with the drawings and they were approved without a single change."

The fact remains that after all those disheartening years of hunting, the women made a superb choice. It was a prime corner on the most exciting new thoroughfare in America. With this single stroke the club's high social profile in Chicago was restored. On July 25, 1927 Mrs. Philip D. Armour, age 85, died at her apartment at 1200 Lake Shore Drive. The day of her funeral the club was closed in her honor. On the following day the WAC's plan to build a streamlined skyscraper along the new Michigan Boulevard was announced to the Chicago press. The era of the founders was over.

COLONIAL SIGNS

WOMAN'S ATHLETIC CLUB OF CHICAGO
PHILIP B. MAHER, ARCHITECT
LUNDOFF-BICKNELL CO.–BUILDING CONSTRUCTION

Brunswick-Kroeschel Co. REFRIGERATION	John A. Boland Company PLASTING	ELEVATORS HAESTNER & WENDT
S. HASKEL & SONS GRANITE	HOLLOW CLAY TILE PARTITIONS METORE ENGINEERING	
ART MARBLE CHICAGO ART MARBLE CO.	CRANE CO. PLUMBING FIXTURES	
	CHICAGO PUMP CO. FIRE PUMP	
CHICAGO	H.P. REGER & CO.	
EASTHOM MELVIN & YEAGER INC. CONCRETE CONSTRUCTION	JULIUS FLOTO STRUCTURAL ENGINEER	PALTRIDGE
	TERRAZZO WORK	
	KALAMEIN DOORS FRAMES & TRIM W.F. OVERLY & SONS	WENDT & CRONE CO. HEATING & VENTILATING

NEW CLUB BUILDING
FOR
**WOMAN'S ATHLETIC CLUB
OF CHICAGO**
FOR INFORMATION REGARDING SHOPS
APPLY TO
BOWES REALTY CO.
664 N. MICHIGAN AVE.   TEL. WHITEHALL 7945

PHILIP B. MAHER
ARCHITECT

THE LUNDOFF-BICKNELL CO.
BUILDING CONSTRUCTION

WOMAN'S ATHLETIC CLUB
PHILIP MAHER,   ARCHITECT
NO. **34**   DATE **9-7-28**
THE LUNDOFF-BICKNELL CO.
GENERAL CONTRACTORS

5

A splendid new Clubhouse

ONCE THE LEGAL PAPERS WERE SIGNED, a thrilling energy began to course through all the club's affairs. Certainly the women were still facing a colossal challenge. The total amount of money needed for the new building was estimated at $1,020,600, and the par value of the bonds set aside for it was only $445,500. Spirits were high, though, and with a fresh confidence the board of directors raised dues and admission fees again and boldly enlarged the Resident Membership to 1,000. Life Memberships were increased from a maximum of 110 to 160 and, with a bit of trepidation, the cost of those pushed up to $5,000 each. The board need never have worried. For Chicago's woman of fashion, excited by the prospect of walking into her own clubhouse on the city's new *Champs Elysée*, the price tag was never a factor. The membership roster immediately filled to capacity, with long waiting lists in every category including the expensive Life. Armed with these figures, the board was able to secure a sizable bank loan. Putting that together with their savings and John Farwell's loan, they now had enough money to meet all their costs.

As soon as the stores on the Michigan/Ontario corner were demolished, excavation for the new clubhouse began. The contractors were the Lundoff-Bicknell Company of Cleveland, who agreed to put up the building for a sum not to exceed $750,000, including their own fee. Completion was originally scheduled for September 1928. As they dug deep, however, for foundations and columns that would support the eight-story building (plus three additional stories, should the building later be converted to some other use—another Farwell safeguard), they encountered unexpected ground conditions. Then a special ordinance had to be passed by the City Council to allow a marquise over the sidewalk to the curb on Ontario Street. Progress was continually delayed and a cornerstone was not laid until May, pushing much of the construction into the following fall and winter.

The Men's Committee headed by Colonel Pelouze continued to superintend the project and okay all bills, but by this time his wife, Helen Pelouze, had been elected president of the club. A daughter of Mrs. William H. Thompson, one of the WAC's five founders, Mrs. Pelouze was clear-eyed, tactful, and herself capable of overseeing every aspect of the job. Someone described her then as "a woman you could go to if you were in trouble." Frank Cooper, a friend of later years, remembered, "She never seemed to get excited. She was always very reserved, very quiet, and very generous." Helen Pelouze was just the woman to pilot the club safely through the inevitable setbacks and clashes that arose around this large undertaking, and throughout her long life she remained one of the most popular presidents ever to hold the office.

Philip Maher's French-inspired building design, with its refined materials and graceful proportions, was universally pleasing. The streamlined facade, clad in smooth-faced light gray limestone with polished black granite at the base and terra cotta accents, had an elegant simplicity. Members viewing the plans liked its Continental aura — the mansard roof with slate shingles and copper cresting, the tall arched windows and wrought iron balconettes. A wealth of decorative ornament mixed classical grandeur with an *art moderne* sensibility. At the top of the building the winged griffins of mythology perched near draperies and garlands carved in stone. Down around the first and second floors, however, Maher used geometric Art Deco detail — spiral scrolling, a wave motif, stylized leaves and vines. Some years later he said, "At that time modern feeling was beginning to creep into design. I felt that a more traditional design was more appropriate to a woman's club. The choice resulted in an awful lot of carving, but then, that was the trend fifty years ago."

PHILIP B. MAHER

PHILIP B. MAHER WAS ONLY 33 years old when he was hired to design the WAC's new clubhouse. The son of Prairie School architect, George W. Maher, he served abroad in World War I and spent a half year after the Armistice sketching the buildings of Paris and the surrounding countryside. His subsequent work on Chicago's new Michigan Boulevard blended a Continental sensibility with the Art Deco forms of a new architectural age. His designs include the Farwell Building (later the Terra Museum), the Blackstone Shop, the Jacques Building, and the now demolished Decorative Arts Building. Also notable was a pair of handsome apartment houses at 1260 and 1301 Astor Street.

Along with most architects of his day, Maher's career was constricted by the difficulties of the Depression and war years. He remained a Michigan Avenue denizen nonetheless. Even into his 80s he could be found in the late afternoons seated at the grand piano in the Tavern Club, playing Rachmaninoff or a cool boogie-woogie. "Phips was dapper and had a dry sense of humor," recalls a friend, "and he loved to reminisce about building the Woman's Athletic Club. This building was really the love of his life."

A newspaper commentator at the time pronounced the building "just the right combination of the new and the classic." Its ultimate destiny as a Chicago landmark and historic link to the sophisticated urbanity of early Michigan Avenue confirms the club's choice of architect. For his work Philip Maher was paid $45,000, plus commissions on the cost of lighting fixtures and kitchen equipment (a contract awarded to Albert Pick & Company).

Even as he was drawing the plans, Maher was adamant that the club select a decorator at once so they could work on the layout of the interior together. Several were interviewed and the firm of Miss Gheen, Inc. chosen unanimously. Originally from Westchester, Pennsylvania, Marian Gheen and her sister Gertrude had come to Chicago around 1915 to assist Elsie de Wolfe with the decoration of J. Ogden Armour's Lake Forest home, Mellody Farm. The sisters established their own firm and over the years furnished many large Chicago houses and apartments. In person Marian Gheen was intelligent and aristocratic, a smart dresser who sometimes wore a lorgnette. Some people thought she was English because so much of her work reflected a British sensibility. Her philosophy stressed beautiful furniture and splendid materials, well and livably arranged. Her watchword was comfort. Her favorite color was apricot. Mrs. Edward McDermott remembered Marian Gheen's reputation well. "She was a woman of outstanding taste. This is the reason she was chosen. Because the club members wanted the club to look like a home, like an extension of their own homes. They did not want to do anything 'New York.' "

Though Miss Gheen felt a budget of one-half to two-thirds the cost of the building would be necessary to furnish the spacious setting Philip Maher was drawing, she was assured that $150,000 was all the club had to spend. She accepted that, though she did insist on a minimum $20,000 commission. Beginning in November 1927 the Decorating Committee met every Friday morning with their "guiding genius," as they called her, in her studio at 163 E. Ontario. The members of this select committee felt it was a real privilege to participate and seldom missed a meeting. Over the course of the project their number included Mrs. H. Newton Hudson (Chairman), Mrs. Frank P. Graves (Co-Chairman), Mrs. Henry Bartholomay, Mrs. Jule F. Brower, Mrs. Allan M. Clement, Mrs. Harry Clow, and Mrs. William Sherman Hay, with Mrs. Pelouze sitting ex-officio.

The committee studied wallpapers, paint samples, different combinations of fabrics and furniture. The process of selection was a ticklish task and Mrs. Hudson reported there was often a "wholesome difference of opinion," but the committee's interest was live and unflagging. There were field trips to showrooms, warehouses, and studios. The local firm of Watson & Boaler made some very good pieces for them, including a beautifully proportioned leather-top kneehole desk. Several local

67

artists were commissioned to paint walls and mirrors, including Nicholas Remisoff, a Russian set designer who was decorating a ballroom for the Casino at the same time. For the ballroom in the new Woman's Athletic Club, the delightful shaggy-headed "Remi" was hired to paint a theatrical pastel-colored mural on the plaster balcony surrounding the floor. Walter Reid Williams, a Hyde Park sculptor, created a large chromium-plated figure for the club's entrance. Intended to symbolize the members' athletic ambitions, this statuette was described then as "a girl running, graceful and restrained but intent on the goal." In time she came simply to be called "our Diana." The committee was also charged with buying large amounts of linen, glassware, and silver, and they purchased $5,000 worth of new china at Tatman's, an exclusive boutique across the street in the Italian Court. From Mr. Tatman they also acquired a brand new supply of finger bowls.

As the plans came together, some members stepped forward to cover the cost of furnishing whole rooms. Mrs. William Sherman Hay paid for the library, Mrs. Charles Morse the modernistic "Mirror Room," and Mrs. William C. Pullman the Pillement Room. In a tremendous gesture of generosity, the George W. Dixon family gave the ballroom in memory of the late Mrs. Dixon who had spent the last years of her life working to find a new home for the club. Marian Gheen chose several paintings at the Chester Johnson galleries, which were then purchased and donated by various ladies. Some members also presented the club with treasures from their own homes. Mrs. Mark Trude brought in some of her precious white Sevre, and the Watkins family gave a pair of crystal girandoles which were placed

THE SECOND FLOOR GALLERY in 1929.

A PAGE FROM A LEATHER-BOUND REGISTER listing many generous donations to the new clubhouse.

Donors and Gifts

Mr. George W. Dixon }
Miss Marion Dixon } Ballroom

Mrs. H. Newton Hudson
  Painting by Sir Peter Lily in Library
  Plants and Flowers at various times

Miss Helen V. Drake
  Crystal Light Fixtures for Hall

Mrs. Joseph O. Watkins
  Painting, Books and Articles for
  Personal Service Department

Mrs. William C. Pullman Toward
  Piellemont Room. Antique Books for
  Piellemont Room.

Mrs. William Sherman Hay Library

Mrs. J. Ogden Armour
  Various Articles – Representing $1,000

Mrs. Frederick H. Rawson
  Various Articles – Representing $1,000

Mrs. Darius Miller
  Large Cabinet in Lounge

Mrs. George M. Reynolds
  Chairs in Natatorium and Bronze Baskets
  in Dressing Rooms and $1,500

on matching pedestal tables in the second floor gallery. Mrs. William Pelouze gave a pair of gilded carved mirrors. Mrs. J. Ogden Armour, just in the process of selling Mellody Farm, donated a pair of gilt wooden brackets for the lounge. Mrs. Harry B. Clow (*née* Elizabeth McNally) gave an atlas and stand for the library, plus a supply of 2,000 cigarettes. Many other members donated assorted vases, lamps, and boxes of detective novels and leather-bound classics to fill the empty shelves in the library.

As the building drew closer to completion, Fred Bowes worked intently to lease the storefronts. Fisher & Spaulding took the north shop and moved in even before the club opened. The next contracts went to Martha Leslie, a millinery and dress shop, and importer Henry Weiner. Some time later Beach and Geils, an Evanston candy firm, signed a 10-year lease, as did Samuel Lee, who opened a little show-room called "Barn Dou" at 638 for the demonstration of Japanese landscaping. The south shop was divided in two and the corner store rented to florist James S. Rhodes.

On the eve of the move a group of members drew up a petition to change the name of the club. There had been agitation on this subject for years, ever since it was clear that, in their haste to reach the dining room, most ladies were bypassing the swimming pool and the gym without a thought. Now a local magazine reported that "the smart aleck young of the best families were laughing openly at the name of mother's club." A visiting lecturer had given a toast: "To the training table diet of the Woman's Athletic Club – coconut cake!" Those who pushed for a change pointed out that fewer women than ever were engaging in strenuous activity. To the older members that was simply irrelevant. The board agreed to take a poll. To the delight of the old guard, 225 voted for a change and 434 opposed it. The Woman's Athletic Club it remained.

On February 22, 1929 a farewell meeting was held in the rooms at the Harvester. Suddenly there was a tearful moment of regret. People looked around and realized how enchanting the old quarters were, not elaborate but full of sunshine and very friendly. An impromptu auction of chairs, pillows, carpets, and curtains brought the rather nice sum of $2,128.10. After the party some remaining pieces were marked for casual use in the new clubhouse and the rest were quickly sent for sale at Barker and Seaverns on Wabash, but this nostalgic mood lingered a few months more.

At last, however, on the afternoon of April 25, 1929, the doors of the new club-house were opened for a glorious housewarming. Chauffeurs circled the block as throngs of women and their husbands crowded in to see the new quarters for the first time. Mr. and Mrs. Scott Durand, just home from Europe, were the first ones through the door. Inside there was music, soft lighting, and flowers everywhere – calla lilies in tall silver vases and great baskets of American Beauty roses. Rather than lining up in the lounge and shaking hands for hours, the directors stationed

MISS HELEN
DRAKE

MISS HELEN DRAKE LOVED TO TELL
the story of the chandeliers in the second floor gallery
and card room. They were made from two old gas
chandeliers which once hung in the John B. Drake
home at 2114 Calumet Avenue. In the early
Twenties this house was rented to a fraternity. A short
time later Miss Drake received a frantic call from
the headmaster to pick up the fixtures at once. "I am
afraid the boys will break them," he said. The
chandeliers were hastily dismantled and packed in ten
large wooden crates. They were moved first to
a warehouse, then to a lighting store where they were
nearly auctioned off in a fire sale, and finally to
the basement of the Drake Hotel, where they lay in
storage for many months.

When plans were announced for the new clubhouse,
Miss Drake offered the chandeliers in memory of
her mother, who had joined the WAC in 1901. Marian
Gheen was enchanted with their antique blue lights
and had the crystal pendants and cut-glass globes
reassembled to suit the style and scale of the
second floor rooms. "It has been a great joy to me,"
Miss Drake wrote in 1932, "to walk beneath them
and think of the many happy family occasions which
they lighted in our dear old home."

themselves at vantage points throughout the building while their daughters and nieces poured the tea. Something innocuous called "Prohibition Punch" was also served from Mrs. Brower's massive Danish silver bowl, and three long pastry tables were set with Mrs. Allan M. Clements' Capodimonte figurines and candelabra. Elizabeth, the longtime head waitress, greeted people at the door of the main dining room in a new modern gown of black crepe.

The guests wandered around every floor of the building, bubbling with praise. Some thought the airy, light, and graceful Adam living room was the finest single piece of decorating. Others decided the little nooks for private entertaining were the true high point. The small and whimsical Mirror Room, with its silver gauze curtains and ebony table, was considered "way out" and made an enormous hit. One of the husbands peddled a mile on the electric bicycle in the gym. The press pronounced the clubhouse a triumph on every count. It seemed, in fact, to satisfy everyone, though true to all such projects, a few could not resist a little needling. One member who identified herself as "a bit of an interior decorator herself" told a reporter the wallpaper in the foyer was quite distasteful, and another complained about the Diana statue in the entrance, which did not entirely fit into its rounded niche. "It is against all the rules of interior decorating for a hand to go out of the picture. Maybe later we can put something really fine in that space."

A tour of the premises in 1929, briefly seen, looked something like this. Coming through the square foyer, a visitor entered a small waiting room. Windows with pierced mahogany cornices opened onto the street. There was a small cabinet near the window with an antique writing box and a book where guests were asked to register. A board near the main elevator listed the entire membership, and when a member was in the club a small gold pin was placed by her name, to help locate her if she received telephone calls, telegrams, or packages from nearby stores.

THE SECOND-FLOOR POWDER ROOM featured silver wallpaper and three tall trompe l'oeil mirrors painted with red draperies.

MIRRORED WALLS in the modernistic
dining room were painted in shades
of gray and jade green.

THE PILLEMENT ROOM was
originally used as a reception area.
The fanciful pictorial decorations
were painted by artist Constant Alex.

WALL PANELS in the main dining
room were decorated by Carl Hollem
in the manner of Pergolesi.

Upstairs on the second floor, one stepped into a gallery papered in a jade green 18th century pattern. The spacious lounge was done in the Georgian manner, with much linen, velvet, and damask upholstery and satinwood tables in the manner of Angelica Kaufmann. (These were made by Cooper and Williams in New York.) Mrs. Raymond C. Dudley, who had recently moved from a large house to a new apartment on Lake Shore Drive, had given the club a Steinway piano, which stood in the corner, draped with black brocade. Mrs. William F. Petersen said, "I think the most extravagant thing we did there was that double sofa which faced in four directions." A little card room just off the gallery featured swags of ivory satin at the window, English hawking prints on the wall, and little nutwood chairs and tables. In the pine-paneled library hung the club's most significant art purchase – a Peter Lely portrait of a court lady which cost $1,800 and was paid for by Mrs. Hudson, the Decorating Committee Chairman. Elsewhere on the floor was a ladies dressing room fitted up with tall *trompe l'oeil* painted mirrors and kidney-shaped dressing tables of Miss Gheen's own design. Along a narrow hall just to the east was the men's washroom and a small men's lounge with leather-covered seats.

The main dining room on the third floor was painted in Miss Gheen's favorite shade of apricot, with gold accents in the moldings and *bois de rose* brocade draperies. A small reception area to the side was marked by the fanciful chinoiserie style of the 18th-century artist Jean Pillemont. In contrast, the fourth-floor dining rooms were intended to express a fresh modern spirit. The popular small dining room featured silvered woodwork, a leopard carpet, and sparkling mirrored walls depicting the splash of fountains and the modern Diana swimming and sailing. Miss Gheen was forced by budget constraints to leave the larger private dining room to the south half finished. Handsome octagonal sconces with frosted glass panels and black glass window rods were the start of something smart. The rest was a mishmash of leftovers and members' hand-me-downs. Mrs. Petersen remembered the room in its first state. "That was the world's ugliest room. The carpets were great big purple flowers, green in between, then yellow. Miss Gheen couldn't have done that. They put all the furniture from the dining room on Harrison in there. Some of it was marbleized. It was terrible." Just to the west of this ungainly space were two offices, one for the manager and the other for the use of the board members.

The fifth floor was the Personal Service space. It was fitted out with rooms for massage, manicures, and hairdressing, where members had their tresses washed in beautiful oyster-shell shampoo bowls. There was a small lunchroom and a shop full of powders and creams. Though the club had originally intended to provide rooms for permanent guests, in the end they did not have the space or the funds for a 24-hour operation. Instead they installed four bedrooms with baths on the south side of this floor. They were meant for the use of suburban members who wanted a place to dress before dinner in town or young ladies who needed a private spot to adjust fancy gowns before debutante parties in the ballroom. (Garbled notes in the club's records suggest that, for a short time after the club opened, these rooms were somehow "misused" during certain young peoples' parties. Whatever that meant, for a brief period the rooms were kept locked, with keys available only from the manager or the board.)

There was a Bath Department on the sixth floor and a gymnasium furnished with exercise equipment. The rest of this floor was a sort of prelude to the ballroom upstairs — a large checkroom for coats, a men's smoking den, refreshment booths, and washrooms for both men and women which wrapped around the southeast corner of the building. A curving staircase led up to the spectacular two-story ballroom, with its ebony floor, silver pillars, and narrow painted balcony. A set of exquisite chandeliers from Paris, "frozen fountains" dripping with crystal, dominated the decor. Adjoining the ballroom in the northeast corner was a red, blue, and black punch room. Along the south side of the floor was an informal solarium with deep-cushioned sofas, tropical plants, and magnificent views.

Equally dazzling was the sea-green natatorium in the basement. Members walked through black carved gates into a room with dark terrazzo floors, walls lined with pink and black tiles, and a vaulted ceiling over the swimming pool. Philip Maher was particularly proud of the magnificent brass and copper light fixtures which added to a chic streamlined spirit, and Constant Alex, the same artist who decorated the Pillemont Room, painted a brilliant scenic mural that went all the way around the room. A dozen black Pompeian arm chairs were placed around the sides, and skylights along the eastern wall brought sunshine and daylight into this windowless space. Adjoining the pool were locker rooms, showers, and 19 small dressing

THE CRYSTAL CHANDELIERS and
sconces in the ballroom were one of two
sets made in France. They were purchased
through Au Paradis, a smart little Rush
Street shop owned by Mrs. Howard Linn
(above), who stocked it with unusual
and artistic furnishings from abroad.

A SELF-PORTRAIT OF NICHOLAS REMISOFF,
the Russian émigré who painted the original
plaster balcony in the ballroom. He was famous
for his fantastic, vividly colored murals. He
also designed stage sets and costumes for dancers
from Anna Pavlova to Ruth Page.

THE RESTFUL SOLARIUM along the southern end of the seventh floor. It featured a dramatic vaulted ceiling and sumptuous upholstery. Note the odd little table near front center — one of a set of colorfully painted drums, refashioned to hold smoking accessories.

THE SPECTACULAR Art Deco
natatorium.

**THE SUNNY SIXTH-FLOOR BALL-
ROOM** was a gift from the George W.
Dixon family in memory of Marion
Martin Dixon, the club's late president.

THE LADIES PARLOR on the sixth
floor featured a gold ceiling and
modern striped wallpaper. Many years
later it was remodeled as the club's
accounting office.

rooms fitted up with black and silver benches and vanity boxes filled with face powder, cold cream, and soaps. There was a hair drying room in the northeast corner and the little "Rooster Cafe" where swimmers could order a bit of lunch.

When all the figures were in, the building and furnishings of all kinds came to a total of $1,204,727.95. Most of the 90 employees from the old clubhouse stayed on and another 35 were hired, increasing the payroll from about $86,000 to something over $120,500. Though the club was able to pay all its bills and its credit standing was high, 15 extra Life Memberships were sold, bringing in another $75,000 to cushion the budget.

The early days in the new clubhouse were gloriously optimistic. During the first full month of operation 6,628 meals were served. The kitchen turned out mountains of lobster salad, broiled squab, and chicken croquettes. Tables had to be moved to relieve congestion in the dining room, and more china was ordered to accommodate all the private luncheons and teas. The new ballroom was sold out for the following winter's debutante balls. There were members-only programs again, and people ate and drank past midnight at evening social affairs. All around it was a season of great expectations. The club was poised for a brilliant future.

GOVERNOR FRANK O. LOWDEN and his wife (née Florence Pullman) with their daughters Florence (rear left) and Harriet. All three ladies were active WAC members. As treasurer, young Florence (Mrs. C. Phillip Miller) watched over the club's Depression finances. "Hattie" (Mrs. Albert F. Madlener, Jr.) gave her first piano recital in the ballroom and later served as president 1945–46.

6

Down time:
pulling through the depression

THE STOCK MARKET CRASH of October 1929 sparked financial chaos and widespread desperation, but at the club's annual meeting a few months later everything was serene. The previous year had brought a record-breaking profit of $156,000. Ladies were still coming every day in droves, having their hair dressed, booking private luncheons for 60 and 70 guests, staying for tea. "There is no reason for any anxiety or apprehension," Mrs. Pelouze assured the Corporation. The House Committee ordered more chafing dishes and another two barrels of glassware.

During the year 1930 there was a bit of worry about some members, with surprisingly prominent names, who were letting their accounts drift unpaid. The flower shop fell behind on its rent. On a prudent note it was decided to hold off buying new WAC swimsuits and not to renew every magazine subscription, but the mood remained optimistic and the club even took in 60 new members, with over 100 names still on the waiting list.

By the following year, however, it was fully evident that the country was in the midst of a calamitous depression. The WAC's membership, which by then was composed largely of second- and third-generation descendants of Chicago's founding families, was hit hard along with everyone else. For many it was no longer possible to belong to every or even any club in town. From a high of 1,770 the membership count began a precipitous slide across all categories. At the board meeting in September 1931 it was noted with concern that it was the first meeting in many years when no application for membership was presented. Instead, resignations were piling in, eight or nine at a clip, then escalating to twenty, thirty, and forty or more a month. Sixty-eight members resigned during June 1932. Most of the women on that long waiting list did not accept election after all, and eventually the list disappeared completely. A Life Membership was sold back to the club for the disappointing price of $1,000, and the next woman requesting same was offered only $500. Another member asked that all the silver she had presented to the club be returned to her.

A DAFFY 1929 CARTOON unveiling
the pleasures of the new clubhouse.

Mrs. Raymond C. Dudley, a charming and brilliant woman whose attachment to the WAC dated from girlhood days under the watchful eye of Mrs. Lyon, was elected president in 1931. She worked hard to stem the club's losses. Mrs. William F. Petersen, who had recently come on the board, remembered Lillian Dudley well and those difficult years in the depths of the Depression.

"We had meetings in that little corner room off the ballroom," she recalled. "It was very bright but bitter cold. But we did not want anyone to hear what we were doing. We took the members who wanted to resign and called on every single one. Mrs. Dudley went to their homes and asked them, please, couldn't they remain. I called on people I would hardly dare call on now. But when you're young, you'll do anything. We lost some of the ones who were on the Children's Memorial board, for instance, because we were charging them for the use of rooms for their meetings and they could get space for free at the Casino. Luncheon here was too expensive. They wanted it for $1.50."

Lillian Dudley and Alma Petersen invented various accommodations to retain members who could possibly afford it and even attract new recruits. Resident initiation fees were deferred, then reduced to $100, and even omitted for a time. Resigning members were carried free for up to three months, giving them a chance to reconsider. In 1934 a new Junior Associate membership was created, limited to 100 young women, with annual dues of $50 and no initiation fee. For regular Juniors already on the rolls, dues were entirely eliminated for the "under 21" group and reduced to $20 a year for those between 21 and 30 years old. Honorary Memberships were offered to a handful of longtime members who in years past had made large donations to the club's treasury. These distinguished ladies accepted gratefully. Consular Memberships were revived. A new Academic Membership was created for the wives of the three Illinois university presidents (Chicago, Northwestern, and Illinois). The board even considered the idea of a Professional Membership but decided it wasn't workable. Though a large chunk of unpaid dues had to be written

MRS. WILLIAM F. PETERSEN, a granddaughter of pioneer brewer Conrad Seipp. She presided over the creation of the Chinese Silver Room.

THE DAUGHTERS OF MRS. STANLEY M. WILEY were presented at a tea dance at the WAC in 1930. "We wore matching dresses of bright emerald green," remembers Mrs. Robert A. Carr (above left), "and the Mirror Room just sparkled."

off and the WAC did lose about 25% of its total membership during the Thirties, the untiring efforts these women made to hold the club together and bring in a new generation of members besides paid off in the long run and must be counted as a great success.

The board members were also forced to shoulder much of the day-to-day administration during this decade. The efficacious Mrs. Draper had resigned in 1928 and unfortunately died of cancer a short time later. She was followed by a series of able managers, but none stayed more than a few years. One of them left after three months. During much of Alma Petersen's tenure as president there was no manager at all, and she spent the large part of every weekday at the club, arriving by nine o'clock in the morning to do all the ordering and write the checks. (During the Thirties the size of the board was expanded twice, from 15 members to 19 and then 21, and the date of the annual corporation meeting was moved from January to April.)

Many economies were introduced. In January 1932 all salaries were reduced 10% across the board. Goods were paid for with cash whenever a discount was available and club announcements mailed out on one-and-a-half-cent open cards to save postage. Service charges were discontinued in every department. Dining room prices were cut, with a new "Dollar Luncheon" at the top of the menu every day. The cost of a swim was reduced to a quarter, and lockers could be rented for $3.50 a year. During the Century of Progress Fair guest cards were handed out liberally, and there were now many regrets that the building design had not included a floor of overnight rooms, which could have brought in significant revenues. Dissatisfaction also developed with the ballroom's location on the seventh floor. The club was losing considerable party business to hotels and other clubs because the dance floor was not close to ground level. Mrs. Henry C. Woods recalled that "Nobody wanted to come here. All because the ballroom's upstairs and the boys liked to wander out, you see, and probably smoke. Nobody wanted to have to wait for the elevator. Young kids don't want to go up and down. So we really lost out on a lot of debut parties."

New Deal taxes and legislation also put new pressures on the budget. When the 3% sales tax became law in 1934, it was first decided the club should just absorb it, so fearful were they of losing business. Various new labor laws altered longstanding personnel arrangements. Staff now had to give an eight-hour day and overtime had to be paid for. The club was compelled to retain the firm of Winston, Shaw & Strong to resolve labor questions. Health care was another sticky issue. Since the years of the founding, when an employee fell sick, cash had been handed out from the Benevolent Fund. In some instances physician husbands of members performed operations gratis, and it was not unusual for an employee to stay two or three weeks in a hospital, courtesy of some WAC member who served on its board. Though the Benevolent Fund was still in existence in the Thirties, discussions were underway about purchasing "old age insurance," and in 1939 the staff was allowed to join a formal hospitalization plan.

Two large business problems hovered over the budget. Despite rosy income projections for the first-floor stores, it was a struggle from the start to collect the rents. Catering to a well-heeled clientele stung by worsening economic conditions, all the little shops gradually fell into arrears, and it wasn't easy to find suitable tenants to replace them. Leases originally signed for $500 and $600 a month were slashed to $450, then $300, then $225. Even so, a collection agency had to go after the payments, and its commissions ate up more of the profits.

High real estate taxes posed additional difficulties. When the WAC signed the ground lease in 1927, taxes on the property came to around $5,000 a year. Upon completion and occupancy of the clubhouse, a tax bill covering 1929 and 1930 was received for $62,000. The Finance Committee was stunned. The club joined a protest organization and withheld payment. In 1932, with the city nearly insolvent and property taxes bringing in about 85% of all its revenues, Mayor Cermak threatened to cut off city services (including water, garbage pick-up, sewer maintenance, and police protection) to owners who did not pay. The protest group countered that 40% of all property in the near north section of the city would be forfeit if exorbitant tax rates were not reduced.

MRS. HARRY B. CLOW, a Life Member, modeling a white satin evening gown and ermine wrap in the St. Luke's Fashion Show. For over sixty years the club's luncheon before the show was one of the biggest events on the WAC calendar.

The Woman's Athletic Club allowed itself to be used as a test case to settle this question in the courts, and the matter was proceeding to trial when Lillian Dudley called a special meeting of the board. In attendance was John Pratt of the Association of Real Estate Tax Payers, who made forcefully clear his opinion that all near north side owners must stand together, firm in refusal, and success would be theirs. Colonel Pelouze, who was also sitting in, concurred with that. Representing government interests, Mr. Sidney Gorham argued that with the city unable to pay its schoolteachers and firefighters, the club had to ask itself whether it was right to withhold its entire share of the tax. Perhaps the ladies would pay something, maybe 50% or 60%. That way, he said, they would "still be acting in the spirit of the Association yet not deserting the city."

After the gentlemen left the meeting, each board member expressed her opinion. It was the consensus of the women to pay some part of the bill, but the whole matter was left to the splendid judgment of Lillian Dudley. Shortly thereafter the club made a special gift of $5,000 to the city's Emergency Welfare Fund. Two months later, under Mrs. Dudley's leadership and as her last act in office, the club resigned from the Tax Payers Association and paid all of its taxes, for every preceding year, in full. Throughout the decade the club continued to seek refunds and adjustments but met all of its civic obligations on time.

The WAC membership overall responded to the general hardship in the city with generosity, contributing cash and many volunteer hours through programs organized by the Red Cross. The best intentions did not always reach their mark, however. Mrs. Petersen told this little story of the Depression. "This fancy head-waitress of ours," she recalled. "When we moved here, she had all the window tables marked right away. For people like Mrs. Armour and Mrs. Valentine. I couldn't get anywhere near there. They were all reserved and usually empty half the time. There was a closet off to the side, and she had a lock put on it. These women she took care of so well would bring down all their old clothes. They would give their old dresses to her and she was supposed to give them to the poor. But she locked them in the closet and then sold them in a very fine resale shop."

Despite endless financial struggles, the Thirties were remembered as a spirited era, when a stream of exciting speakers brought huge crowds into the club on Tuesdays mornings. The events themselves were like fashion shows. Half an hour ahead of time the ladies would start filing into the ballroom, dressed in smart tweeds and wool crepe, with long sable scarves, pearls, and fresh flowers pinned to their lapels. Everyone wore gloves and a hat. By the time the speaker walked to the podium, the room was a sea of bright turbans, smart little berets, velvet tams, straw boaters, toques, quills, and bright feathers. A few of the dowagers still wore hats with plumes. Every silver chair was usually taken, with latecomers hanging over the balcony rail upstairs.

MRS. HENRY C. BARTHOLOMAY, a frequent hostess at the club's morning programs. Gracious and well read, she brought many friends, both as speakers and as guests.

Sunlight streaming into the room, the audience would listen intently. (In those days the ballroom windows were clear, with a million-dollar view of the city.) Some ladies knitted and crocheted. Others sat with hands folded in their laps. Many of the programs lasted as long as one and a half to two hours. Afterwards the crowd would descend in elevator loads to the dining room. The lucky ones lunching with the speaker got to hear stories "off the record," many of which would then appear in print the following day. As part of the club's revival efforts, the Press Committee, which for years had kept the WAC *out* of the newspaper, was remade into the Publicity Committee which worked hard to get back *into* it. (The old "No Photographs" rule was rescinded too.)

The society editors had a field day because the programs were fresh, intelligent, and full of flair. Book reviews ranged from Nathaniel Hawthorne's works to *Life Begins at Forty*. The elegant Bostonian Edward Weeks, editor of the *Atlantic Monthly*, assured the ladies that the "shocker novel" would soon be out of vogue. Princess Te Ata, daughter of the last Chickasaw chief, wailed, chanted, and beat the tom-toms. A Southern chorus sang spirituals. Rudolph Ganz tried to interest the WAC ladies in modern music. After he finished playing one of his own compositions on the piano, one member said, "My dear, [it] gave me exactly the same reaction as I get scratching my nails along tin." Christopher Morley, a New York City raconteur, told the crowd of his wonderful discovery that when he submerged himself completely in a tub of hot water, he could hear conversations in the apartment downstairs. "I know you don't like to get your coiffeurs wet," he told them, "but my system is well worth trying some time."

MRS. GEORGE L. CRAGG (near right), a longtime "bridger" and the club's first and only Ping Pong Chairman. Her grandfather was a Chief Justice of the Illinois Supreme Court who rode the circuit in his younger days with Abraham Lincoln.

MRS. CHRISTOPHER J. ("MOGS") CHAMALES, a great all-around athlete and winner of the club's first squash trophy.

Political topics drew the biggest audience. They pondered such subjects as "Labor's Fight for Power" and the "Maladjustment of Wealth." This latter speech contained the warning that President Roosevelt's New Deal was saving the members of the Woman's Athletic Club from something much worse. Better get used to the idea that their current fur coats might be their last, the speaker told them. Dr. T. Z. Koo played the flute and described a new unified China, and another speaker talked about the rising tide of Japanese nationalism. Maybe the most prescient talk was that of Colonel R. Stewart-Roddie, a young Scot who warned of a bombastic European politician named Hitler. To convey the appeal of the new Nazi party for the youth of Germany, Stewart-Roddie gave a speech in the manner of Hitler and played a stirring Nazi song on the piano. It was marching music, he told them, a battle march.

By the late 1930s morning programs and the lunches after had become the heart of the club's existence. Some husbands worried that the women were succumbing to "lecturitis." Every so often a firm resolution would be made to "go athletic again." In 1935, for the first time in the history of the club, the pool was opened at night, and husbands and beaux, who had never been allowed near it before, were invited to swim. Mrs. Avery Brundage brought in the beautiful Olympic champion Eleanor Holm one evening to give an after-supper diving exhibition. The men apparently showed "more than mild enthusiasm." The pool enjoyed something of a renaissance after that, and Miss Schendel, who had taken charge of the natatorium, organized children's relay races and water ballet with great success. She staged a lovely water pageant in March 1939.

There were tap dancing lessons, ping-pong tournaments, and classes in corrective posture taught by Miss Helen Rockwell of the Wellesley College Department of Hygiene. The big new attraction of the Thirties was the Squash Court. During the club's first several years in the building the eighth floor attic had been used as a laundry, with a large unfinished space where the housemen repaired furniture and stored old tables and chairs. Mrs. Stanley Zaring, daughter of the club's late president Mrs. Dixon, had the idea of taking out the laundry and installing squash and badminton courts, with a pleasant lounge to the side. Casting about for ways to bring young people into the club more often, the board decided the $2,000 project was worth a try. Upon completion of the courts in December 1935 the new Junior Committee gave a buffet supper followed by five thrilling exhibition matches. The headline in next day's society column: "Woman's Athletic Club Holds Athletic Event At Last."

John Danielson, a pro from the Chicago Athletic Club, was hired to teach squash racquets two days a week, and he set up a series of ambitious invitational tournaments with eastern women's teams, local men's teams, and players at the Winter Club in Lake Forest. Young women like Mrs. Zaring, Mrs. Franklin G. Clement, Mrs. William B. Freer, Mrs. Arthur M. Wirtz, Mrs. Horace W. Armstrong, and Mrs. T. Lloyd Kelly were playing three or four times a week. Mrs. Christopher J. Chamales received a silver trophy after she won the club's first championship match.

In 1936 the badminton court was enlarged. By way of celebration a door was built leading out onto the roof, and the badminton players and their rivals from Winnetka, Evanston, and Barrington could step up a little tulip-carved stairway and outside for summertime "garden parties."

The club charged 35 cents for the use of either court, and a book of tickets included four 15-minute rub-downs as well. This brought the players down to the sixth floor Bath Department, where many members, athletes or not, enjoyed an exquisitely relaxing ritual. Mrs. Huntington Eldridge remembered, "Mother and I came in for years. You'd take a hot bath first. Then this wonderful old Swedish masseuse – oh, she was so marvelous – would rub you all down with a mat, and you'd get in a hot box like a sauna." Others recall this steam cabinet too, and a strong hose "which the masseuse would run up and down your back." In 1938 the club began to offer a "face-lifting mask" from the Hungarian Cosmetic Company and a collection of rare Garden Fragrance perfumes, both of which made a perfect finish to this pleasant routine. It's not surprising that a news article of the Thirties identified the club as the place where "where Chicago's most prominent women go to get cleaned up."

Without a doubt the "sport" that really succeeded at the club was the game of bridge. In January 1934, at the suggestion of Helen Pelouze, the board announced a series of duplicate contract bridge games to be held on Tuesday mornings under the direction of an expert, Mrs. Richard F. Peyton. Duplicate play began promptly at 11 o'clock, prizes were awarded, and members could invite one guest. It was another experiment to bring people in, and the special luncheon served afterward cost just a dollar. Some board members felt the idea would flop because the game was too difficult and nerve-wracking, and in the beginning it was only the club's little band of card intelligentsia who did attend. The game caught on though, and Mrs. Peyton's contract was renewed for several seasons. She added a brief talk and demonstration hands, and beginners began flocking to the sessions as well. Mrs. Peyton was succeeded in this job by Maxine Miner, who taught bridge at the club for a dozen years till she moved to Peoria in 1948.

In January 1936 the bridgers, sixty or seventy strong by now, took a long hard look at the gymnasium. The board made a fateful decision. The rowing machine was taken away, the athletic horse given to a school, and the gymnasium was redecorated as the lovely and official "card room."

On the evening of April 20, 1938 the first World Bridge Olympic was held at the club, beginning at one minute past eight o'clock. At this international event 16 prearranged hands were played in competition with players all over the world, who began bidding at precisely the same time. The WAC held a dinner beforehand, most of the players brought their husbands, and the event was such a success it was repeated for several years after, with Mrs. Pelouze winning many of the little blue and silver buttons awarded to those who bid and played their hands correctly.

Ordinary after-dinner bridge games had been introduced well before the "Olympics," but evening events in general did not succeed until the club had got past a big bombshell of the Thirties. With few exceptions, from the days of Mrs. Lyon forward, the club had never served alcohol, even at dinners and dances, with predictable results. Mrs. Henry C. Woods remembered, "Men didn't want to come in the evening if they didn't serve liquor. Then we had all those years of Prohibition. In the men's clubs they had it in their lockers, but here they didn't."

The repeal of the 18th Amendment brought this question to a burning head. A coterie of ardent Prohibitionists, none more staunch than Mrs. Charles Ward Seabury, was deeply opposed to any change in policy. Many others, however, pointed to the club's impoverished bottom line. A poll taken by the board revealed that "30% of members take a cocktail before dinner or luncheon." On December 19, 1933, the board voted that all kinds of beverages could be served in the club. Years later Mrs. C. Phillip Miller, who was club treasurer at the time of the policy change, recalled with dry amusement, "The finances improved right away."

The new rules did cause something of a ripple in Chicago society circles. "Dear me," one reporter exclaimed, "imagine the conservative Woman's Athletic Club putting in a bar and serving cocktails in the lounge! And combing the city for the best bartender and cocktail mixer. I remember when it was a major offense for a lady to light a cigarette in the dining room."

A second-floor service pantry was equipped to serve drinks, and Mrs. Henry Bartholomay loaned the club a portable bar. Feeling that they "ought not to go into

PORTRAIT OF

MRS. PHILIP D. ARMOUR

THIS POSTHUMOUS PORTRAIT of Mrs. Philip D. Armour was commissioned in 1939 by her two daughters-in-law, Mrs. J. Ogden Armour and Mrs. Patrick A. Valentine. It was painted by Charles Sneed Williams, an Indiana artist who took his training in London and Edinburgh and became so Anglicized Mrs. Valentine later remembered him as an Englishman. Over the course of his career he painted many international society figures and aristocrats including the Duchess de la Rochefoucauld and Princess Marie Louise, the granddaughter of Queen Victoria. This oil portrait showing Mrs. Armour in the pearls she always wore double-looped about her neck was probably based on an old photograph. It was sent directly to the club from Williams' studio in the Fine Arts Building and hung in the drawing room and then the library for many years before it was moved to its present location.

it too heavily at first," the board ordered a supply of eight-ounce glasses (instead of the usual ten or twelve-ounce tumblers). Martinis, Whiskey Sours, and Old-Fashioneds were the big favorites, and even after the club hired John Koch, its first bartender, some of the members liked to go back to the pantry to mix their own. A husband of one of the members who was thought to be a real connoisseur bought the club's first cellar, and wine lists soon appeared on the dining room tables.

Drinks before dinner proved so popular that the following year the officers considered moving the accounting office, which at that time was located in a space just to the west of the second-floor powder room, up to the sixth-floor gymasium and converting the office space into a cocktail lounge. The idea proved too expensive (and besides, the bridgers wanted the gym), so instead a small men's lounge down the hall from the telephones was made into a bar to more easily accommodate a large number of patrons in the drawing room.

By early 1937 the club was doing well enough to put some money into the stock market, order new gold-trimmed china, and think about finishing off the large fourth floor dining room. Marian Gheen was not around to carry out her original scheme for the room. She died in 1932. So the Decorating Committee had to come up with a plan. Alma Petersen was president at the time.

"Once I invited Rue Shaw over," Mrs. Petersen said. "She was later head of the Arts Club. I said, 'What would you do with this room?' She said, 'I would have to throw it out.' Well, I do not remember who handled it, but we had the room

MRS. FRANKLIN G. CLEMENT
(far left) pouring tea at the club's fortieth anniversary party. The table was set in the Victorian style with satin bows, silk-shaded candles, and a large silver bowl of pink roses.

MRS. BRUCE MACLEISH, president 1939–40, served on the board of directors for almost 40 years.

measured and sent the figures to China. In China they had this silver paper, and they put the designs on it according to where the windows were and so on. Then the [Sino Japanese] war started and we couldn't get it. All of a sudden in the middle of the war a Japanese ship picked up our paper and brought it over. They must have wanted that money very much. So then we put that paper in. It was very expensive, all of it. I paid for the screens. I wanted them to match the wallpaper, so we could use that room as part dining room and part sitting room." Two years later the necessary tables and chairs were purchased, and for a long time after this space was referred to as the "Chinese Silver Room."

Plans were also made to redecorate the ballroom. The architect David Adler was asked for a proposal, and he suggested remaking it into an elegant library. His reputation was enormous, and several ladies were inclined to let him carry out his ideas carte blanche, but the estimate was high — about $25,000, plus his 25% fee. By now Mrs. Bruce MacLeish, the club's longtime decorating chairman, was in the president's chair. Her husband was a vice president of Carson Pirie Scott & Co. In the end the committee simply selected new paint colors and fabrics themselves. The old plaster balcony rail, by this time faded and crumbling, was replaced by new ironwork from Carson's, handwrought right here in Chicago.

At the club's 40th anniversary celebration on December 13, 1938, there was a note of triumphant survival in the air. The drawing room was set for a gracious Victorian tea, and a long table was covered with an old lace cloth with pink satin bows hung at each corner. Atop the silver candelabra were pink candle shades dripping with bugle glass fringe. Old-fashioned chicken sandwiches and candied rose leaves were passed on trays, and punch was served from a mammoth silver bowl. It was a sentimental hour. Grandmothers brought daughters and granddaughters and reminisced about the first clubhouse. The officers, swathed in orchids, reminded reporters that earlier in the year they had held another tea — their first-ever New Members Tea — at which 135 new recruits were welcomed into the fold. The club had come through the worst of the Depression intact.

A few months later another party was held at the club, a glorious private reception for the Danish Crown Prince Frederik and Princess Ingrid. The royal couple was dashing — he in white tie and tails, she in taffeta and diamonds. In attendance were many admirals and generals in full dress uniform, chests glittering with medals and decorations. Ladies floated about in bouffant tulle, black lace, and purple satin. The Prince and Princess stayed late to shake hands and talk cordially with every last guest, impressing all those present (who had worried about whether and how to curtsy) with their democratic friendliness. The atmosphere was enchanting, with a feeling that good times had finally returned. Few in the room that evening could have foreseen the events of the following spring, when Hitler would launch a lightning invasion of Denmark and Norway, easily overrunning those ancient monarchies, setting Europe and the world on the path to war.

DURING WARTIME a Red Cross flag was flown alongside the American flag on the club's rooftop in honor of the WAC's hard-working Victory Unit.

7
the WAC goes to War

ABOUT 300 CHEERFUL LADIES turned out for the season's first program in the fall of 1940. They were eager to see the redecorated ballroom, which was thrown open that morning for inspection after a summer of renovation. The room had turned out quite well, and the fresh silk upholstery, mirrored windows, and marbleized pillars (now black, to match the new ironwork) were much admired. The audience was also eager to hear Pierre van Paassen, a Flemish reporter who had been one of the first to interview Mussolini and Hitler. The ladies were anticipating van Paassen's famous charm and a few off-the-record stories. Instead he gave them a disturbing hour and a half. Mussolini and Hitler were just limbering up, he said. He had seen maps in Munich dividing the United States in two, half to Germany and half to Japan, with Chicago on the dividing line. He predicted the Italians might take the Suez by Christmas. "If Britain falls," he told them, "we will have to face the Axis alone." There was much rustling of skirts and shifting of handbags during his talk, and by the time the crowd filed out of the room they were agitated and angry with him. At lunch some naive soul suggested that perhaps van Paassen's new book should be available for sale at the club. "Absolutely not!" she was told.

There was more bad news a few weeks later when Martin Dies, Chairman of the House Un-American Activities Committee, arrived. He gave an inflammatory speech decrying the Fifth Column — Germans at work in Los Angeles aircraft factories and thousands of black-shirted Fascists in New Jersey who "all take Uncle Sam for an old goof." The chief menace was the danger from within. "Now I'll ask you a question!" he thundered at the members of the WAC. "What are *you* going to do about it?"

As the war spread and the reports became more bleak, many foreign correspondents, ambassadors, and refugees were added to the club's speaking calendar. In those pre-television days, when lecture appearances presented a rare opportunity to see such people in person, the crowd grew larger for every program. Reservations were often closed a day or two after announcement cards went into the mail. The club could only accommodate about 350 diners. More people would arrive anyway, as many as double that number, just to hear the talk. All chairs in the ballroom were usually taken a full hour before a program started, and latecomers were sent to the solarium or out to the hall. Even standing room was at a premium. After-dinner lectures were also packed. Some of the city's most eminent citizens, too anxious to wait for an elevator, would be seen pushing and shoving up the stairs to grab seats in the ballroom. One society reporter wrote that attending a dinner program at the club was now like going to a football game. After one chaotic gathering a ruling was issued that no one could sit on the up or down stairways while an event was in session.

Maybe the most emotionally fraught evening in the club's history was the night of the Clifton Utley–Sterling Morton debate on "America's Big Issue." Both men were husbands of WAC members. Their duel was held on January 9, 1941, and described in next day's paper as "a tense affray in which one needed life insurance." England had just been pummeled the day before with another air attack, and during dinner before the program the first call for mobilization of American manpower went out over the radio. An hour later a reported 800 men and women, dressed to the gills, crushed onto the seventh floor, where Mrs. Bruce MacLeish, president, delivered a deliberately bland introduction. Clifton Utley was at that time director of the Chicago Council on Foreign Relations. Speaking for the William Allen White Committee, he painstakingly made the case for all-out aid to Britain. He received polite applause. Sterling Morton then took the microphone on behalf of the America First Committee, which favored nonintervention. He said the possibility of a German invasion of the United States was "hooey." In a short while their prepared remarks were tossed aside, and accusations about "a shooting war" and "fighting our own fight" started flying. Hecklers shouted questions from the floor. Mrs. Utley tried to remain composed even when her husband was hissed from the back row. Someone thought he heard Morton call Utley's group the "America Last Committee." (This was later denied.) Mrs. MacLeish did her best to look soothing throughout. It was agreed afterward that though no verdict had been reached and no minds were changed, the issues had been clearly and fairly argued.

However members may have differed about America's entry into the war, after Pearl Harbor the club mounted a united defense effort. Right away they put on "Navy Night" to honor the nation's naval forces and inform the membership of the Navy's relative strength and state of preparedness. Ten-week courses in first aid, nutrition, home nursing, and life saving were given in the ballroom. A Red Cross Victory Unit was organized, chaired first by Mrs. Earle J. Zimmerman (and after she left the city to join her husband and son at Fort Warren, by Mrs. Fremont A. Chandler). Lounge chairs and bridge tables were taken out of the solarium, which was made over into a prim businesslike workroom with ironing boards, sewing machines, long tables covered with green oil cloth, and utilitarian black chairs.

The club was able to secure only one direct-current iron, which was guarded like a precious jewel.

The workroom was open to members and friends on Mondays, Wednesdays, and Fridays from 9:30 A.M. to 4:00 P.M. About 40 or 50 women came in on an average day. They wore white pinafores and headdresses and worked all day with just a half hour off for a 60-cent lunch of coffee and sandwiches. Making surgical dressings was meticulous work, the gauzes having to be folded on a hairline. The ladies knitted sweaters, kneebands, socks, and afghans for soldiers, nurses, and orphans. Since there was a shortage of yarn, much of it was donated by the members themselves. They also sewed many pairs of pajamas, army kit bags, rompers, snowsuits, and even tailored tweed coats. Ingenious garments were created from the pieces of wool saved by the ban on men's trouser cuffs. Mrs. William S. Jenks held the Chicago record for making buttonholes (over 7,000). Needles clicking, sewing machines whirring, the atmosphere was grim and determined. After D-Day, with the "wounded in action" lists mounting, an emergency appeal was sent to all members to come in and roll bandages: "We need the help of everyone NOW."

The Victory Unit was in operation from January 1942 through December 1945. During those four years volunteers gave 110,551 hours of service. They made a total of 92,608 surgical dressings, 8,814 sewn garments, and 2,320 knitted items. At least 63 members received 500-hour certificates from the Red Cross. Many earned 1,000-hour commendations, and a few sewed 3,000-hour insignias onto their uniforms. One of these last was Mrs. Reimund Baumann, wife of the Danish consul, whose son

97

GUESTS AT THE CLUB were impressed by the number of members in uniform. Miss Sue di Lorenzi (right) was Chairman of the Lounge for Women Officers at the Bismarck Hotel. (She later donated the bishop's chair used every Christmas by WAC Santas.)

MEMBERS OF THE CLUB'S VICTORY UNIT at work in 1944. Headdresses were required when making surgical dressings.

Harald was missing in action for a good part of the war. Mrs. Baumann seldom missed a day of work with the Unit. Watching newsreels one night at the movies, she and her husband spotted Harald among a group of German war prisoners. With the aid of the filmstrip they were able to locate their son and send food. In the fall of 1945 a famous photograph showing the entrance of the first American division into Paris was made into a new 3-cent stamp. The day it was issued Mrs. Baumann brought the stamp to the club and showed it to everyone who came in. With the use of a magnifying glass, Harald's face could be singled out in the victorious crowd. For many of the workroom regulars it was one of the proudest moments of the war.

Remembering the club's felicitous dinners for servicemen during the First World War, it was decided to put on a series of supper dances for the midshipmen at Abbott Hall. These events were organized by Elizabeth MacLeish's daughter, Mrs. John Dern, whose late father-in-law had been Secretary of War in FDR's 1933 cabinet. The first such affair was held in January 1942, when 125 young ensigns arrived to party with a like number of pretty girls rounded up from all over the Gold Coast and North Shore. At the piano, Mrs. Robert Biggert led a community sing to break the ice. After the fellows found their partners by a numbered-ticket scheme, the couples paired off and went in to a buffet table groaning with hams, salads, cheeses, and warm apple pies, a heavenly feast for stomachs used to a steady diet of Navy rations. Swing music for dancing was provided by Fletcher Butler's orchestra, a great favorite with the young crowd. The men in uniform had sent word ahead that they didn't want a long stag line, and in fact, all the cutting in was done by extra females so that no midshipmen was ever left without a partner. Mrs. Otto Madlener demonstrated her exotic version of the rhumba and led a snaky conga line around the ballroom. Beer and cocktails were served, which revived a Prohibition storm of protest from the club's teetotalers. Letters of outrage were read at the next board meeting. However, since the boys were marched right back to the campus at the end of the evening and the girls saw themselves home, the parties were continued and warmly appreciated as a great boost to morale on the home front.

Throughout the war the club invested substantially in U.S. Defense Bonds, but its money troubles were back. With many members now stationed elsewhere several months of the year, the board (fearing another wave of resignations) had to be flexible about granting Non-Resident status and carrying back-due accounts. Some of the staff left to serve in the armed forces also, and it was a job to retain good employees and hire suitable new ones. Salaries were raised again and again, sometimes with the caveat that they might have to come down after the war. (They never did.)

Food and materials were in short supply. Mrs. Edward McDermott remembered, "We were frugal. You got along with less. You didn't use the towels. You patched things up. You were careful with everything." Coffee and sugar were rationed. Mrs. James K. Logsdon recalled that saccharin tablets were placed in sugar

bowls in the dining room. The kitchen cut back on coconut cake, making only one cake on every other day, and many of those went out to army and navy posts. (Any dessert, however, would be made to order if a member brought in her own sugar.) Linen placemats were replaced by paper doilies. A service charge of ten cents was added to every drink. In 1943, for the first time in the club's history, cold chicken salad was the entree luncheon of the day. As time went on members got used to a main course of Baked Cheese Sandwich or Creamed Eggs on Toast Points. A poster went up in the pantry: "Food is War Material. Don't Spoil It."

The annual yearbook was not reprinted, and the club's comprehensive monthly calendar was scotched for a simple list of outstanding events, mailed out with the bills. The chandeliers in the ballroom were dimmed to use less power, and the club closed earlier in the evening to save on fuel. By the end of November 1942 there was not enough oil to heat the pool, so it was closed for five months and through the following winter as well.

An interesting budget note from those days was the insurance policy the WAC took out for war damage. It protected the clubhouse against losses from bombing attacks, fires, explosions, military invasion, and enemy sabotage. (After a careful check the directors found that harm from riot and civil commotion was already covered in the club's fire insurance.) In conjunction with the terms of this special policy, which was carried through the club's agent W. A. Alexander, sand, water, and shovels were placed in appropriate spots throughout the building, in the event of a surprise air raid. This insurance policy was renewed once and remained in effect till after D-Day, when the course of the war turned firmly in the Allies' favor.

A parade of outstanding speakers brought the real sights and sounds of the war home to the membership. There was Sigrid Undset, the Norwegian novelist who had escaped to America via the Arctic Circle. The aeronautic designer Alexander P. De Seversky presented his plan for victory through air power. Dr. Reinhold Niebuhr discussed the religious implications of the conflict. Helen Kirkpatrick, stationed in London for the *Chicago Daily News*, recounted tales of the 50,000 women in Britain working the railroads, driving buses, and laboring in the docks. Ely Culbertson, the bridge expert, described his elaborate 11-zone plan for world peace. Sigrid Schultz, the former head of the *Chicago Tribune*'s Berlin bureau, gave intimate glimpses of many Nazi figures she had interviewed before the Anschluss. Her story of feeding snails to Herman Goering to the limit of her expense account brought down the house. (If he had any redeeming qualities, she added, they were nowhere in evidence.) The wife of General Mark Clark read her husband's letters home, in which he extolled the bravery and courage of his troops. Jay Allen described the months he spent in a concentration camp. "You meet the nicest people in Europe in jail," he told them.

All the great questions of the day were considered. "Is China a Worthy Ally?" "With DeGaulle and the Fighting French in Africa." "What About Japan?" "Russia Is No Riddle." The exiled Archduke Otto of Austria was mobbed. An Allied victory was imperative, he said, or "the next Pearl Harbor is Chicago." Otto was outdrawn only by Pierre Clemenceau, grandson of the great "Tiger of France," who had escaped to Africa in 1940 and was the first to drive a motor car from the Persian border to Kabul. Clemenceau drew so many reservations the club barred the program to all but members.

Men were coming into the club regularly now, certainly at night to hear these war reports, and increasingly for luncheon programs as well. In September 1939, after considering the matter carefully, the board had voted to offer admission cards to husbands, fathers, unmarried sons, and brothers of members, who could then use the lounge and dining room on their own. Now whenever some midday event was

THE PUNCH BOWL

THIS ART NOUVEAU PUNCH bowl and a matching ladle were presented to the club by the family of Mrs. Joseph O. Watkins. A longtime member, she lunched at the same table every day for years with her sister, Mrs. William C. Pullman. They were daughters of Billy Pinkerton, the famous detective, and it is likely this lovely piece of hammered silver probably came from the old Pinkerton family homestead on Ashland Boulevard.

thought to have a special appeal for men, potatoes would be added to the special luncheon. Portions would be larger and served with a rich dessert. Men were also coming to swim and play squash. In fact, the WAC organized a men's squash team which played matches for a time against the men of the University, Lake Shore Athletic, and Union League clubs.

Still, it was an awkward moment when William Stanton Picher wished to continue using his guest card after his mother's death. She was Mrs. Oliver Sheppard Picher, a Life Member who had joined around 1915. (Her late husband was president of the Eagle-Picher Lead Company.) In April 1940 Mr. Picher and his partner Joseph Faulkner, both of them just graduated from the University of Chicago, had leased the club's northernmost shop at 638 North and opened the Main Street Book Store. It was a smart little shop, stocked with serious American literature plus all the books of the moment, and it quickly developed a reputation among Chicago's carriage trade. Mrs. Picher died a year and half later. When the question was raised, the board decided that Mr. Picher was no longer eligible to come upstairs for lunch under his mother's dining room privileges. After his three-year lease expired Mr. Picher moved his books and metal cases to a larger space in the building next door. Down the years the Main Street Book Store (and later on, its novel art gallery) became something of a legend on Michigan Avenue and a bit of a loss for the club.

Few festivities as such were held during the war, but there was a concerted effort to maintain a close-to-normal calendar for young people. Mrs. Rawleigh Warner, Mrs. Telfer MacArthur, and Mrs. Nicholas Starrosselsky put on spring dances for sub-debs, festooning the ballroom with fresh forsythia and winding magnolias round all the pillars. There were lots of dance exhibitions, when the holiday college crowd was taken through the intricate steps of the Viennese waltz, the tango, and something newer called the jitterbug. One of the Navy glee clubs put on a show. Sometimes a party simply consisted of bridge and keno games in the lounge. To save on food, the menu was often limited to tea or punch and appetizers.

A delightful innovation of this period was the Children's Christmas Party. In December 1939 Miss Emily Goehst had the idea of renting some new "Walter Disney films" for a late-afternoon showing to youngsters 3 to 14 years old. The invitation brought an enormous response and grew into an annual event, of which Miss Goehst took splendid charge for a dozen years. There were many sorts of entertainments. One year she brought in trained animals, then a magician and a Punch and Judy show. There was a ventriloquist and a silly clown named Happy Hi Ho. Even when supplies were short she was able to secure at least a few dozen balloons, which were tied to sticks and propped in vases at the tables, like flower arrangements. There were always hats to put on and favors to take home after the hot chocolate, ice cream, and Santa Claus cookies were consumed. The party was described once as a Lilliputian riot, the wired-up offspring always outlasting their mothers and grandmas at the end of the day.

MRS. ARTHUR W. WAKELEY
took charge of first aid classes
for members. During her
presidency dining room and pool
privileges were extended
to officers of the WAVE, WAC,
and SPAR.

MISS EMILY GOEHST, creator of the annual children's Christmas party. She was a lively master of ceremonies and engaged novel entertainments for these three-generation affairs.

FROM 1944 THROUGH 1959 the club sponsored annual parties for wounded servicemen, for which it received several citations from the Veterans Administration. Most memorable was the 1950 jamboree in the Vaughan Hospital gymnasium, which featured a boxing match between Golden Glove fighters refereed by heavyweight champion Jack Dempsey. Pictured below are Mrs. Wilson J. Killough (second from left), perennial chairman of the veterans parties, with two patients and some other members of her committee.

FOR A DOZEN YEARS after the war the club made annual cash contributions to the Red Cross High Seas program. The money paid for gifts, which the members also helped to wrap, that were then mailed to American soldiers who would be on the high seas – or somewhere overseas – for Christmas.

All in all, the club came through the war sounder than ever, and among the reasons was the arrival in August 1942 of one of the strongest managers in its history, Miss Winifred Greely. She was then already well known to Chicago society, having managed the Cordon Club in the Fine Arts building during the Thirties. At the start of the war Miss Greely was operating a tearoom in the old Chase and Sanborn house on Cape Cod. Mrs. Bruce MacLeish found her there and talked her into coming back to Chicago. At that time the WAC had been without a real manager for about five years.

"Miss G." took charge with dispatch. Though she impressed some reporters as "an indolent Southern charmer type," she was an experienced businesswoman who combined grace and efficiency to superb effect. She arrived at the club every day at 6:00 A.M. and left some time after five in the evening. She knew the members by name and got around all eight floors quickly and often, ever on top of the day's events and problems. Almost immediately the board gave her the authority to determine all salaries, raises, overtime pay, and vacation days. She could limit members' reservations. When she said the bar was closed, the party was over. Sylvia Besser, who came to the club in 1939 and had charge of the second floor for almost 40 years, remembered Miss Greely as a fine person. "She had class. She was of the same caliber as the members. She belonged in the club."

May 8, 1945, was V-E Day, celebrating Germany's unconditional surrender and the end of the war in the West. Several clubs in the city were closed. The WAC would have closed also except for the practical difficulties of reaching 350 women who had signed up to hear Margaret McWilliams, wife of the governor of Manitoba. A flood of cancellations was expected. Instead the telephones rang all morning with requests for extra places. Throngs of women arrived in bright colors and splashy prints. Many wore corsages of lavender peonies and violets. Hearts were happy all around. Mrs. Payson Smith's fresh spring bonnet said it best — a raffia straw hat with a tiny man bicycling his way through a field of brilliant flowers.

LITTLE MARGARET KRAMER beside the WAC's 20-foot Christmas tree. At the close of the war Miss Greely was able to secure a shipment of the new Madame Alexander fashion dolls and some baby dolls with real hair. They sold out in one day.

ARTHUR ELLIGAN, the club's doorman 1937–77, at the front entrance. The WAC address and logo were traced in gold leaf on the glass panels under the canopy.

8

Dining In:
the fabulous fifties

THE POSTWAR YEARS took off in a mood of uplift and renewed prosperity. The club was still a favorite with old Chicago families, and the 50th anniversary was marked with a year of special events celebrating the city's history and high cultural rank. The 1948–49 season opened with a brilliant dinner for Artur Rodzinski, the new conductor of the Chicago Symphony, and closed with an old-fashioned tea commemorating the club's founders. Long tables were covered with gold candelabra, satin streamers, and delicate floral bouquets under glass. The party napkins were paper, edged in gold (in strict keeping with Victorian custom), and the programs were scented with violet. Waitresses maneuvered through the crowd passing the club's renowned coconut snowballs, 50 to a tray, each lighted with a tiny birthday candle.

Almost 700 members came to this party, including an astonishing number of oldtimers. Among the club's most pleasing benefits was the opportunity to meet these distinguished ladies and their energetic descendants. In 1945 George M. Pullman's granddaughter (Mrs. Albert H. Madlener, Jr.) stepped into the presidency, and the chair was occupied not too many years later by Charles H. Wacker's daughter (Mrs. Earle J. Zimmerman). There was a delightful sense of ongoing traditions. It was nice to be greeted by venerable employees too. Minna Kenburg, the bath attendant, had been hired before the turn of the century, and Mae Woltersdorff was still at the switchboard. Mae had joined the club in 1907. (Or was it 1905 or 1903? Nobody including Mae herself was absolutely sure of the date, but in 1955 she was given a gold watch.)

During these years the WAC solidified its reputation as a great luncheon club. Members would always point with exasperation to the swimming pool whenever jokers poked fun at their "fork-lifting exercises." The truth is, however, that by the Fifties the squash court was filled with broken furniture and the exercise horse had long since been donated to a children's camp. Food was now the major draw, and there was a general consensus that the WAC's kitchen was the best in town.

This unexcelled reputation was largely due to the taste and skill of the club's longtime chef, Ione Rhynsburger. She came to the club in 1936, a recent graduate of the University of Iowa with a degree in dietetics. She received $25 a week to start. Delicate, wiry, indefatigable, Miss Rhynsburger managed the club's kitchen for 37 years. In that time she developed a certain style of cooking and service to a high art — simple flavorful dishes that were never contrived or chi-chi, made from all fresh ingredients, served in modest portions. She introduced many recipes (none of them dressed up with fancy names) that became staples of the club's menu. Tomato bouillon with horseradish cream. Mushroom sauce on artichoke bottoms. Grilled Roquefort and chicken sandwich. Pecan rolls. Tomato aspic salad. The three-decker 50th anniversary sandwich. Grilled cheese and tomato with crisp bacon. Lobster Alaska. The sight of her Chicken Amandine on the day's menu (slices of white and dark meat deep-fried in an ambrosial almond batter) shattered any diet resolutions. With no trepidation Miss Rhynsburger cooked a formal four-course luncheon one day for Dione Lucas, the famous Cordon Bleu chef, who was in the dining room with a group of Smith College alumnae. Their meal was finished off with a favorite WAC dessert — ice cream balls rolled in toasted almonds, topped with Ione Rhynsburger's exquisite hot butterscotch sauce.

A member could count on certain rituals. Every Saturday noon she could get fresh apple pie with cheese. On Wednesdays lunch was buffet-style with sumptuous salads and casseroles laid out on a long table. At evening events Lobster

THE CLUB'S LONGTIME CHEF
Ione Rhynsburger (fifth from left) with her staff at a picnic in the park.

SOCIETY REPORTERS at the WAC's 50th birthday party snapped Mrs. Nicholas Starroselsky pouring tea for (below, left to right) Mrs. Earle J. Zimmerman, Mrs. William O. Hunt, and Mrs. Bartholomay Chapin.

The SMART SET

Thermidor was often served in addition to ham and a standing rib roast. For a period of at least fifty years the club had a collective addiction to lobster. Miss Rhynsburger once recounted the two things that impressed her most when she first came to the club. The first was that every grape was peeled for fresh fruit salads and the second that lobsters were steamed every single day. Even into the Fifties the kitchen received an order of fresh lobsters, flown in from Maine, at least three times a week. People came from all over for the lobster salad. It was a special favorite with the men. Mrs. Henry C. Woods ordered it almost every time she came into the dining room. In the Sixties, when the price of lobster began its climb to prohibitive heights, a small salad with mayonnaise dressing was still available most days, though it might cost as much as four dollars a plate.

Back in the kitchen everyone had a special job. There were two pastry chefs. One did the breads and rolls, and the other did the cakes and pies. For years, until wartime rationing cut baking supplies, there was a cook who did nothing but make coconut cakes, four a day, six days a week. Every couple of weeks a sack of two dozen coconuts would come in, to be cracked, peeled, and shredded by hand. Salad girls made all the molds and also the dressings and ice cream toppings. Another cook would come in at eleven and, with the help of the sandwich girl, make finger food for tea. The menu was printed every day by the storeroom man on his small hand printer. The house-men took turns busing trays at noon, and the cleaning ladies came down and helped with the dishes.

The staff also made rolls, pastries, and salads to go, and the celery seed salad dressing was available in bottles. Orders taken before 10 o'clock would be delivered the same day. Mrs. Joseph E. Magnus told a reporter, "I can't resist the bread the club bakes, even though it costs 75 cents a loaf — and I'll probably spend $75 getting those bread and butter calories off!" The kitchen could make up a "college spread" for children away at school or a boxed meal for a friend in the hospital. A Wheaton hostess credited Ione Rhynsburger with saving her reputation and sanity when several dozen thimble-sized biscuits and lobster sandwiches were produced posthaste for a last-minute cocktail party. (At that time members could also buy liquor by the case through the club.)

Though homemakers in the Fifties were using lots of new kitchen shortcuts, Miss Rhynsburger never compromised on ingredients. There were no packaged soups or powdered mixes. "Everything was fresh," she recalled. "Nothing was canned. No leftovers in any form were ever served." Later on in the Sixties when the club was casting about for ways to cut food costs, it was suggested she buy pre-grated coconut in plastic bags. It would have been a sacrilege. "They even tried to get us to use frozen egg whites," Miss Rhynsburger remembered, "and someone wanted to bring Mrs. Smith's Pies into the club and serve them in the dining room. I refused."

Food was serious business at the club, but Ione Rhynsburger could have fun with it too. Hedda Hopper came to speak at the club shortly before Easter one spring, wearing a flowered hat about a foot high, dishing all the latest Hollywood gossip. Miss Rhynsburger sent a special dessert into the dining room that day, little white meringue nests filled with lemon custard. She perched a yellow toy chick on top of each nest. Hedda Hopper loved the furry little birds, kind of a hint about her own cackling. She promptly snatched the birds off all the desserts at her table and stuffed them into her purse. For a grandchild, she explained vaguely.

The dining room itself was an important social experience, run by a series of ladies with firm standards of comportment. The hostess always wore black or navy blue crepe, and the waitresses were also dressed in black, with white bibbed aprons and headbands. Irene Zeissler, a longtime waitress who came to the club in 1940 as a "pool girl," recalled the formidable Miss Helen, who trained the wait staff. "She was tough," Irene said. "Years ago they were *all* strict. We couldn't talk to the members. We could only say hello. You had to stand to the side while they filled out their own checks and then leave right away."

Mrs. Philip L. Cochran added, "I can remember coming as a very little girl with my grandmother. You *never* came without your velvet dress and your white gloves and your Mary Janes. And when you walked into the dining room, Miss Helen was very austere. You just always felt as if your stocking seams had to be straight and your white gloves had to be immaculate. I was scared to death of her until I was 30."

Irene remembered that many kinds of dishes in different patterns were used, and members often requested special table linens and exotic silver and porcelain decorations. Whenever the supply of finger bowls ran low, more were ordered immediately. Miss Greely, the manager, was a constant presence in the dining room as well. She did all the flowers herself (a favored arrangement was yellow roses and pansies in a silver epergne), and she planned the menus for special parties too. In the fall of 1956 she obtained Mamie Eisenhower's recipe for pumpkin tarts, and for two months leading up to the election enormous numbers of these tarts were consumed every lunch hour.

MISS GREELY touring the kitchen before a large party. Members and staff agreed: "Her word was law."

MRS. GEORGE RICH, III (left to right), Mrs. Edward E. Gardner, III, and Mrs. Paul Butler making plans for the club's 50th anniversary.

Seated in the dining room, it was not entirely surprising to spot the likes of Mrs. Wendell Wilkie, Alexandra Tolstoy, Burton Holmes, Cornelius Vanderbilt, Mary Garden, or Ogden Nash at a nearby table. A member could feel confident that any visiting celebrity would be well taken care of. One could also be fairly sure of seeing certain members who lunched at the club almost every day. Many widowed ladies had their dinner at noon, meaning they wouldn't need more than consomme and toast for supper. Mrs. Charles Garfield King (whose daughter Ginevra was F. Scott Fitzgerald's model for Daisy in *The Great Gatsby*) was often seated at a table near the window. Mrs. Henry Russell Platt came every Friday before the concert with her daughter, Mrs. George G. V. Bobrinskoy. Mrs. Platt was quite deaf and would have family letters read to her in a loud voice while she ate her meal. On the way out she would be unable to find her coat check. After a while Sylvia Besser stopped giving Mrs. Platt any ticket at all and simply hung her coat at Number One.

There was a large class of grandmothers. The beautiful Angelina Leicht might be there, much older now, swathed in lovely mauve chiffon scarves to cover any signs of aging at the neck. The remarkable Mrs. Patrick A. Valentine (Mrs. Philip D. Armour's surviving daughter-in-law) sparkled with vigor and was treated by all with reverent affection. Mrs. Beverly W. Pattishall recalled, "I think Mrs. Valentine was about 90 then. Her hands were still so beautiful. She told me once, 'My dear, I sit at home with my hands in two large jars of Vaseline and listen to the radio.'" Mrs. Valentine often covered *her* neck with a pearl and diamond dog collar, and many people were very disappointed to hear after her death that this spectacular choker had been a piece of paste jewelry all along.

Outside Michigan Boulevard (redubbed "The Magnificent Mile" by Arthur Rubloff in 1947) was blooming. In 1949 the North Michigan Avenue Association planted a 40-foot elm tree across the street, the first real note of greenery on the avenue since the old houses and their gardens had been torn out in 1918. When it was clear the new foliage could thrive, the WAC invested in trees, shrubs, and grass on its own "front lawn." Upkeep was not an easy matter. Oyster scale infections, heat from the pavement, and poisonous exhaust fumes meant frequent replantings, but at its best the new landscaping made a nice complement to the club's handsome limestone facade.

The NMAA also organized cohesive Christmas decorating schemes for the whole avenue. In the early years, starting around 1939, plans were quite simple. The club chipped in $10, and someone came around to wind boughs of holiday greenery around the lamp posts out front. Over the years the NMAA grew much more ambitious. Whenever feasible the club went along with its suggestions for stars, lights, and fancy fabric swags on the building exterior. One year some handsome Christmas angels were mounted on the building's facade. Back in the Fifties, though, even those elaborate decorations never came to more than a few hundred dollars a season.

The festive trimmings were important to the club's store tenants too. After the war a pent-up demand for luxury goods brought many newly prosperous shoppers to Michigan Avenue, where a mix of stylish boutiques sold the finest clothes and housewares in the city. (Suburban malls had not yet stolen away large parts of this carriage trade.) The club's smart little storefronts were prime territory, and each tenant had a special retail niche. After the Main Street Book Store moved next door, the northernmost unit ("638") was occupied for a few years by the photographer Merrill Chase. In 1946 that space was leased to Jeannette Gaffin, sister of the more famous milliner Bes-Ben, who ran her own hat salon there for almost 20 years. While her brother's eccentric chapeaus were tricked up with such items as teaspoons, dust-mops, and plastic turtles, Jeannette Gaffin specialized in simple expensive classics. In those days before bouffant hairdos, when a woman never came into the WAC dining room without a hat, Miss Gaffin did a land-office business.

Metcalf's, a deluxe stationery shop that also carried cards and Christmas wrappings, was another longtime tenant. Its owner, Henry Rosenthal, printed the WAC directory for many years. Over a long period a number of charming little stores which sold dresses, scarves, and handbags moved in and out. When two adjoining tenants left in 1946, Mr. Sidney Bayer took both spaces and opened the exclusive Franklin-Bayer linen shop, a North Michigan Avenue fixture for almost 40 years. At that time the corner unit was occupied by the Vocational Society for Shut-Ins, which sold expensive hand-made goods. When the Society moved out in 1955, Mr. Bayer expanded into that space as well. Rents were very reasonable. During the war

PARADE-WATCHING was fun from the club's second-floor balconies. Waiting for Queen Elizabeth's motorcade in 1959 were (left to right) Mrs. Gordon Shorney, Miss Leslie Van Vlack, Mrs. Henry C. Woods, Mrs. Joseph Magnus, and Mrs. Philip Van Vlack.

JEANNETTE GAFFIN'S HAT SALON in the club's northernmost storefront was a great favorite with WAC members. Miss Naomi Donnelley saved this delightful peach and silver hatbox.

the shopkeepers typically paid about $150 a month (and some less than that). In the Fifties, even at double and triple the price, the shops were still a bargain.

Programming at the club took on a decidedly international cast. Reporters like William Shirer, Daniel Schorr, and Harrison Salisbury dissected Moscow, the atom bomb, and the war in Korea. Dr. Tom Dooley talked about the fight for democracy in Southeast Asia, and Austin Kiplinger summed up the view from Washington. Thor Heyerdahl showed movies of his voyage on the Kon-Tiki. The Arctic explorer Donald McMillan predicted that space travel would be the frontier of the future. It may have been possible for a WAC member to be thoroughly *au courant* without ever picking up a paper or turning on the television. Seated in a silver chair in the ball-room, she was hearing up-to-the-minute news on the Filipino cabinet, Colonel Juan Peron's latest maneuvers, and the fate of Chiang Kai-shek as reported by his former secretary. The question which floated above all the lectures of the Fifties was posed one morning by the WAC's perennial favorite, Clifton Utley: "What Does Stalin Want?"

An astonishing parade of celebrities livened up the entertainment calendar too. Bennett Cerf told members what to read, and Mortimer Adler mercifully assured them, "You're Never Too Old to Learn." Richard Gump outlined the basics of good taste, followed by Oleg Cassini who deplored extreme fashions as a Parisian plot against the American woman. Dorothy Draper, decorator of the outrageously bold Camellia House in the Drake Hotel (described by her critics as "an exercise in trop-ical baroque"), advised her audience to forget the old rules, wear a redder shade of lipstick, and upholster an old chair in yellow. Ilka Chase pointed out that a woman with aspirations now needed a wife herself to manage this new "do-it-yourself" era.

Stage and screen personalities performed at the club every season. Margaret Landon told how she came to write *Anna and the King of Siam*. Claude Rains gave a dramatic reading. Cornelia Otis Skinner did her famous character sketches, and Elsa Lanchester sang bawdy old ditties from the English music halls. There was much philosophical advice. Mrs. Dale Carnegie told WAC members, "Don't Grow Old — Grow Up!" Alistair Cooke warned them to be at least a little worried about the beat generation. "It's all right to be a juvenile delinquent," he complained, "but it's a pity to be a *snob* about it." Dr. Norman Vincent Peale was probably the biggest draw of the decade. He told the crowd to throw out their aspirin tablets and sleeping pills and just start living.

Casting about for ways to bring more people into the dining room on off days, Mrs. Charles M. Sailor suggested that a small fashion show during the noon hour might be just the thing. This was in May of 1956. Some of the women thought this was a radical idea. At any rate, it had never been done before. "I went to Mrs. Dudley," Gladys Sailor recalled. "She had been on the board a number of years. I asked her if people would accept it. She said, 'Well, why don't you try it?'"

BRUCE DERN (far right) and Wade Fetzer, III, signing the dance cards of Meda Moulding (left) and Dorothy Simmons at a holiday party for teenagers in 1952. Bruce Dern, who moved on to a stellar career in Hollywood, was the grandson of WAC President Mrs. Bruce MacLeish.

So one day the next September a few models from Martha Weathered's dress shop strolled among the tables in the latest fall and winter fashions. The price of lunch was upped to $3.50 for the occasion, and no one seemed to mind. Saks Fifth Avenue organized a much larger show the following January, with models parading on two floors. An accordionist played in the main dining room and a pianist played on the fourth floor. The day was such a success that a whole series of these events followed, with stores like Bonwit Teller and Stanley Korshak also participating (though Saks put on every other show). Eventually these programs were moved to the ballroom for better viewing, and sometimes a Stauffer consultant was also present, dispensing posture tips and reducing secrets.

The Fifties were great party years at the club. In an effort to encourage the younger generation to make more frequent use of it (beyond all the debuts, weddings, and the kiddie Christmas blow-out), a committee of Juniors invented the Younger Members Dance. The first one was given in October 1952. The ballroom was decorated in red and black, with lots of shiny leaves scattered around a virtual barnyard of ceramic roosters. A daring feature of the party was a dance contest, with a bottle of champagne for the winning couple.

This cocktail supper dance drew so many reservations it was henceforth put on the calendar every autumn and spring. Bill Otto's orchestra, a cotillion fixture that specialized in moody renditions of songs like "Embraceable You," played every year for a crowd in crew-cuts and rustling taffeta. Droves of young women arrived in the new "After Five" dresses, and one year Miss Lita Sullivan made a sensation in a bare-back sweater. The parties broke up around ten o'clock to accommodate the suburbanites who, as one committee member said, "have to get home and pay off the babysitter." This early-evening feature appealed to a lot of older folks too (the ones over 40). They started crashing the party, and by 1959 the Juniors were forced to relent and extend invitations to the whole membership.

These little galas were the birthplace of a grand WAC tradition. The supper dance held in the fall of 1956 was billed as the "Harvest Home" party. The ballroom was decked out in cornstalks, pumpkins, and baskets of gourds, and Ione Rhynsburger laid out an especially lavish buffet. It is very likely that duck was served, because the party then became the "Harvest Home Duck Dinner" and eventually, the incomparable, one and only "Duck Dinner," an annual sold-out autumn ritual for over 40 years.

Another popular staple on the entertainment calendar was the Thursday night travelogue. After a long hiatus during the war, many members were vacationing abroad again, planning to fly for the first time. These after-dinner armchair trips, with professional travelers showing color films of places like Paris, the Alps, Hawaii, Japan, and Australia, drew a capacity audience. Sometimes first-run movies were shown too, with Philip K. Wrigley bringing in his own projector because the club didn't have the right type.

It was Mrs. Wrigley who first suggested the consular dinners, an extravagantly successful series of exotic meals hosted by the club's five consular wives. (At that time there were only five such members, coming from Sweden, Great Britain, Belgium, France, and Canada.) The idea was to honor the diplomats, promote a feeling of international *bonhomie*, and venture a bit into foreign food. The first one, "A Delicious Swedish Royal Dinner," was scheduled for October 23, 1958. Fingers crossed, the board decided to charge an astronomical $5.75 per person (but that, of course, included the wines). Consul and Mrs. Goesta Oldenburg helped plan the menu, which featured Scandanavian delicacies like potatoes rolled in crumbs and sugar and tiny Mazzarines. Both the Oldenburgs arrived in formal dress, and the head table was covered with a shimmering gold cloth. Dinners of similar elegance were held for the other consuls.

These distinguished "Old World" gatherings, forerunners of the international evenings held in later years, were recalled by many members as the high point of the Fifties. Each party was a novel experience carefully plotted beforehand at intimate little dinners in Helen Wrigley's apartment. The most memorable event may have been the British affair, when Consul Robert Whyte Mason invited the English cast of *My Fair Lady* to join the WAC members for saddle of beef and Yorkshire pudding. The Duke of Bedford, scion of Woburn Abbey, was also present. The first nobleman to install hotdog stands, a trolley ride, and souvenir shops on his staggeringly taxed estate, the Duke was in town to drum up tourist business. He was a great showman with a wry sense of humor about his predicament. His fellow

A LETTER to Miss Greely from Mrs. Philip K. Wrigley, who took meticulous charge of arrangements for all the consular receptions and dinners.

Mrs. Philip K. Wrigley

1500 Lake Shore Drive, Chicago 10, Illinois

Dear Miss Greeley;

This is the menu as specified by Mrs. Mason who said they never serve salad with the main course, so we shall omit it entirely as she really made no further mention of it. I wonder if we should add rolls, or other little odds and ends such as horse radish or something like that? She said by all means to have the rolls in the napkins and by the way, do you suppose we could have the napkins specially starched like they were for Sweden? They did look so cripp and beautifully white and glistening as we walked in.

Will see you soon.

Save Thursday, February 17, 6:30 p.m.
for dinner at the
WOMAN'S ATHLETIC CLUB
•
FASCINATING TRAVEL TALK
First public showing of the capture and transport out of Assam to the Brookfield Zoo, of the two new armor-plated Great Indian Rhinoceroses. Only pair in any zoo in the world outside of Calcutta.
By RALPH GRAHAM
Assistant Director, Zoological Park, Brookfield
whose daring and ingenuity brought these "Rhinos" here alive. This successful expedition is of special interest to club members since it was made possible by MR. GEORGE B. DRYDEN.
•
Telephone for reservations. WHitehall 4-6123
No cancellations after February 16th
$3.75 per plate

THURSDAY NIGHT TRAVELOGUES were a staple on the club calendar. A large crowd came to see pictures of the Brookfield Zoo expedition to India, which was financed by a WAC husband, George B. Dryden.

aristocrats frowned on him, he admitted. When pressed about reports he had rented the grounds of his stately home to a nudist congress, he reminded WAC members of the rainy English climate. Confidentially, he told them, "It really looked more like a plastic raincoat convention."

Almost every area of the club was refurbished during the Fifties. Forced to postpone repairs and let rooms go shabby during the war, the board took on extensive building and redecorating projects as soon as quality goods became available again. In 1946 the accounting office was moved to the sixth floor. It was originally situated in an odd two-story space just to the west of the second-floor powder room. There was a small cage near the cloakroom where members came for cash and stamps, and behind it Mr. Johnson and Helen Fahrenbach had their desks. Coats and supplies were stashed on a back-room balcony, a cramped but efficient arrangement. It was finally decided to move the whole department to the sixth floor, where the ladies checkroom and a small but pleasant lounge next to it were remodeled as an office suite.

Soon after that the original *trompe l'oeil* mirrors were removed from the second-floor powder room, which was then done over in a completely new style. The Silver Room was redecorated. The foyer doors to the Mirror Room, originally curtained, were now painted silver. Large panels in the main dining room were replaced by antiqued mirrors (to make the room seem larger), and the ceilings were sound-proofed then as well. In the ballroom all the glass doors overlooking Michigan Avenue were painted black and the balcony windows upstairs replaced with mirrors, to facilitate darkening the room for daytime programs. The second-floor gallery was repapered using the last rolls of the 1929 order. "One thing that always amazed me," Mrs. Sailor recalled, "was that Miss Gheen had ordered so much of this wallpaper. There was enough to do everything over — that was an outstanding break — and Miss Greely knew where it was."

THE DUKE OF BEDFORD (far left) was amused by the centerpiece on the head table at the English consular dinner – a red velvet crown trimmed with gold braid nestled in a bed of roses. He was seated with WAC President Mrs. Charles M. Sailor (center) and Consul Robert Whyte Mason and his wife.

Most exciting was the restoration of the camphor-crystal chandeliers in the ballroom, which by then were coated with 30 year's worth of Chicago dust and grime. Mrs. Henry C. Woods remembered, "The ballroom got very sad looking. Everybody kept saying, 'It's so grim up here, kind of gloomy. What is it?' And that was it. The fixtures had never been cleaned since they were put in."

An industrial designer from the School of the Art Institute was called in to examine the fixtures, and under his supervision Leon Mendelsohn and a crew of eight men from Steel City Lighting spent the summer of 1957 bathing more than 100,000 eroded and encrusted beads and crystals in a special cleaning fluid. Dangerously rusted rods were replaced, and the beads were restrung on resilvered wires. The whole precarious operation was insured by Lloyds of London for $20,000. By October the chandeliers and sconces were shining again with a fairytale sparkle (all of this work paid for by a generous contribution from Mrs. Woods). The lights were so dazzling, in fact, that a month later the Younger Members Committee had trouble dimming them to a suitably romantic level for their annual supper dance.

During this period the second, third, and fourth floors were air conditioned, a controversial innovation greeted by many as a calamity. Mrs. Woods recalled, "People weren't used to air conditioning. They said it would ruin the club, they were going to resign. But the board elected to do it because other people weren't going to come if they didn't. The machines were put in those big square boxes in the living room ceiling. It didn't blow on anybody at all. People were going to resign, and they didn't."

An automatic telephone system was installed, the boilers were reconditioned, and new exit and emergency lights were put in place to meet the city fire code. The building was tuckpointed twice. The most expensive undertaking of all was the 1959 conversion from DC to AC electric current.

An altogether disruptive event was the widening of Ontario Street in 1952. Though plans for a new "super-highway" with Ontario as its feeder street had been on the drawing board since 1939, no one was really worried until the City cancelled the WAC's sidewalk canopy permit in 1950. After a futile legal challenge, the club was forced to accept this unwelcome development. Because the pool would now be situated beneath a heavily trafficked public roadway, it was necessary to move pipes, wires, and ducts in the vault below. Under Philip Maher's supervision two new support columns were constructed at the south end of the pool. The skylights along its eastern border were an ongoing source of trouble downstairs. Cracks, leaks, and uneven settling of the glass blocks had meant endless repairs and created a public hazard besides on the sidewalk above. In 1959 the skylights, such a nice amenity for thirty years, were removed, and a brand new pavement was laid at the club's expense.

All these extraordinary expenditures put intense pressure on the treasury. Senior Resident dues were raised twice in five years to a high of $17.50 per month,

MRS. PHILIP R. CLARKE, president 1953–54, often brought flowers from her Hinsdale garden for the Wednesday buffet table.

and the club levied the first assessment in its history to cover the conversion to alternating current. At two financially delicate moments Philip R. Clarke, whose wife was president 1953–54, made the club interest-free loans (requesting in return only that he be served a plain grilled cheese sandwich whenever he sat down to one of the club's fancy lunches).

There was a 10-year window when the club had a legal opportunity to buy the land underneath the clubhouse. The option was seriously considered. The members even had the courage to contemplate building additional stories to enlarge their floor space. However, John Farwell had stipulated a boom-year price of $975,000 in the 1929 contract. Though near north real estate values were now climbing fast, that price was still exorbitant in 1957, the year of decision. Indeed, the six-story Decorative Arts Building across the street had sold for only $343,000 in 1944, and the Kiwanis bought the old Anita McCormick Blaine mansion around the corner at Rush and Erie (a lot similar in size to the WAC's) for even less money in 1956. The club was advised to invest its capital in liquid assets and let the option expire.

It was a colossal challenge every year, but the ladies always found a way to make the ends meet the middle. In 1955 the bottom line even showed a net profit, after depreciation, for the first time since 1932. Mrs. Charles M. Sailor closed one of her presidential newsletters to the membership with a paean to the WAC's eternally balanced budget. "Business men, husbands of members who read the Club's annual fiscal report, don't see how it is done. Never in the red. Bow deeply in courtly admiration."

MRS. WILLIAM WRIGLEY
(left to right), Mrs. Rudy L.
Ruggles, and Mrs. Burton W.
Hales in the second-floor
drawing room, where ladies met
often for cocktails and
conversation.

9

Grace under pressure

THE SOCIAL UPHEAVALS of the Sixties left their bewildering mark upon the Woman's Athletic Club. Gracious living was everywhere under siege. The dignified matrons in flowered hats and mink stoles were off the fashion pages, replaced by young swingers in beehive hairdos and miniskirts. Daughters, always the promise and future of the WAC, were now inclined *not* to follow in Mother's footsteps. During the bra-burning stage of the women's movement they were on their way to sit-ins instead and marching against the war in Viet Nam. They were not flocking to join a club the newspapers now referred to as "Sleepy Hollow." Friendly society reporters, their own columns dwindling, still tried to give the club an occasional flattering boost. A depiction of the WAC from one such story: "The casual visitor sees a most unathletic scene. Elderly women sip sherry in high-ceilinged quiet lounges." With friends like this, who needed enemies?

Pressure was coming from other directions as well. After the Fifties' migration to the suburbs, many women came into town less and less. They lunched at the country club and did all their buying at new shopping centers. When they did drive into the city, they had to cope with more congestion on and around Michigan Avenue. Between 1957 and 1963 over $500 million was committed to new construction along the boulevard, the John Hancock Building going up at the north end and the Equitable Building to the south. The last of the townhouses, those enchantingly remodeled remnants of old Pine Street, were disappearing. The Italian Court across the street, that little web of shops and studios where so many Chicagoans had been introduced to French cooking at Le Petite Gourmet, where Irene Castle had once taken a *pied-a-terre* upstairs, was demolished. A tall concrete office building went up in its place. The scale of the neighborhood was changing rapidly.

Traffic was fierce. During the Forties, even on crowded program days a member could count on having her car whisked off to a nearby lot and delivered promptly after lunch (for the munificent sum of 25 cents). In the Fifties many of those parking lots became building sites. With Ontario Street revamped as a main artery to the

Northwest Expressway and meters installed on nearby streets, parking became a serious problem. Thus some suburban members decided that coming to the club was for special occasions. The dining room and all the departments felt the subsequent pinch.

The WAC wasn't alone in these difficulties. Clubs all over the country were trapped in a financial squeeze. In the wave of the colossal postwar monetary expansion, the problem of inflation was acute. In 1962 it was calculated that the club's operating expenses had increased by about a third in ten years, but there was no corresponding rise in income. The payroll spiraled up and up. With a rambunctious building boom underway on Michigan Avenue, the assessed valuation of the clubhouse and land rose accordingly. The club had to meet steep real estate taxes and cope with new I.R.S. rulings besides, which now put a limit on revenue from outside groups (which had otherwise been a potential new source of support). Another revision to the Code in 1969 obliged the club to pay federal taxes on its rental and investment income, screwing the vise even tighter. It's no wonder that the club began running deficits again, though astute management of its investment portfolio helped ease the pain. One of the Finance Committee's proudest buys was 15 shares of a hot stock called I.B.M. It shot up 69 points shortly after purchase. What to do, they wondered. It was a volatile stock with no income. They took the profit and put it toward new draperies in the Silver Room.

Meanwhile, the price of meals and services at the club was unavoidably pushed up. The entree luncheon of the day was $1.25 in the Forties. By 1960 it cost $3.50. A slice of coconut cake was up from 20 cents to 45 cents. A swim cost two dollars instead of one, a massage four dollars instead of three. Initiation fees and dues were reluctantly increased. Senior Residents now paid $350 to join and $35 in monthly dues. Several special assessments were also levied, and a new 15% service charge was added to bills for wedding receptions and other large parties.

The budget difficulties were considerably compounded by the high number of outstanding Life Memberships. Though none of these perpetual memberships had been issued outright after 1931, the original agreement had stipulated that they could be passed once (with a transfer fee) to a descendant or sold to someone else for whatever the market would bear. Thus in 1961 fully 15% of the club's roster were still "Lifers" who paid no dues. The board discussed the possibility of assessing this group. Mr. Edwin Austin, the club's attorney, advised against it. So the transfer fee was raised instead, from $700 to $1,000 and eventually all the way up to $10,000, which did bring in a modest amount of additional cash.

The departure of Miss Greely was a poignant moment. Always a quiet knowing presence in the background, steering day-to-day operations with tact and finesse, she had over time become the club's invisible rudder. Now the popular manager announced her intention to retire and move to Seattle. Many members were near hysteria. Some tried to talk her into staying on in some kind of reduced capacity,

124

inwardly sensing she would never do anything halfway. "In all my 20 years here," she reminded them, "I've only been in the swimming pool twice and then both times I had to get out because I was called to the phone!" Reluctantly, a search for her replacement was organized, and Miss Anna Mae Magee, assistant manager of the Skokie Country Club, was hired in the spring of 1962. To Miss Greely the board paid a unique farewell tribute. Besides giving her a handsome "appreciation purse," the directors changed the by-laws to make her a Guest for Life, entitled to all the privileges of the club, without limitation, any time she chose to return.

The real challenge of the Sixties was to meet a radically new state of affairs — both inside the club and out — with courage and imagination. No member was more valiantly devoted to this task than Miss Frances Hooper, who was surely one of the most energetic promoters the club ever had. An advertising pioneer who founded her own agency in the mid-Twenties, she handled all of the Wrigley Company's magazine advertising for more than 30 years. She once mailed an advance order for ad pages to *Harper's Bazaar* in Paris by carrier pigeon. In her private life she was an enthusiastic collector who at one time owned the diaries of Emily and Anne Brontë. Her Kate Greenaway watercolors eventually went to the Carnegie-Mellon Institute and her Virginia Woolf papers to Smith College, of which she was a 1914 graduate.

"She was a character!" is the almost unanimous reaction from those who knew Frances Hooper. Her answer to any problem was "Think Big!" Her vision for the Woman's Athletic Club was that it should cease to be merely a club and become a bona fide cultural institution alongside the Chicago Symphony, the Art Institute, and the Museum of Science and Industry. She believed the WAC was a natural showcase and proving ground for top-drawer women doing important things. It may be that some of her ideas went over the edge. Feeling the club ought to have its own

MISS FRANCES HOOPER, a pioneer Chicago advertising woman. As program chairman, she brought many world-class personalities to the club podium.

INDIRA GANDHI (far right) is welcomed to the club in 1962 by Mrs. Burton W. Hales (left) and Mrs. Allin K. Ingalls. "Women are a tremendous talent force," Madame Gandhi told her WAC audience. "They should be allowed to do what they are able to do."

MRS. DONALD F. CARNE swimming with her daughter Elinor while Mrs. Herman T. Van Mell lounges nearby. The Pompeian wicker chaise is a piece of the club's original pool furniture.

auditorium, she pressed the idea of opening an entrance from the west side of the clubhouse into the Kungsholm Theater next door and renting the premises as needed. When the club was later presented with an opportunity to buy that property, her immediate response was typical. "Look into it!" She was restrained only when outside advisors gently suggested the idea was ridiculous.

Nevertheless, in her sense of the changing social landscape and the renewed effort needed to carry the day, she was right on the mark. She was always a champion party planner. Under her aegis the club hosted many novel entertainments. Among the most memorable was "The Jolly Christmas Supper Dance," for which she designed the festive invitations herself. Another time she organized a Halloween luncheon around the pool, appointing the club president "booby trap chairman." Mrs. Sailor recalled, "Frances knew how to put a party over."

During her term as Program Chair, Miss Hooper brought many outstanding women to speak at the club. Working with the Canadian Consul, she secured the dynamic Ellen L. Fairclough, the only female member of the Canadian cabinet and Canada's Woman of the Year, for an after-dinner talk. The club heard from Laurel Van der Wal, a top-ranking 6'2" scientist in the space program. Agnes Moorhead, the Academy Award–winning actress, gave a reading in the ballroom. Baroness Maria von Trapp appeared while *The Sound of Music* was running on Broadway. Local heroines were invited too. Carol Fox, the astounding young founder of the Lyric Opera who had brought Maria Callas to Chicago for her American debut, gave the members a moving account of her early struggles. Carol Fox spoke first in 1964. Three years later it was Miss Hooper's idea to bring her back to receive the club's first Distinguished Woman Award, honoring Fox for her cultural contributions to the city.

Maybe Frances Hooper's most spectacular *coup* was the visit of Indira Gandhi in April 1962. As the official hostess of her father, Jawaharlal Nehru, Mrs. Gandhi was then First Lady of India and president of the Indian National Congress as well. Diminutive, dressed in a delicate sari of yellow silk, she dazzled the 300 members who turned out for the lecture. (Her son Rajiv, traveling with her, was sent to opening day at Comiskey Park.) There was fervent applause when Mrs. Gandhi recounted the buoyant welcome Jackie Kennedy received when she toured India. Though many women in that country held high office, Indira Gandhi's concern was the dismal plight of the average woman. She drew quite a gasp from the crowd when she recalled that, before Independence, widows were not even allowed to inherit their own jewelry. After her talk she was entertained for lunch in the Mirror Room where she was pleased to autograph the placecards, which were saved by all those present as treasured souvenirs of a great occasion.

The traditional programs were still popular, and there were many of those. Winston Churchill (the younger) told of his African journeys, Cleveland Amory dissected high society, and Ginette Spanier, director of the House of Balmain in Paris, talked about the fascinating world of haute couture. (Aside from the Gabor sisters, she confided, beautiful women had little confidence in themselves. Pay careful attention to gloves and shoes, was her advice, and stay away from those awful pointed toes.) It was a splendid morning when Mrs. Edward Marshall Boehm, wife of the sculptor, brought a huge porcelain eagle into the ballroom and told how her husband made his famous birds. "This was before the days of Styrofoam," Mrs. Thomas A. Kelly recalled, "and all the pieces she brought, including that enormous eagle, came packed in popcorn. Real popcorn. For protection. It stands out in my memory as one of the most fabulous programs we ever did."

Still, the drift of the programming had turned in a new direction. At the instigation of Mrs. Burton W. Hales and Mrs. Earle J. Zimmerman, a series of personal financial planning seminars was organized. They were able to pull in high-ranking officers of the top Chicago banks to discuss stocks, bonds, and estate planning. So much for the old canard about the unseemliness of ladies discussing money in public. The Program Committee tackled all the big subjects – the Middle East, the C.I.A., Red China, low-cost housing in Chicago. Robin Moore defended the Green Berets, the crack U.S. defense teams fighting in the jungles of Viet Nam. Through the years WAC speakers had always addressed the pressing questions of the day, but never had the issues seemed as contentious or divisive. It's interesting to note that during the summer of 1952, when both political parties held their conventions in Chicago, the club remained open in the evenings for members who wanted to drop

127

by for drinks or conversation. During the 1968 Democratic convention the club was shuttered early at the request of city officials, who asked all owners along Michigan Avenue to provide extra security. (As an additional precaution the head houseman slept overnight in the clubhouse, though the property never suffered any damage.)

The club held its first "physical fitness" class in the fall of 1961. There were ski warm-up sessions and films of Stein Eriksen on the slopes in Australia and New Zealand. The pool enjoyed something of a renaissance, especially after the arrival of the effervescent Irene Webb, a swimming instructor who came to the club through the Red Cross in late 1963. Mrs. Webb taught countless WAC children to feel at home in the water, somehow imparting to each one a special self-confidence. Until the Latin School built its own pool in 1970, hundreds of pupils were sent over for afternoon swim lessons. Everyone agreed this new coach was a real "live wire," organizing relay races, diving contests, and charming water ballets. She hooked up a record player near the pool which would spin out songs and marches while little arms and legs splashed in unison.

There were many, many birthday parties and weekend water shows put on for proud parents. After an extensive redecoration of the locker and changing rooms, a lovely show of new swimwear was held on a Saturday in January 1967. Saks Fifth Avenue agreed to furnish the teenage models, and a young woman named Nena Ivon arrived to coordinate the proceedings. Husbands and sons were welcomed, and the grand finale was a spectacular swimming exhibition featuring the Tiny Tots, Olympic champs, and a troupe of teenage "Cowgirls" in fringed skirts and kerchiefs.

At the same time there was more adult interest in swimming. In April 1965 Mrs. Gerald Sivage displayed a new silver bowl intended to reward those members who completed a 50-mile swim. The following January the first trophy, suitably inscribed, was presented to Mrs. Charles R. Aiken. The next recipient was Mrs. Donald F. Carne, another one of Mrs. Webb's "regulars," usually seen paddling about in a faded blue suit and men's socks under her flippers. In February 1969 three more trophies were given to Misses Martha Miller and Dorcas FitzGerald and Mrs. John K. Diederichs. A large Red Cross chart was posted near the pool so swimmers could mark their progress, and Eleanor Page, the longtime *Tribune* columnist whose mother was a member for many years, donated a plaque to honor the youngsters for mileage goals too. For a few delightful seasons scuba diving lessons were also offered. Janet Kelly and her family signed up. "We took it for an hour after the club closed at night. I have my little certificate. Qualified Scuba Diver! It was a nice safe place to learn."

A really astonishing project of the Sixties was the installation of indoor golf links on the eighth floor. The WAC's answer to suburban pitch-and-putt, this compact course was quickly redubbed "WAC whack." The old squash and badminton courts were cleared out and redesigned, with the help of Jock Hutchison, Jr., a pro from the Skokie Country Club, into a golf practice range. The floor of the squash court was covered with grassy indoor-outdoor carpeting. This was the driving range. Seven tons of sand were hauled up the back elevator and dumped in the badminton court. This was the bunker, a sand trap with a putting clock, pitching basket, and chipping practice area. The walls were repainted a soft green and a mural of a golf course was stretched across one side to suggest the feeling of the great outdoors. There were lockers, buckets of balls — everything short of golf carts to lure the lady golfers back downtown.

Mrs. Thomas Lyle Williams, chair of the new Golf Committee, launched the venture at a cocktail "Par Tee" on October 27, 1967. Jock Hutchison offered weekly lessons, and husbands were allowed to play on Saturdays. For five or six years a small but devoted little band was quite attached to this penthouse golf studio. Even those who wandered up infrequently had to admit that gazing out the window at the new Lake Point Tower and then looking down to line up a shot was a pleasant and novel experience.

Many windows at the WAC were opened, administratively speaking. From the days of the founding there were women who had occupied seats on the board for as long as 35 or 40 years. Now it was voted to rotate the board and also to include more members from the club's younger echelons. (When Mrs. John Trumball gave birth in 1965, little Mark Trumball was celebrated as the first "board baby"!) Corporation members were asked to serve on committees to get more familiar with club operations. When the yearbook was reprinted in 1967, it had a suddenly super-digitized look, introducing zip codes, apartment numbers, and all-numeral telephone numbers. "Whitehall 6123" — the club's historic exchange — disappeared forever.

Almost all areas of the club were refurbished during the Sixties, and the rugs, which had suffered ten cruel years of spiked heels, were extensively repaired.

BASIL BROWN, a top designer and presiding genius behind Marshall Field's Trend House. He was a great favorite with WAC members and was selected for the first major redecoration of the clubhouse since 1929.

Though the club employed several decorators, the large part of the work was supervised by Basil Brown, Marshall Field's top interior designer. When Brown extended the sixth floor card room 18 feet and installed a Verte-inspired wallpaper mural, it was decided to rename it the "Venetian Room." In 1963 the Life Members paid for the restoration of the Mirror Room. The first-floor entrance hall was redone in yellow and white with a generous gift from Mrs. Edward Blake Blair. At that point the vestibule windows were sealed to shut out street noise and dirt. During the holidays the whole decor took on a spectral glow under the direction of Mrs. Hays MacFarland and her "Glitter Girls." This group of ingenious ladies (which sometimes included Mrs. James Ward Thorne, creator of the popular Thorne rooms now on display at the Art Institute) met at the club for years to sew for the Presbyterian–St. Luke's Christmas sale. They also made many ornaments and wreaths which were hung every December to sparkling effect all over the clubhouse.

The Gift Shop blossomed into a full-scale boutique. For about 30 years it had been part of the Personal Service Department, a counter-top operation on the fifth floor where members could pick up little sachets or a bottle of cologne. There were some fragrant hand creams bottled under the WAC name and boxes of Meta's Chocolates, delicious hand-dipped candies Meta made in her South Side basement and delivered to the club herself. Lifesavers and cigarettes were available in the second-floor checkroom. Sylvia Besser, who had charge of that checkroom, remembered, "It was Miss Greely who instigated the gifts-for-Christmas idea. She would go to the Little Traveler in Geneva to get things to sell. Sequined trees, lapel pins, wreaths. They were so pretty. People bought them like mad."

In the mid-Sixties Mrs. Kenneth Covell, who was then Chairman of the House Committee, set up a case near the pool to sell bathing caps, party favors, and water toys. Miss Besser recalled Mrs. Covell, who was "tall and blonde, a very good dresser. Her husband was tall and good-looking too. He used to come into the club evenings and occasionally for lunch. One summer he built a display cabinet — the big yellow one with the fancy top and glass shelves. It was a pastime for him. The two of them set it up in the hall on the second floor. Mrs. Ruggles, who was the president, bought some merchandise, and her daughter Jean Ramoser made a lot of men's silk ties

MRS. JAMES WARD THORNE beside one of her famous miniature rooms in the Art Institute. During the 1950s and 60s Mrs. Thorne kept half a dozen enameled wood chests stored in a cubicle on the WAC's fifth floor. These were filled with intriguing bits and pieces she used to make new Thorne Rooms every year for the Presbyterian-St. Luke's Hospital Christmas sale.

130

Woman's Athletic Club of Chicago
AN EVENING DOWN EAST

 DELECTABLE YANKEE DINNER IN INFORMAL NEW ENGLAND ATMOSPHERE

MARSHALL DODGE
MONOLOGIST RACONTEUR

 HE WILL SPLIT YOUR
SIDES
～ WITH ～
LAUGHTER

MENU

Boston Clam Chowder
Yankee Pot Roast
Boston Baked Beans

Brown Bread
Crisp Green Salad
Blueberry Crunch

Thursday November 6, 1969

COCKTAILS 5:30   DINNER 7:00

$5.00 PER PERSON MEMBERS MAY INVITE GUESTS
RESERVATIONS 944-6123
CANCELLATIONS UNTIL NOON NOVEMBER 4

THE YOUNGER MEMBERS COMMITTEE put on an old-fashioned "church supper" in 1969. Five dollars a head covered drinks, dinner, and hilarious entertainment.

HARVEST HOME DUCK DINNER
By CANDLELIGHT

FRIDAY, NOVEMBER 1, 1968 AT 6:30

This Autumn dinner is being repeated by request. It is a delightful way to entertain . . . Members may invite guests. Come for cocktails at five thirty.

Woman's Athletic Club of Chicago

THE DUCK DINNER

Poached Filet of Sole, Chantilly	Roast Duck a l'Orange	Bibb Lettuce, wine dressing
Bernkaster Riesling	Hunter's Baked Rice	Herb Rolls
Meister Kroner	Pommard	Peach Melba
Intermezzo	Clos de la Commaraine	Demi-tasse
	Domaine	
	Jaboulet — Vercherre	

DINNER $8.00

Call 944-6123 for reservations / Cancellations accepted until Wednesday, October 30

AN INVITATION TO the popular Duck Dinner.

and Ascot scarves. She was very talented and sewed them herself. We sold quite a lot of those ties."

After the Covells moved to Texas, the Gift Shop was separated from Personal Service. Under the direction of Mrs. Bentley G. McCloud, sales efforts were shifted to the second floor where that handsome yellow cabinet showed a variety of goods to very nice advantage. Mrs. Hays MacFarland designed some elegant new gift wrap, and before long more cupboards were installed to accommodate the increase in trade.

The Consular Dinners continued. Now that relations had eased, countries like Germany, Austria, and Japan were feted too, and members had a chance to sample their native dishes. (The club kitchen balked, however, at serving seaweed and raw fish.) For the Italian evening Consul Giacomo Profili promised an after-dinner talk about his impressions of Italian women. "Oh really?" his wife said when she heard the topic. "I will like to hear that too."

Partly to promote the sale of vintage wines from all over the world, the club also offered a series of gourmet dinners with international themes. There was a Mexican Fiesta with Flamenco dancers and an Italian harvest dinner, the *Sagra dell'uva*." The Entertainment Committee was bold enough to charge $15 a person for an evening of French cuisine. Americana was part of the program too. The ball-room was draped with fish nets and lobster pots one night for a New England Shore Dinner, complete with oysters and clams on ice, steamed lobsters, and "Fisherman Sam" wandering the floor taking tintype pictures of guests. The Harvest Home Duck Dinner was repeated every autumn, by request.

The 70th anniversary season made a memorable splash and did much to weave fresh contemporary voices into ancient club traditions. For the first time a serious effort was made to assemble old records and memorabilia into a respectable archive. Mrs. Philip R. Clarke donated funds to organize scrapbooks and rebind an album of early members' photographs by Matzene. Frances Hooper put together a 70th anniversary booklet that was not just a calendar of events but a celebration in brief of its founders, customs, and most spectacular treasures. Mrs. Edward McDermott sent a thousand-dollar gift to benefit "the true treasures of the club – the employ-ees." After the Director of the National Portrait Gallery in London affirmed that the club's signature *Portrait of a Lady* was indeed an authentic portrait from Sir Peter Lely's studio, Mrs. Henry Woods contributed funds (yet again) for its restoration by the Art Institute's conservator.

A glittering series of programs brought hundreds of long-lost members back into the clubhouse every month. Mrs. Harold F. Grumhaus, a director whose hus-band was president of the *Chicago Tribune*, arranged for the syndicated columnist "Suzy" to speak. It was her first appearance before a woman's club. Bright and vivacious in her Arnold Scassi kilt, Suzy brought inside news of the Beautiful People. The audience plied her with questions, most of them about the impending marriage

MRS. PHILIP K. WRIGLEY (left), Clare Boothe Luce (center), and Mrs. Thomas A. Kelly (partly hidden) greeting Mrs. Joseph Nellis (foreground) at the club's 70th anniversary dinner. Mrs. Luce was wearing the jeweled Count Sarmi gown she commissioned for President Nixon's Inaugural Ball the previous month.

of "Jackie and Ari." "But who else is there for Jackie to marry?" Suzy countered. She had loads of fascinating dish to spill. A reporter covering the event wrote that if the members hadn't prized their ballroom chandeliers so dearly, they would have been hanging from them.

Another glorious event was the Zodiac Luncheon in January 1969, a members-only celebration of astrology. All the Virgos sat together and the Scorpios and so on around the zodiac, dining in a darkened ballroom lit only by a revolving crystal ball flashing moonbeams on the walls. Irene Hughes, the famous mystic, rose after luncheon to interpret the stars. Among her predictions that day: Richard Nixon would not have a second term in the White House. No Kennedy would ever again win the presidency. Jackie Kennedy would have three years of marriage with Mr. Onassis. ("Three years of *happiness*," she clarified, "but I do not wish to embellish on that.") Not a bad record for a seer.

Ruth Ruggles and Marion Hales co-chaired a luncheon for Sir John Wedgwood, who brought from England many rare pieces of 18th-century china and silver, all duly guarded by private detectives. Members who owned Wedgwood of different colors, patterns, and periods brought examples from home, which were laid out in table settings with lush flower arrangements by the WAC's Garden Club members. Frances Hooper herself gave a slide show on Founder's Day featuring "Treasures and Traditions," and many handsome gifts presented in years past were on display that day in the solarium.

All agreed that the season's star turn was the black-tie dinner for Clare Boothe Luce, an evening which drew coverage from several magazines and major newspapers across the country. Mrs. Luce, then a recent widow, was billed as "the most distinguished woman in America." She had a long record of accomplishment — bestselling author, playwright of that smash hit *The Women*, congresswoman, war correspondent, U.S. ambassador to Italy, and not least, wife of the preeminent Henry Luce, founding publisher of *Time*, *Life*, and *Fortune* magazines. Letitia Baldridge, then a young Chicago career woman who had served as her social secretary in Rome, was in attendance at the dinner.

Swathed in a gown of rainbow-colored chiffon, the blue-eyed Mrs. Luce pronounced the clubhouse "the most beautiful feminine fortress in existence." She then gave voice to the perplexing identity problems facing the American woman. Now that "The Pill" had completed the task of emancipation, women were free to earn their own living, to choose marriage or not, children or not. Mrs. Luce challenged the playgirl philosophy of Helen Gurley Brown. Low necklines and short skirts, she cautioned, were not the way to go. But was the erasure of all sexual distinctions a desirable idea? What would happen to the once-sacred institution of marriage when women, literally and figuratively, were wearing the pants? Mrs. Luce acknowledged that she herself rather liked "doing her own thing."

If she did not lay out any precise solutions to these large social questions of the day, Clare Boothe Luce seemed to suggest ways that women could draw on the past to translate old social arts into agreeable new forms. Among the members of the audience that night there was likewise a feeling that the club was back on track, weathering change without losing sight of civilized traditions. Still ladies, after all those years.

CARVING OF AN OX SKULL draped with garlands, one of several architectural ornaments that frame the club's seventh-floor windows. During the Sixties, as new construction began to alter the original style and scale of Michigan Boulevard, such classical decorations were an increasingly rare sight along the avenue.

LITTLE AMANDA SENIOR
whispering to Santa at the
Children's Christmas Party. Ralph
W. Applegate, Jr., donned
his Santa suit and whiskers every
year and always sat in the
club's old-fashioned "Santa
Claus chair."

10
in the *Swim Again*

AFTER YEARS OF SUBURBAN EXODUS Chicago residential trends reversed again in the 1970s. Many newlyweds stayed in their city apartments or moved to some once-elegant townhouse on the North Side, a section of the city fast becoming known as "rehab heaven." A whole string of near-seedy neighborhoods was transformed with fresh paint, resanded woodwork, and brand new kitchens. It's not surprising that these inventive young families, who wanted to stay connected to all the excitements and resources of the city, also rediscovered (as one young lady dubbed it) "the dear old Woman's Ath."

Mrs. Thomas Z. Hayward, Jr., who joined the club right out of college in 1965, never forgot that Arthur, the club's venerable doorman, recognized her without fail from the day she arrived. "I couldn't figure out how he remembered my name," she recalls. He said, "'You're the only one who never wears a hat.'" By the mid-Seventies the club was alive with hatless young mothers and exuberant children on their way to swimming lessons, squash games, and classes in everything from backgammon to Chinese brush painting.

The biggest draw for these new junior members was the pool. Though generations of schoolchildren had learned to swim there, over time it had taken on a grim complexion, rather like some below-stairs tank in an English public school. The original wicker furniture, once so chic, was now looking very sad. There were mysterious splotches of black paint on the walls, and the plumbing was in such poor repair it was hard to get enough hot water for a shower. "Myrtle Rose asked me to serve as Athletic Chairman," Mrs. Charles M. Dykema recalls. "I think it was the very same day I was elected to the board. I went down to the pool and I thought, 'Oh dear.'"

Under Clarice Dykema's energetic direction, this department was redecorated and thoroughly resuscitated. Working with a small committee on a tight budget, she bought a set of sparkling white Brown-Jordan patio furniture. The walls were repainted. The dressing room stools were reupholstered, and Mrs. Robert Maher sewed special tablecloths for use at splash parties. They even hung fresh plants near the water, which had a kind of sultry charm but didn't live very long.

The ever-magnetic Irene Webb still had a reputation as the best swimming teacher in Chicago. Even suburban members were driving their children downtown after school two and three days a week for the prized lessons in the WAC pool. Along with new classes for Tiny Tots, expanded hours (including Early Bird swims), and intensive use by the Francis Parker School summer camp, the pool was quickly used to capacity again and generating a handsome profit for the club.

A chorus of voices recalls the delights and friendships of those years. Charlotte York, then one of the Tiny Tots, remembers that Mrs. Webb was equally encouraging to all the youngsters, whether they were good swimmers or just fair. "I was learning to dive," she says today. (Back then there was a diving board, since removed.) "I can still hear Webby saying, 'Oh-oh. Almost. Try again, try again.' There were different levels of tests. Swim Unassisted. Dive. I think Life Guard was the ultimate. When you passed a test, you got a little red and blue patch which was sewn on your bathing suit. It was the biggest honor you can imagine."

Children liked the warm water. Even babies could swim in it. In fact, Mrs. Webb believed in getting babies into the water as soon as they emerged from the womb, an idea which horrified some older members. "That was *unheard* of in my day!" said Mrs. Sailor, but the young mothers were willing to try it. Melinda Martin Sullivan (then Mrs. Herbert A. Vance, Jr.) remembers, "Mrs. Webb had a theory that babies were used to the sound of the fluid. My daughter was born in December, and she was in the pool by February. Where do you get a swim suit for a two-month-old? Several mothers did this. You got into the water with the baby. Mrs. Webb stood four feet away from you. You pushed the baby toward her and let go. She was ready to catch them. It must have worked because my oldest loves water."

MRS. CHARLES M. DYKEMA (far left), who revived the club's athletic programs. She founded the Family Olympics, which featured water games, relay races, and poolside buffets.

MRS. WEBB, the club's longtime swim instructor, in the pool with Alison Vance, aged four months. Mrs. Webb believed in getting newborns into the water as soon as possible.

Highchairs and playpens were brought in for the toddlers, and Mrs. R. Thomas Howell remembers the sense of freedom this gave to all the new mothers. "I could have the baby in a crib next to the pool and do laps," she says, "and when I swam past the baby, I would wave." Karen Howell eventually organized a nursery and baby-sitting service in a small inner room near the pool. "It had been part storage room, part office," she adds. "It was located where the Cafe is now. Karen Hunken and I went to thrift shops and bought cribs and toys. Later Charles Webster did a really wonderful storybook mural on the walls."

With a first-rate staff, this nursery became so popular members had to make reservations to use it. Mrs. Ralph W. Applegate, Jr., was a frequent customer. "Yolanda was the first baby-sitter," she recalls. "I would bring Trey down there, and she would say, 'Oh hi, Mrs. Pineapple, how are you?' She was so cute."

Many adults were swimming in the pool's new "lap lane," marking their progress in red squares on the big Red Cross "Swim and Stay Fit" chart. Members who swam 25 miles a year had their names printed in the club newsletter, and many were eligible for silver bowls at the annual athletic luncheon. Mrs. Lee H. Strohl, Mrs. Richard H. Schnadig, Mary Beth Beal, Mrs. Charles E. B. Jessop, Mrs. Charles N. Granville, III, Mrs. John J. Bransfield, Jr., and Mrs. Duncan Y. Henderson (who followed Clarice Dykema as Athletic Chair) were all regulars down at the pool. Mrs. Robert E. Molumby, who came down from Evanston to swim several days a week, says, "I don't know how many silver bowls I have, maybe six or eight." Everyone knew David Clarke, who was in the lane almost every day and was the first man to complete the 50-mile swim. When he passed the 400-mile mark in 1975, he received a silver tankard.

Lunch at poolside was reward for the morning's workout. Charlotte York echoes the reminiscences of many longtime swimmers. "You would be in the water, and you would hear this rolling and rumbling. It was Irene, wheeling the cart across the tiles, bringing your tray to your table. Finally you could get out of the pool and have your lunch!" For children it was traditional peanut butter and jelly or maybe a "drug-store cheese sandwich," otherwise known as "Breezy Cheesies." These were grilled cheese sandwiches cut in squares and served with matchstick fries and bread and butter pickles. The mothers consumed endless sprout salads, egg salad sandwiches with crumbled bacon, and broiled tomato, cheese, and bacon platters. Mrs. Jon N. Ekdahl remembers she did laps even when she was expecting. "I did the back stroke, little things," she says, "just so I could get the cinnamon toast."

Family Olympics on Saturday mornings brought fathers down to the pool as well. There were relay races and games, with ribbons galore for the winners. (On the subject of contests, the club actually fielded a swim team that traveled to points around the state and into Wisconsin for meets.) There were poolside buffets and Halloween parties too, but the greatest swimming event by far was to have your own birthday party at the WAC pool.

Mrs. Clayton Edward Whiting, Jr., remembers, "In those days you could take over the whole pool for a party, have it all to yourself. What was so amazing was that Mrs. Webb would ask you about the age group of the kids, and if they were small, maybe five or six years old, she would lower the water in the pool!" For Kathy Whiting and others who wanted it, Mrs. Webb would plan all the games — blowing balloons to the opposite end of the pool or racing with kickboards and inner tubes. Sometimes she would toss coins in the deep end, and the boys and girls would dive for them. At the finale she might set a dish of birthday candles sailing on the water, and the birthday child would blow out these floating lights one by one — a magic moment that still lives in the memories of many grown-up children.

The prize for the most exciting splash party in the club's history, however, might yet belong to Mrs. John K. Notz, Jr. "This was back in the Fifties," Jan Notz says. "My best friend Susie Veeder and I had the same birthdays, and we had a party down there. Our mothers were patrolling things, walking around the side of the pool in their suits and hats and gloves. All of a sudden a child started gasping and choking in the deep end. Without a second's hesitation Mrs. Veeder, who was a very good swimmer, dove into the water. With all her clothes on. She pulled this child out of the pool and up onto the side. She still had her hat on. We just loved that party."

Along with the blossoming "gentrification" of near-downtown neighborhoods, another broad social trend that worked in the club's favor was the growing interest in women's sports and physical fitness. At that time squash seemed to be the coming game for women. Clarice Dykema recalls, "Oh, I loved to play squash. I used to go with Charlie to watch exhibition games at the C.A.A. And I thought, maybe it's not quite regulation, but we do have a court! I talked to Tom Johnson, the squash pro at the C.A.A., and he agreed to come every Friday morning to coach our ladies."

Once the sandbox, driving net, and all the other golf paraphernalia which no one had used in several years were cleared out of the court, it was repainted and a schedule of squash classes and tournaments was organized. "We had a number of instructors," says Karen Howell, who played often in the Seventies. "There was a woman from South Africa, Annette Seegers, who was one of the top players in the United States." There were special clinics and a series of evening exhibition matches to pump up interest in the game. As many as 125 guests sometimes squeezed into the gallery, sipping wine, watching Tom Johnson compete with other "A" players in the city like Charlie Murphy and Dick Campbell. Clarice Dykema set up a squash ladder and "round robins" for the members. She played with Mrs. James G. Reese three times a week, and for a while there were a fair number of other regular players too, including Ann Rohlen, Mrs. Frank T. Padberg, and Mrs. Robert Palmer. Mrs. Peter Reese was then club champion, and Derry Henderson captured the title a few years later.

Around the same time Clarice Dykema brought in a lively young aerobics teacher, Andrea Clark. Already known to several members from her classes for the

Lake Shore Park District, Andrea Clark helped the club build a program of exercise instruction and eventually became its first Athletic Director. "Andrea put the 'athletic' back into the Woman's Athletic Club," says Helen Applegate. She brought aerobics. She did swim-and-trim classes. She hired high-end teachers."

Clark's enthusiasm brought many members into the club for regular workouts, and the therapeutic routines she developed to alleviate arthritic conditions and different kinds of spinal problems attracted even more converts. "Andrea put the mirror and the ballet barre in the Venetian Room," Mrs. Ellis B. Rosenzweig remembers. "She started with one session in the morning and one in the afternoon. We would drop off our children at school or at the pool and then go up there for a class."

Even more popular were the girls' ballet lessons, also held in the Venetian Room. "It was called 'Dance,'" says Marcia Ekdahl. "Andrea brought in this wonderful gal with red hair – Mary. She was small and sprightly, and she motivated those kids to learn things they never had any idea they could do. The girls wore leotards and pink tights and slippers, and they worked at the ballet barre. They did some tap-dancing too. I remember we needed to buy heeled tap shoes." There were also tumbling classes, originally for boys only, up on the eighth floor. A lovely graduation of sorts was held every May, when the little ballerinas and gymnasts would perform their cartwheels and somersaults and walk on the balance beam to the enthralled applause of mothers and grandparents. This annual production, which was staged

MRS. S. AUSTIN POPE in one of her favorite Bes-Ben hats.

in the ballroom and entirely choreographed by Andrea Clark, continued through the Eighties and was a highlight on many family calendars.

The spirit of participation carried over into the WAC's general programming as well, with lectures and seminars turning the club into a little university. Numerous art experts discussed contemporary painting, African sculpture, Old Sheffield Plate, and English furniture. Clement Conger, Curator of the White House, paid a visit, as did Rosamond Bernier, who had known Matisse and Miro in her years as an editor in Paris. Local dealers like Paul Franklin, Helen Findlay, and Richard Himmel appeared for panel discussions on art and antiques, and a man from the Victoria and Albert Museum demonstrated how to spot pottery and porcelain fakes. Books of tickets were sold for these workshops and small glasses of sherry served during the question-and-answer period. On several occasions Mrs. James W. Alsdorf, one of the club's own members, recounted tales of her travels in India and Nepal, where she and her husband purchased many superb stone and bronze sculptures. WAC members got an early glimpse of their fabulous collection, which grew to number several hundred pieces and was later presented as a major gift to the Art Institute.

There were lessons in flower-arranging, art-buying, interior decorating, plant-growing, weaving, quilting, and chess. Wednesday morning needlework courses were popular, and another handful of ladies set up their easels in the attic for weekly painting lessons. Mrs. Gordon Lang remembers, "Penny de Young and I took art classes on the top floor where the fitness equipment is now. We each bought a little tin box for our paints. It was a still-life class. The teacher put a pot of geraniums on a chair by the window, and we had to paint that. Penny is very artistic to this day and had all kinds of ideas. I was busy just trying to get that flower down."

THE CLUB'S

ANTIQUE CLOCK

THIS QUEEN ANNE CLOCK was a gift to the club in 1977 in memory of Mrs. S. Austin Pope (far left), a Life Member and president during the WAC's 50th anniversary year. The black and gold lacquered case was made by Joseph Bates in 1695, and the silver dial, signed in a handsome script by Thomas Jenkenson, is dated 1725.

Ada Pope's great interests were decorating and gardening, and in these she was a thorough perfectionist. She supervised much of the club's redecoration in the 1960s and even in her later years could often be found adjusting some small but telling detail in one of her favorite rooms. After her sudden death in 1975 a group of friends purchased this exquisite antique as a tribute to her taste, talent, and devotion to beautiful surroundings.

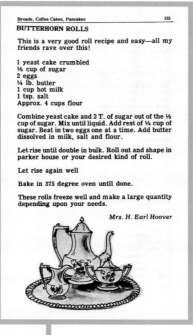

Breads, Coffee Cakes, Pancakes   155

BUTTERHORN ROLLS

This is a very good roll recipe and easy—all my friends rave over this!

1 yeast cake crumbled
½ cup of sugar
2 eggs
¼ lb. butter
1 cup hot milk
1 tsp. salt
Approx. 4 cups flour

Combine yeast cake and 2 T. of sugar out of the ½ cup of sugar. Mix until liquid. Add rest of ½ cup of sugar. Beat in two eggs one at a time. Add butter dissolved in milk, salt and flour.

Let rise until double in bulk. Roll out and shape in parker house or your desired kind of roll.

Let rise again well

Bake in 375 degree oven until done.

These rolls freeze well and make a large quantity depending upon your needs.

Mrs. H. Earl Hoover

96   Pies and Cakes

W.A.C. COCONUT CAKE

1½ cups granulated sugar
½ cup butter (flavored with a little grated orange peel)
1 cup milk
2¼ cups cake flour
2 tsp. baking powder
5 egg whites—large (6 if small)

Cream butter and sugar and add orange peel, milk, 2 cups sifted flour and beat well. Add remaining ¼ cup of flour into which the baking powder has been sifted. Last—fold in whites of eggs, beaten dry. Bake in 3x9 inch layer pans 25-30 minutes. Before frosting cut all the brown crusts off to make the cake completely white.

COCONUT FROSTING

2 cups granulated sugar
½ cup water
2 egg whites (beaten dry)
1 tsp. vanilla
Juice of ½ lemon
1 whole fresh coconut grated. Let stand 2 hrs. or so after it has been grated and shake roughly several times to dry it out. (Substitute canned sweetened coconut if fresh not available.)

Boil together the sugar and water until it spins a thread. *Slowly* beat this into the egg whites, lemon juice, and vanilla.
To Frost Cake:
Spread frosting on bottom layer and sprinkle with grated coconut. Place center layer. Put frosting on both sides of top layer and sprinkle top heavily with coconut.

Gourmet cooking was all the rage, and renowned chefs drew an eager audience. Louis Szathmary of The Bakery passed out restaurant secrets and discussed his philosophy of food. Ruth Ellen Church presided over a "Sparkling Evening with Wines," and members felt honored to get French cooking lessons from Alma Lach, a local expert with a national reputation. Perhaps the most enjoyable culinary moments took place in the club's own kitchen, when Marla Schachtel and others on staff did the teaching. "We watched Freddie make pecan coffee cake," says Karen Hunken. "She rolled out the dough and put in a layer of butter. Then she rolled it out again and put in another layer of butter. That's when I knew why those coffee cakes were so good. I remember she made them only on Saturdays."

Those WAC recipes would never have been available to earlier generations of members. Even the most persistent, who had chalked up hundreds of wasted hours trying to duplicate the club's salad dressings and pastries at home, could not pry those secrets out of Ione Rhynsburger, the WAC's longtime kitchen manager. In 1973 it was decided to publish a 75th anniversary cookbook, a project chaired by Mrs. Thomas D. Hodgkins with Melinda Sullivan at her right hand. Miss Rhynsburger, then a few years from retirement, graciously cooperated by at last supplying recipes for many of the club's longtime dishes, some of which had never been written down before. This friendly unpretentious book had a yellow cover, enchanting pen and ink drawings by A. Philbin Schulz, and a section of members' own favorite recipes as well. It cost $5.95 and sold out within a few years. It may have prompted the request from *Gourmet* magazine in 1977 for permission to reprint the club's orange roll recipe. In 1979 a second edition was published under the aegis of Mesdames William G. Dubinsky and Richard J. L. Senior. Some recipes were revised, and Diana Senior prepared a spectacular 40-page index that listed entries not only by food type but by contributor's name as well.

A club travel program was organized by the redoubtable Anne Nicholson, known to her fellow members as Chicago's foremost theater devotee. A playwright herself and a force behind the preservation of the Goodman Theatre, she had an unusual number of friends. Karen Zupko Stuart, a kindred spirit, still conjures up the sight of Anne "steaming up Michigan Avenue in her kilts, her Ferragamos, and a butter-soft red leather jacket which Leslie Hindman and I persuaded her to buy."

With the help of agent Josephine Barr, Anne Nicholson led two trips abroad, the first to England and the second to France (where WAC members and their spouses went to Giverny the first year it was open to visitors). Peter Dagnall, the model of a Cambridge gentleman, served as shepherd on both tours. In England there were several nights of theater and some spectacular dining in stately homes. "We went to the Old Vic," Mrs. John B. Wright recalls, "where we met *every*body." Some people still smile about their visit to Broughton Castle. Crossing the moat, the group was greeted by Lady Saye and Sele, who expressed many regrets that her husband could not be present. There was a tour of the house and a wonderful buffet. Lady Saye and Sele admired the Chicago Symphony and was admired in return by all the Chicagoans. As they were leaving, the friendly hostess confessed that her husband had escaped over the back hedge shortly before the group arrived because he did not, he said, fancy spending his lunch hour talking to a bunch of ladies with hockey sticks.

As always, the club calendar included many full-dress fashion shows. Bill Blass himself appeared on the runway in 1977. Some of these fashion events now had a charming new "family" spin. Frances Hooper may have inspired this trend when she hosted Kate Greenaway Day in 1972. This beautifully executed program included an exhibit of Miss Hooper's original Greenaway watercolors, sketches, and books. After readings from the author's letters and stories, some of the WAC's petite ladies, aged four to ten, marched about the solarium in little Kate Greenaway gowns and bonnets. A few years later Mrs. Andrew McNally IV chaired a special Family Valentine Party. She displayed a selection of her father-in-law's antique Valentines, an exquisite collection that has since been exhibited at venues like the Chicago Historical Society and the Newberry Library. There was a family fashion parade of moms, dads, and offspring modeling sporty clothes from Saks, a show carried off with special elan by Nena Ivon's lovely narration.

Members were often surprised at how pleasantly their children took to the club-house and its rituals. Remembered with special affection are the now-demolished little dressing rooms near the pool. "You remember those rooms had a small shelf and a mirror," says Edie Molumby. "When my girls came down with me, they would

147

each want their own room. Then they would close the door, sit on the little bench, and comb their hair." Matthew Hunken remembers how much fun it was simply riding up and down in the elevator with Howard, "who was always the gentleman." Carey Lennox seems to speak for many grown-ups when she recalls childhood excursions to the club with her grandmother, Mrs. Hays MacFarland. "We'd be all dressed up and have our little drinks and hors d'oeuvres in the lounge," she says. "Then we'd go upstairs to the dining room. My sister and I loved the pockets in the tables where you put your gloves and purse. And oh, the finger bowls! People think kids get bored with formal stuff like that. We loved it."

In recognition of the growing participation of women in the larger world, the club continued its presentation of Distinguished Woman Awards to high achievers. A series honoring Great Ladies was begun in January 1975 with a luncheon honoring Lady Valerie Solti. Nancy Dickerson, the first woman correspondent to cover a national political convention on television, received a citation the following year. Anne Armstrong, U.S. Ambassador to the Court of St. James, was another honoree, as was the legendary Helen Hayes, who was also presented with an Honorary Membership. Chicago's own great ladies were remembered too. Ardis Krainik and Lee Phillip Bell received awards, and Margueritte Stitt Church, a longtime WAC member who represented the 13th District for a dozen outstanding years in Congress, was given a Distinguished Citizen Citation.

Barbara Bush was another red-letter guest. Coming in the spring of 1979 at the invitation of Mrs. Philip L. Cochran, Mrs. Bush talked about their tour in China, where George Bush was then the U.S. government's official liaison. Mrs. Earnest E. Christensen remembers that during the question-and-answer period following her slide talk, Mrs. Bush looked out at the crowd and said, "Doesn't *any*one want to ask me about the most important event that occurred yesterday?" This was her husband's announcement that he was entering the race for president. Ronald Reagan, of course, got the nod that year instead.

In an amusing postscript to the Bush event, a few months later Nancy Reagan attended a private party Daniel Terra held at the club. Mrs. Reagan felt quite at home, having been a guest at many WAC teas and dances during her debut years. Several people still remember that as Nancy Reagan walked out onto Ontario Street that afternoon, bidding farewell to a host of generous supporters, she turned around one last time for a word with Wilbert Williams, the club's longtime doorman. "Goodbye, Wilbert," she said, "and you be sure to vote for my husband in November." Reagan already had his vote, Wilbert says, as Loyal Davis, Nancy Reagan's father, was his doctor of many years.

The club was always celebrating gala anniversaries – the Diamond Jubilee Ball, Edwardian Day, Dorsey Connors reflecting on a century of elegance in Chicago. In 1978 Franz Benteler and His Royal Strings played for an 80th anniversary black-tie dinner dance. Perhaps the most memorable parties of the Seventies,

LADY VALERIE SOLTI accepting the club's Distinguished Woman award. Over 300 people attended a luncheon in her honor in January 1975.

MRS. PHILIP L. COCHRAN (left)
and Mrs. Robert C. Gunness
(right) flank Anne Armstrong (center)
at a reception in the drawing room.
The first American woman to be appointed
Ambassador to Great Britain, Mrs.
Armstrong regaled members with tales
of life at court.

however, were the sold-out children's Christmas parties, held *twice* every year, on the first two Saturdays in December, to accommodate the large number of families who made it an annual ritual.

"Those parties were quite the thing," says Judy York, onetime chair of the event. "You made your reservations the minute the announcements came out or you didn't get in. They were so fancy and so much fun. A total madhouse. The clothes were amazing. You have never seen more magnificent dresses and bows on little girls than the ones they wore. Beautiful taffetas and those Florence Eiseman dresses with all the smocking and embroidery. The boys in their cut-off pants and saddle oxfords. People would have tiny, tiny babies in these gorgeous outfits."

There were sing-alongs, puppet shows, dog shows, magic acts, and long lines to see Santa. The role of Santa was played by Norman Clarke for five years. As he told Mrs. Richard W. Hurckes, he felt Santa should not wear glasses, so he removed his and even his own son did not recognize him. After he retired the role was taken on by Bill Clark, Philip H. Kemper, and Ralph W. Applegate, Jr. Sitting on Santa's knee, each child would get a small gift and a chance to whisper what he really wanted for Christmas. ("And what would you like to find in your stocking?" Phil Kemper asked one little miss. "Emeralds," she answered without missing a beat.)

Part of the WAC Christmas tradition was having a Stuart-Rodgers family portrait taken by the fireplace in the lounge. Betty Rodgers (now Mrs. Lyman Wood Jeffreys) was expert at composing these pictures, with everybody's socks pulled up, ankles crossed, faces smiling. Many of the photographs are now family heirlooms. "Those 5 x 7's in their mahogany frames go all the way up our second-floor staircase and around the wall on the third floor," says Marcia Ekdahl. "We started taking them at 18 months and did it through senior year in high school. Even when the kids were too old for the party, the five of us would still dress up and go over there for a photograph. That's been one of our happiest moments, having that picture taken."

Underpinning all these enjoyments was a sturdy administration. Helen Miley (who later remarried and became Mrs. Rowntree) was appointed manager in December 1971 and did much to square prices with usage. During her term as president, Mrs. George S. Chappell, Jr., streamlined board operations, with committees now reporting to four vice-presidents. Her truly signal achievement was to introduce, at long last, a modern pension and health insurance plan for employees.

When Mrs. James D. Baillet assumed the presidency in 1976, she organized a Long-Range Planning Committee, chaired by Mrs. Lawrence J. Lawson, Jr., which worked to promote member services. This group published a booklet on planning private parties and issued for the first time a price list of fresh and frozen carry-out foods. A monthly calendar full of news and information replaced the individual program notices. Thursday night dinners were brought back, and they even tried a "Buffet-Bus" on Symphony Nights. (The first buffet was successful, but the bus broke down on the way to the concert!) The club's rooms were opened more often to outside groups, and at the invitation of Mrs. William F. Petersen and Mrs. Philip H. Kemper, both the Chicago Columbia Club and the Chamber Music Society established a regular calendar of meetings and recitals which continue to the present day.

In spite of renewed vitality and very active management, the club's overhead continued to grow faster than its revenues. Possibly the worst financial decade in this century for all clubs, the Seventies brought inflationary increases in the cost of food, labor, and materials, along with crippling tax and insurance bills. The national fuel shortage made matters worse. Adding to the WAC's own difficulties, the upgrading of its security and building systems could no longer be deferred. Though Mrs. Philip L. Cochran did a superlative job rounding up outside consultants who provided advice (gratis), repairs to fire doors, stairways, wiring, and pipes were numbingly expensive. The days were long gone when such measures as switching to paper placemats and doubling the price of cola would make a meaningful difference in the budget (though both were done). Dues and initiation fees were raised. There were special assessments and a new 15% service charge on meals in the dining room. Still, the deficits kept growing, and the forecast was bleak.

Few of those lighthearted members splashing about in the pool or leaping around the squash court ever knew how close the club came to collapse. They were unaware that speculation in city financial circles put its survival at an outside limit of three years. Almost completely forgotten was the darkest shadow of all. The clubhouse was sitting on leased land, a Michigan Avenue property growing more valuable every day. The calendar was now rolling perilously close to the time when the possibility of buying it would disappear forever. When the lease expired, the clubhouse and virtually everything in it would be lost.

Most white knights exist only in books. It was the club's great good fortune to meet a real one in the nick of time.

DANCERS SWEEP ONTO THE FLOOR at the 90th Anniversary Ball. Couples (left to right) are Nena Ivon and her escort, Mr. and Mrs. Francis J. Klimley, and Mr. and Mrs. R. Thomas Howell.

11
Titles and Trust

IN THE WINTER OF 1977 Mrs. James D. Baillet asked Wayne Maxwell to come onto the Long-Range Planning Committee as real estate consultant and review the club's store leases, which for years had been managed in an almost casual way. Long leases had been granted at old-fashioned rates with little thought to actual operating costs or inflation. It was a sleepy situation, with some tenants occupying prime space on the most elegant street in Chicago for not much more than the price of a nice two-bedroom apartment in a good neighborhood.

Wayne Maxwell, then retired, had been in the real estate business all his life. His wife Gigi was a member of the WAC board. "Gigi brought me into this," he said later. "She was developing great fears for the survival of this club. I became very much enamored of it, and after I met with the Planning Committee and understood the problem, it became a personal effort of ours to see that something was done."

Both the Maxwells worked to bring the storefront rents in line with current values and, as they put it, "make our income property produce." It was a long campaign. Its particulars must remain sealed, but the log of rising receipts alone can never reflect the true dimensions of that struggle — the hundreds of phone calls, long meetings, blind alleys, surprises, disappointments, legal jousting, and down-to-the-wire negotiating that finally achieved a proper and stable tenant base.

When he first tackled the situation, Wayne Maxwell remembers, "I found the club was in a difficult position. Nobody had any recent information. I had to make pencil sketches and measure the square footage myself because no one had any idea where the blueprints were. There were plans all over the basement. I finally found the original tracings crushed at the bottom of a big wooden bin."

He was also astonished to encounter resistance not from a tenant but from someone at the club. The first time he proposed a modest rent increase, one woman pronounced the new rates "Immoral! Absolutely immoral!" (Fortunately, she was outvoted.) The stores changed hands several times. As the years went by, there were festive moments too. When Sidney Bayer retired after 40 years on the Avenue, he held a grand going-out-of-business sale, pulling out long-stowed-away boxes of breathtaking laces, linens, and silks. WAC members snapped up this cache of gorgeous merchandise.

It was a glorious match when Cartier, the legendary French jeweler, leased the anchor store in 1984, opening with a splash at the height of the Christmas shopping season. Wedgwood, seller of fine English china, took another storefront the following year. Over time the club was able to boast an appealing mix of prosperous shops with character and cachet. All it took to accomplish this dramatic turn-around was fortitude, patience, and extraordinary savvy. Wayne and Gigi Maxwell possessed them in abundance.

They were also exceedingly generous. Wayne Maxwell never collected his due brokerage commissions. He donated them instead to the club, with the stipulation they be managed separately and used as seed money to buy the land. In a few years' time this fund passed the $100,000 mark and kept growing. In 1983 it was renamed the Maxwell Fund. In 1987, when the bylaws were amended to permit the admission of men, Wayne Maxwell was elected the first male member of the Woman's Athletic Club.

All along, though the average member was never aware of it, the time was running closer to the expiration of the ground lease. On different occasions some tentative overtures were made to bank officials by the Maxwells, Mrs. Dykema, and Mrs. and Mrs. F. Richard Meyer, but in truth the club was still in serious financial difficulty. In fact, it was tacitly acknowledged that the Maxwell Fund might have to be used instead to cover the costs of relocation. "Who would have given us a mortgage then?" asks Mrs. Lawrence J. Lawson, Jr., who assumed the presidency in 1980. "We had an operating deficit. What I did my two years in office was work on finance. The whole business of buying the land was a far-off dream."

From the early 80s onward, however, the club's financial picture did improve. The store leases made the biggest difference, but the introduction of new programs and services plus a minimum restaurant charge added a good deal of ballast.

MRS. WAYNE MAXWELL (center) and Mrs. Earnest E. Christensen (right) look on as Mrs. Lawrence J. Lawson sets fire to the WAC's 1929 lease agreement at the Buy-the-Land Luncheon in April 1986. As the club's guiding spirit in this historic purchase, Mrs. Lawson was presented with a silver compact engraved "To Our Negotiator."

Through the presidencies of Mrs. Maxwell and Mrs. Earnest E. Christensen the budget moved firmly into the black.

Meanwhile, Barbara Lawson was appointed the club's first Real Estate Chairman. A longtime WAC member who had celebrated her 16th birthday at an elegant luncheon in the Mirror Room, Mrs. Lawson was determined to see the club somehow achieve that "far-off dream." She remembers now, "If we wanted to, we could not have forgotten about it. Wayne kept needling us, and he was like a father, in that you wanted to rise to his expectations."

On May 21, 1985, the fateful season began. "I approached the board that day," Barbara Lawson continues, "and proposed that we begin negotiations with The Northern Trust Company, as Trustee of the John V. Farwell Trust, to purchase the land beneath our clubhouse. Everybody was thrilled with the idea, of course, and agreed that it should be done if at all possible. But many of them were just a little pessimistic, particularly the women who had come through the hard times. There was a long discussion. Pinkie [Christensen] called for the vote. It passed unanimously, and that was a really big step. Then I brought in an advisor, Harold W. Perry, Jr., of Pannell Kerr Forster, our club accountants. Skip Perry knew Chicago real estate extremely well. He was professional, understated, supremely competent. He contacted The Northern Trust Company and we began."

There followed a long silence of several months. Members of the board had agreed that confidentiality was paramount. They heard nothing about the negotiations in progress, and no one asked a single question. Behind the scenes Perry and Lawson worked together with remarkable skill and sensitivity to achieve a positive outcome. In the late fall the club was offered a chance to buy the property at a price it could afford to pay. Barbara Lawson brought this offer to the board on November 19. "People couldn't believe it!" she remembers. "They were ecstatic. Of course, it was all contingent on our getting a mortgage approved by mid-January. We all worked very hard to get that done – the lawyers, appraisers, myself, and the people at the Washington National Insurance Company in Evanston, which gave us our mortgage. It was an amazing Christmas holiday."

The decision to purchase the land was ratified at a special meeting of the Corporation on March 14, 1986, and the closing was held on March 21. Thus the land and virtually the future of the club were secured. "That was the day we knew it wasn't too good to be true," says Barbara Lawson. "It was a mix of the right people, the right time, the right balance sheet. We finally joined our land with our building, and that marriage, of course, was the happiest news we'd had at the WAC for a long time."

An important factor in winning that mortgage was the club's fresh and attractive appearance, much to the credit of Mrs. Harold T. Martin, the Decorating Chairman. "She wanted the club to look exquisite," recalls Barbara Lawson. "She was discerning and also bountiful, and she had the kind of genteel taste that everyone liked."

Eloise Martin refurbished the ballroom, hung cream and moire paper on the fourth floor, and resilvered the Silver Room doors. She had the courage to remove Marian Gheen's original ivy and cream wallpaper in the dining room foyer (which by that time had gone very shabby) and paint it a soft green. She also purchased a large antique screen, circa 1830, to complement the new color of the wall and better balance the proportions of the long and narrow space. "That screen came right out of a chateau in France," says Mrs. Martin. "It was imported by Richard Norton. I remember I loaded it into the station wagon and drove it down and hung it myself on a 95-degree day."

In 1984 the old wallpaper was also removed in the second-floor gallery and replaced by a light yellow glaze under the direction of Chicago decorator Bruce Gregga and his colleague, Mrs. Edward R. Weed. "We were worried to death," says Lawrie Weed, who is also a longtime WAC member, "that everyone would have a heart attack when the last of that paper came down. But Elouise Woods liked the project and agreed to cover the whole cost of redoing it." Another prominent "angel" in those years was Mrs. Charles F. Grey. After the ballerinas and the gymnasts took over the Venetian Room several days a week, Josephine Grey paid for new draperies, chairs, cabinets, and other amenities to maintain its gentle charm for Monday bridge.

Once the land was secured, the long-deferred matter of air conditioning the ballroom was taken up with new enthusiasm. "We could never book any programs or private parties there in the summer," says Mrs. Lee W. Jennings, who was president at the time of decision. "And you were never sure about May or September either. Suddenly it's 90 degrees one day and everybody is sweltering. People were pushing for air conditioning. But it cost a lot of money, and we really dreaded it because we didn't know what we were going to run into up there. I was on the ladders, climbing behind walls, looking at the wiring in those attics. We were very careful."

An excellent water-cooled condenser system was finally installed in 1988, with unobtrusive vents which blended right into the design of the rooms. Because the seventh floor would now be in use year round, the solarium was entirely redecorated as well. At that time the long sun porch was still filled with a sea of furniture — divans, bridge chairs, little jardinieres, and drum tables that gave it the look of a 1920s house party. Lawrie Weed introduced a new simplicity and style with tall mirrors, a pair of parsons tables, chic black-and-white striped curtains, and some unusual topiary plants. Mrs. Howard J. Trienens suggested renaming this pleasing new space the Presidents' Room. Accordingly, pictures of the past presidents were rounded up by Mrs. Richard W. Hurckes and Mrs. David C. Hilliard and hung on the north wall.

THE OLD SOLARIUM was reborn as the Presidents' Room at a tea in October 1988. A cluster of WAC presidents surround their senior colleague, Mrs. Charles M. Sailor, who had recently celebrated her 94th birthday. From left to right: Mrs. Wayne Maxwell, Mrs. James D. Baillet, Mrs. Sailor, Mrs. Lee W. Jennings, Mrs. Lawrence J. Lawson, and Mrs. Joseph Andrew Hays.

An inaugural tea honoring contributors to the new Presidents' Room was held in October 1988. Throughout this decade many members continued to make generous gifts of cash and family heirlooms, and some of the club's nicest silver and linens were acquired through bequest. A fine French lyre clock came from the family of the late Mrs. Clifford Barborka. Mrs. Lawrence O. Holmberg left an ivory-handled tea set, Mrs. John W. Clarke a sterling silver punch bowl with a dozen cups and a footed tray. The sister of Miss Helen MacNair donated her monogrammed wooden chest of silver flatware, and Mrs. Charles J. Gallagher herself gave a cloth handmade in Spain and a large supply of matching tea and dinner napkins. These and many other exceptional gifts are often laid out for special events, to which they lend incomparable grace and glamour.

So the club's formal quarters were resplendent again. A concerted effort was also made to modernize services and programs to attract "the new woman" in a rapidly changing society. The Personal Service Department had been in a moribund state for years. Into the Fifties and Sixties a good part of the fifth floor was used for storage, and a shampoo and set could take an extra hour if the water went out. Miss Helena, the manicurist, was the only operator booking regular appointments. Business was so slow that suggestions to turn the space into an art gallery or a travel agency were given serious consideration.

Clarice Dykema held fast to her conviction that the department was necessary to the versatility and future of the club. A plan commissioned during the Seventies for a state-of-the-art fitness facility had proved too rich for the club's foundering budget, but Mrs. Dykema did hire away two masseuses (Estelle and Velma) and a receptionist from the Lake Shore Club when it closed in 1977. Business tripled in 1980 with the arrival of Donna Montewski, hairdresser to a whole generation of WAC children. She could charm a weepy toddler into his first hair cut and give his mother an expert facial an hour later. She made appointments on Saturdays to accommodate businesswomen. When Helen Applegate took over as Personal

Service Chairman, she started to promote specially tailored Spa Days. "You could sign up for a day or a week," Mrs. Applegate recalls. "There were exercise classes, massage, facials, pedicures. We wore you out and pampered you back."

With the aim of making the Personal Service quarters light, airy, and inviting, a modest in-house remodeling was undertaken during the Dykema regime. Six old "Silence Cubicles" were rebuilt as four resting rooms, a hair salon with new shampoo bowls and chairs was organized in the northwest corner of the floor, and a shower room was installed in place of an ancient service kitchen. Lost along the way was the old wooden steam cabinet, a big white box with a hole on top for milady's head. Mrs. William D. Staley still misses it. "You just opened it up, sat down, and closed the lid," she says. "It was on a timer, like the ones at Maine Chance. The steam would come up and all the oil from your massage would get into your skin. It was wonderful."

Members could still get a sense of the old Turkish Bath Department on the sixth floor, though this area too was reorganized with new lockers, lights, make-up mirrors, and a small sauna. The steam and salt showers, where long-ago members were packed with mud, hosed down, and rubbed with salt, still retained a touch of their old magic. The original Hot Room, however, was filled with boxes by then and the blue-tiled Scotch Douche converted to a huge liquor closet.

The fifth floor bedrooms were made over as day rooms for meetings and bridge games and renamed for three notable members — the Armour Room, the Lyon Lounge, and the Maxwell Room. The large square room at the east end was completely transformed. "Do you remember when it looked like a hospital room?" asks Mrs. Donald J. Hindman. "It was all white. There was an old sink in the corner and a massage table and a screen that always had a towel thrown over the top of it. It was very depressing."

CELEBRATING AT THE GRAND REOPENING of the pool in March 1990 were (bottom row, seated left to right): Dr. Teresa Berry, Mrs. Lee H. Strohl, Mrs. Robert E. Molumby, Marion Elmquist; (middle row, standing) Mrs. James P. Elmes, Mrs. O. J. Heestand, Jr., Edith E. Trutter, II, Mrs. Michael L. Keiser, Mrs. John J. Lynch, Jr.; and (top) Mrs. Carter H. Manny, Jr., who contributed funds for the pool's new water filter system.

A trip to the furniture stacks in the attic produced four Chinese red card tables. Mrs. F. Lawrence Alberti, First Vice-President and a lady of fastidious taste, had the idea of putting Formica on the tops and then painting the tables white, so they could be easily cleaned. The wash basin was torn out, chair rail moldings installed, and new carpeting and fabric for chair pads selected by Nancy Vert. Pat Hindman knew a shop in Key West that still had some Audubon prints from the Amsterdam Series, which she purchased and hung on the walls. *Voila*, the large, light, and serene Audubon Room – one of the best loved rooms in the club.

Toward the end of the decade it was at last financially possible to renovate the pool. Thomas Hickey of Weese Hickey Weese worked with contractor John C. Telander to bring it functionally up to date and legally up to code, while maintaining its architectural integrity. A new tile floor was laid. The dressing rooms and showers were entirely redesigned with an eye toward easy flowing spaces and enhanced lighting. Not in the least, a brand new attraction was born – the Cafe 626.

"We had to change," says Mrs. Joseph Andrew Hays, who presided over this project. "We're a woman's club, but we had to be there for families. There had been only a small room with two lockers in it for men. Husbands and sons wanted to swim here too. We never had a casual eating area. If you weren't dressed up, there was nowhere you could stop for a quick bite, nowhere you could eat comfortably with children. If you did order something by the pool, it took forever. So we installed this new cafe and put together a menu of things that kids like – those chicken pieces and hamburgers and ice cream. And salads and yogurt for the moms. I go down there now and see a bunch of young women with children and somebody's husband slipping in for a quick bowl of soup and I am thrilled. For a city club, this is the future."

Programming was updated as well. Nena Ivon founded a new group called Network in 1982 for the club's growing cadre of working women. "At the time this was really something different," she recalls. "We started at noon, we listened to the speaker while we ate lunch, and we were out by 1:15 p.m. The idea was to give professionals more access to peers, to talk about successes and failures and problems in a small setting."

Issues went way beyond "What Color Is Your Parachute?" (though someone did take up that hot topic too). Members learned how to start a business, manage time, read a balance sheet, negotiate a divorce, and pick a stock. Over the years many of the speakers were members already flourishing in their own careers – Margaret McCurry, Pamela Bardo, Laurel Bellows, Peggy Snorf, and Leslie Hindman among them. Virginia Wolff, one of the city's top floral designers, recalls that her audience was most impressed by the fact that she had started her business later in life, after her children had flown the nest. Pamela Bruce Cronin, one of the first women vice-presidents at the First National Bank of Chicago, was invited to talk about money management. (She was not a member at the time, though she soon joined and chaired the Network herself a few years later.) It was a case of Network in action.

159

"THE BRIDGERS"

DURING THE 1920S, 30S, AND 40S just about everybody played bridge. In 1981 Daisy Kuhlmey recalled her introduction to bridge at the WAC; "When I first joined the WAC in 1935," she wrote, "Mrs. William Nelson Pelouze and Mrs. Richard C. Cragg invited me to join the bridge group." Players met in the ballroom for a lesson followed by lunch and adjourned to the sixth floor card room. In the summer months they played at the Glen View Club. (In the early years, Mrs. Pelouze supplied the group with gorgeous prizes and other luxury items.)

The Venetian Room, on the sixth floor, has been home to the Duplicate Bridge Group for many years. Decorated with wallpaper murals of Venice and engravings of Venetian scenes, it was an elegant venue for bridge and private parties alike.

When aerobic exercise became more popular in the early 1980s, it was discovered that the parquet floor (this room was the club's original gymnasium) underneath the soft gray carpeting provided the necessary cushioning for these classes. The carpet was taken up and mirrors and a barre were installed on the long wall covering the

Venetian murals. Since mirrors are taboo in a card room, gray silk curtains were hung so the mirrors could be covered on bridge days. (In 1994 the bridge players tried Tai Chi in the Silver Room before sitting down to a long afternoon at the table.)

The pre-game lesson has been an important part of the bridge experience at the WAC. In 1936, Mrs. Minor became the club's first bridge instructor. "Never show the texture of your bid by the expression or tone of voice," she would remind her students. She was replaced in 1948 by Mrs. Paul Marks. Other principle instructors included D. J. Cooke and Betty Gordon. Today's WAC bridge players are taught by Richard Strauss and Michael Papangelis. Kay Hathaway has been the director for more than ten years.

Since 1960, the "bridgers" have had an official chairman. They are, in chronological order: Ann Alexander, Marguerite Williams, Lura Holmberg, Mary Allen, Pattie Bennett, Helen Huff, Cynthia Rummel, Bundy Lind, Oogie Buenz, Nancy Wright, and Jane Hand.

In 1990, Carol Hays, then club president, reported that Mrs. Josephine Gray celebrated her 90th birthday at the club. Josephine, known to many as "Mrs. Bridge" was responsible for the

refurbishing and decorating of the Venetian Room including new tables and chairs (as well as giving the club its first computer). In thanking the club for the birthday celebration Josephine noted the exquisite "shoulder bouquet" that she had been given. "This gracious, generous lady plays bridge most Mondays – and still wins," Hays wrote, "Josephine can't fib about her age for we all remember she's a year younger than our club."

For special occasions such as the 90th birthdays of Gertrude Sponsel and Daisy Kuhlmey and others, the bridge group held Dutch-treat luncheons to which Faith Vilas (former club president and long time WAC board member) brought her legendary Pink Petal Cake – a white cake with rich pink frosting topped with numerous pink-frosting petals.

Many WAC members have achieved Life Master status with the American Contract Bridge League, among them: Mary Allen, Lee Fitzgerald, Alice Foy, Shirley Gately, Miss Elizabeth Hoffman (a WAC Life Member since 1935), Mary King (one of Chicago's outstanding players), Cynthia Rummel, and Faith Vilas.

CYNTHIA WALKER RUMMEL

CYNTHIA RUMMEL
(Clockwise from left), Kay Hathaway, Marie Fazio, Patty Bennett, Thelma Craft, Bundy Lind, Faith Vilas, and Helen Huff at a spring luncheon.

KIRSTEN GULEV AND MRS. CHARLES F. GREY.

"You may laugh now," she says, "but in the early days, before all that dress-for-success stuff, I'd had Nena talk to my female officers about suits and accessories and make-up. So then she asked me to speak at the WAC. I tried to gear it toward different types of investments and financial instruments, and I worried, 'What if nobody comes?' But there was quite a good-sized group." In fact, Network quickly developed a reputation for good talk on timely subjects and attracted participants across the whole spectrum of the membership.

Then there were "the ladies who read." A literary discussion group was also founded in 1982 by Mrs. John B. Wright, Club Librarian, who always carried two or three novels in her capacious handbag. These members met one afternoon a month in the club library to review the literature of their choice. On occasion authors and professors were invited to speak, but in the early years these bookish ladies did most of the talking themselves. Fittingly, the group was launched with Anne Nicholson's review of *The Grande Dames*. Books under consideration ranged high and wide, from *Hollywood Wives* to M. F. K. Fisher's *Consider the Oyster* to *Memoirs of Hadrian*. There were movie nights in the Venetian Room too, complete with popcorn. It is fair to say the group tended toward a certain Anglophilia and was always ready for another tome about Churchill, Henry VIII, or the Queen Mother. Mary Beth Beal held the group captive one afternoon with her account of *The Lisle Letters*, a scholarly history of one English family through its correspondence. All agreed they hit the jackpot the day that Mary Mills Dunea gave an account of her attendance at the wedding of Prince Andrew and Sarah Ferguson. (Whether this meeting included a review of a book is not clear in the records.) Anne Nicholson so enjoyed this cozy gathering of friends that after her mother's death she redecorated the library in her memory, a commission graciously carried out by Robert Turner.

Among the cornucopia of services was a revitalized gift shop. Pinkie Christensen set its operations on a more businesslike course and introduced Crane stationery and invitations, Gordon Fraser greeting cards, and a variety of novel items, including some on consignment. "When we went to China in 1981," she recalls, "I bought a lot of small items there. Tiny porcelain amulets on braided cords. Petit point eyeglass cases. Cinnabar bracelets. Little folding scissors no bigger than a couple of postage stamps. Those giant-size teacups with the lids. Now they're everywhere. At that time they were something new and they sold very fast."

Mrs. Christensen organized the club's first real Christmas bazaar in 1981, when a rather nice profit was realized from the sale of WAC baked goods, handmade placemats, baby clothes, cheese spreads, jellies, and decorations. This whole shopping service, including the second-floor store and holiday boutiques, expanded manyfold in the hands of subsequent Gift Shop chairmen, each of whom put her own stamp on the merchandise. Mrs. Richard D. Gifford introduced designer dresses and playsuits for children age one to eight. "We brought in toys for children too," remembers Mrs. David L. Conlan, "and small hostess and wedding presents. We bought lots of things for the bazaar ourselves – wrappings, advent calendars, stocking stuffers. One of my favorite shoppers was Verna Stovall. We'd have a dozen of this or that, and she'd buy them all."

Another appealing amenity was developed by Mrs. John C. Kern, a cosmopolitan traveler who forged reciprocal ties with clubs all over the world. Members traveling on business or pleasure could now get modestly priced rooms and meals in gorgeously appointed settings, many so fascinating they were destinations in themselves. The Paul J. Millers brought back tales of the Royal Selangor Club in the center of Kuala Lampur. "It was behind a big gate in a pretty park," Michal Miller reports. "Very colonial, with a long wooden bar that could serve a regiment." Its delightful opposite was the quaint and charming Women's University Club in London. "The front door was very obscure," recounts Mrs. Jeffry J. Knuckles. "It was on a street so tiny the taxi driver never heard of it."

The Cosmopolitan Club in New York quickly became a frequently used favorite of many WAC members. Mary Louise Fazzano recounts a weekend visit there some years ago. "I heard there was a winter hurricane coming, a bad Nor'easter. New York was clearing out. I called ahead to the Cos Club and said, 'This is Miss Fazzano. Would you mind putting two chicken sandwiches in the refrigerator for me?' Sure enough, the whole city shut down. And there I was, with ten floors in Manhattan to myself. But I had my sandwiches. The idea is, they care about you. I am a Non-Resident, and one of the reasons I keep my WAC membership at full tilt is the reciprocity. It is very reassuring to know that when you're in a strange city, you can go to a place where you'll meet like-minded people."

The program calendar still featured big names and intriguing stories. Among the most notable were P. D. James, Kitty Carlisle Hart, The Honorable Richard B. Ogilvie, Lilli Palmer, Mike McCaskey, Ruth Page, and Yue-Sai Kan, a Chinese TV star with the largest television audience in the world. Jazz pianist Art Hodes, a legend in himself, came several times to play "Gershwin and All the Greats." Every

MR. AND MRS. JOHN C. KERN, world travelers, at one of England's stately homes. As WAC Reciprocity Chairman, Anne Kern established ties with almost 50 clubs in the U.S. and abroad.

PAULINE TRIGERE, center stage, with models at a fashion retrospective in the autumn of 1992. For many years Miss Trigere opened the club's fall season with a showing of her latest collection. The program was always a sell-out.

August Genevieve Buck closed the season with a slide preview of fall fashions. Many years the club reopened in September with Pauline Trigere in person, commentating her own style show, entertaining an enthralled group at lunch in the Pillemont Room with her worldly anecdotes. "She did not do that many shows," says Nena Ivon, who brought the famous designer to the club. "I think she liked the elegance of the WAC, the sense of the Old Guard, the clientele she knew for a million years. Being French, she wanted things to be very lovely and feminine, but with tradition."

Astrid Bidne, who cooked at the club for 30 years, was still turning out the old-time dishes. "Nothing left the kitchen unless it was perfect," declares Hattie Egan, who has spent nearly twenty years on the third floor herself. "Astrid did those chicken crepes, so light and thin. Her favorite was the mushrooms with Mornay sauce and bacon on artichoke bottoms. She served that a lot on Club Days. The grilled Roquefort sandwich. The 626. The 50th anniversary sandwich. The Protein Luncheon. People still ordered cake. We had to start making two cakes a day because sometimes we would run out."

The dances were never more elegant, many of them arranged with taste and flair by the club's accomplished party-giver, Mrs. Francis J. Klimley. Invitations were engraved, dress was black tie, and tables were made up to suit the size of one's group. Marguerite and Bob Merriam were often at a romantic table for two.

"We did have nice parties," Nancy Klimley reminisces. "We had fish courses and favors and beautiful flowers. I bought long cloths in white silk damask. We had great music – Stanley Paul, Bill Scott. I invited Shelley MacArthur Farley to sing. She was singing then at the Gold Sardine Bar. So we had her at the WAC. It was a sell-out. We would have three kinds of wine at those dinners, and then we just drank champagne for the rest of the evening. People stayed overtime till we had to tell them the elevator operators were leaving. They just danced and danced."

There was always a holiday luncheon and a Dickensian family feast preceding a performance of *A Christmas Carol* at the Goodman Theatre. In 1980 a stellar new tradition was born, the International Christmas evening. This was organized by

LOVELY LADIES at the 90th Anniversary Ball. (Left to right) Mrs. Philip H. Kemper, Mrs. Robert E. Merriam, Mrs. John B. Wright, Mrs. Edward R. Weed, and Mrs. Russell O. Bennett.

Woman's Athletic Club of Chicago

*20th
International Evening*

Weihnachtsgrüsse Aus Deutschland

*A Christmas Celebration
in the German tradition*

*Thursday
December 14, 1989*

Menu

Bunter Salat mit Lachs und Weissem Spargel
Salmon and White Asparagus on Bed of Greens

Leberknödelsuppe
Liver Dumpling Soup

Gänsebrust mit Bratapfel
Breast of Goose with Baked Apple Slices

Rotkohl
Red Cabbage

Kartoffelkroketten
Potato Croquettes

Brötchen
Miniature Rolls

Aachener Printenauflauf mit Zimtschaum
Aachen Gingerbread Pastry

Mokka
Demi-Tasse

Wines

1985 Trabener Würzgarten Auslese
Riesling (Mosel)

1988 Grossbottwarer Wunnenstein
Trollinger (Württemberg)

Mrs. Philip H. Kemper, longtime shepherdess of the WAC's consular program, who worked with Chicago-based diplomats and their spouses to create a festive night of food and music celebrating cultures all over the world. The first was an English evening with roast beef, Yorkshire pudding, and English madrigals. As the years went by, these events grew more and more splendid, with the consuls contributing fine wine, artistic menu covers, and fabulous door prizes. Countries without Christmas traditions sponsored dinners throughout the year. The Egyptian Escapade featured a belly dancer and is probably the only time a lady with an exposed navel ever sashayed around the WAC drawing room. "The German Christmas in 1989 was really special," adds Pat Kemper, a native of Germany who lived through the bombing of Berlin and worked as an interpreter after the war. "I was able to get up and say, 'We bring you greetings from Germany, East and West.'"

The Eighties saw many dreams fulfilled and the beginnings of some wonderful new traditions. It was also perhaps the end of an era, the last of the ladies who arrived week in week out, sipped their cocktails or mineral water, always lunched at the same table, and settled into a gentle rapport with the staff, whose courtesy and devotion made this graceful routine possible.

Once upon a time, of course, the second-floor lounge had been a far busier place. Bartender John Cusack, who started working at the WAC in 1962, recalls the Club Days of yesteryear. "All the ladies came down for cocktails before they went up to lunch. The library and the drawing room would be packed. I'd have to bring in extra help for the day. They drank dry and sweet sherry straight up and a lot of Bloody Marys. We'd go through nine or ten quarts of Bloody Marys when they'd come down from those fashion shows."

HOWARD CAMMON, the club's senior elevator operator. He retired in 1997.

JOHN CUSACK, the club's longtime bartender. He came to the U.S. from County Meath in 1950. When he started work at the WAC, there was no bar at all, he recalls. "We used to serve drinks from tables in the hallway."

THE PERSONAL SERVICE DEPARTMENT flourished under the care of this dexterous trio. (Left to right) Regina Grach, Ursula Gaworski, and Donna Monteweski.

By the early Eighties the veterans of those crowded days, much older now and smaller in number, were still noontime regulars. Wilbert was waiting to help them out of their cars, and Mary Barrow or Kay Razor would greet them at the elevator. They might stop upstairs to order a box of stationery with Nancy Swan or talk to Adrienne Carleton about a special tea for a visiting granddaughter. Then they would make their way to their own chairs on the second floor, and Johnny would bring a little dish of trail mix and their favorite cocktails.

Johnny still recalls those ladies very well. There was the tall Mrs. Copeland of aristocratic bearing who sat every day by the round table in the drawing room. "She liked a split of Cold Duck," he says. "I had to get it for her special. She was the only one in the club who drank it. Mrs. Saunders is another one who was here all the time. When she came in for Club Nights, she'd bring 18 or 20 people. She would take the whole library and ask for two private waitresses. She'd have that radio announcer, Paul Harvey, and he always ordered a very fine champagne. Then there was Mrs. Windsor, who used to come in the afternoon. She was a volunteer at the Art Institute, and she'd walk all the way up here in the summertime. And she'd say, 'Johnny, what have you got that's cool?' I'd squeeze a couple of fresh lemons and take a good heaping teaspoon of sugar and some ice and put it in the blender. I'd add a little water and blend it for just a second or two. That's how it started, that lemonade people like so much. I made it for her, and she recommended it to other people."

Mrs. Henry C. Woods, one of the club's great benefactors, remains a vivid memory. "She used to get in at least three days a week," Johnny recalls. "She and Mrs. Kemper, the wife of the head of the insurance company, would sit out there at the first table at the end of the gallery. Sometimes Mrs. Webster would join them.

OLA MAE WILBURN (near left), who reigned over the second floor for more than 15 years.

WILBERT WILLIAMS, guardian of the club's front door. The policeman at the corner was once overheard to say: "Hey, I know what 'WAC' stands for. Wilbert's Athletic Club!"

MRS. HENRY C. WOODS, a generous benefactor and loyal member for more than 50 years.

Once in a while Mrs. Webster brought Buddy Rogers, the actor who was married to Mary Pickford. Mrs. Woods would love a Whiskey Sour and was very particular about the way it was made. She would tell Mrs. Kemper about sailing to Europe to meet the troops at the end of the First World War. They were all young brides then or about to be married to officer husbands. Mrs. Woods came back on Pershing's flagship. She was a very great lady."

Upstairs in the dining room Doris Norman, the hostess, gave them all a warm welcome. "Mrs. Woods always sat at the little deuce by the mirror," she recalls. "Mrs. Shedd was another grand person to visit with. Mrs. Sill was a very special lady. Her husband built the Sky Ride at the Century of Progress. Then there was Mrs. Eckhart, who had a whole floor at the Drake Towers and a house in Palm Beach and a place in the Adirondacks. Twice a year she would be in Chicago for two months, and then she came for lunch every day. I'll never forget, she had covers for the handles of her canes crocheted to match all of her hats."

Little Miss Helen Miller arrived without fail, even in the worst weather. She was a "bridger" and left a bag with her name on it in the checkroom where she kept her own deck of cards, scorepads, and three pillows. She ate the same lunch every day — a cup of mushroom soup and a sliced chicken sandwich on homemade bread, cut very thin. Doris still talks about the Saturday of the fire at the FCB construction site behind the club. Exploding gas heaters atop the half-finished building sent burning metal shards flying across Michigan Avenue. A ring of fire circled the 12th story, and scaffolding was dropping to the ground in flames. "The fire department ordered us to evacuate our building immediately," says Doris, "and I went around asking all the ladies in the dining room to leave. When I got to Miss Miller, she just looked up at me and said, 'You mean before I have my sandwich?'"

Kathy Grenier, manager of the club 1985–94, was a constant and affectionate support to many members who were very alone in their later years. When they missed a few days in the dining room, she would call to check on them. If they were ill, she would find a way to send over a pint of soup or a slice of cake. They delighted in this tender care.

Ola Mae Wilburn, who had charge of the second floor for 15 years, thinks back on it all. "Those were the good old days," she agrees, "and they were *really* good. I remember Mrs. Gilbert, Mrs. Wright, Mrs. Porter, and tiny, tiny Mrs. Schmick. They came six days a week. When they got off the elevator, I would go to Johnny and say, 'They're here.' In the winter, by the time they checked their coats and stopped in the ladies room, we would have their drinks set out in the library. And they just loved that. Then they would go upstairs and eat fast so they could play bridge. Sometimes they went to the movies. On Saturdays they would stay with me all day, until ten minutes to five.

"And you know, when they didn't come in anymore," Ola Mae adds with a touch of sadness, "it was very lonesome."

JOYOUS WAC PRESIDENTS
at the Mortgage Burning Ball.
(Clockwise from back row left):
Mrs. Richard D. Gifford, Mrs.
Lawrence J. Lawson, Jr., Mrs.
Faith Lehman Vilas, Mrs. Wayne
Maxwell, Mrs. Earnest E.
Christensen, and Mrs. Joseph
Andrew Hays.

12

Celebrating a Landmark

IN THE LAST QUARTER of the twentieth century an extraordinary real estate boom transformed North Michigan Avenue into one of the world's most populous shopping streets, with sales topping a billion dollars a year. In the name of progress many old buildings of grace and distinction were demolished, one by one, until the boulevard's stylish Parisian ambiance was clearly in danger of disappearing altogether. A sense of alarm spread through the city's preservation community, with a growing insistence that the last of these original structures be saved. Among those handsome remnants, the Woman's Athletic Club was a crown jewel.

In the early 1980s the State of Illinois had made efforts to designate the entire North Michigan Avenue area as a historic site. This nomination was opposed by both the city and most of the property-owners along the street and failed. The WAC, sitting on leased land and fearful of piling additional economic hardship on top of its already teetering budget, also registered a protest. So when the club's president, Mrs. Faith Lehman Vilas, received a letter in November 1990 from the Commission on Chicago Landmarks saying the club was under consideration for landmark status, feelings on the subject were still mixed and the first instinct was to resist. With the intention of opposing it, Mrs. Vilas and Mrs. Richard D. Gifford went down to City Hall for the Commission hearing. Adulatory speeches were given. The clubhouse was pronounced a benefit to the neighborhood, and the alderman declared its interior to be "gorgeous." The Commission unanimously approved preliminary designation. Joan Gifford remembers that, leaving the meeting that day, "Faith and I felt like we'd been swept away."

Armed with a 120-day extension, the club's board reviewed the pros and cons. Some like Mrs. Howard J. Trienens and Mrs. Carter H. Manny, Jr., were very much in favor of landmark status from the start as a matter of civic and cultural pride. Moreover, it could cost a lot to fight it, and the club was still laboring to pay off a hefty mortgage. There was no question, on the other hand, that the value of the

171

property would be considerably reduced while the taxes on it might continue to increase dramatically.

"The board was split," Faith Vilas recalls, "and we had a lawyer who advised us to fight. And I think what really happened is that the ones who very much favored designation convinced the others that it was an honor and a way to maintain the integrity of the club. And since the members do not, as persons, own the building, no one was hurt if it could not be sold for a large profit. In the end we were all delighted about being named a Chicago landmark. It has turned out to be a very favorable thing."

A Landmark Committee chaired by Mrs. John C. Telander worked with preservation attorney John York to hammer out an agreement whereby the club retained control over the building's air rights and its interior. Once this amended document was approved by the Corporation, the Woman's Athletic Club of Chicago was named an official landmark by the full City Council on October 2, 1991. The designation was celebrated with great fanfare the following spring at the Landmark Luncheon and the Landmark Ball, and since that time the building has garnered increasing admiration from architects, preservationists, students of the decorative arts, and tourists just sauntering up the avenue.

Another momentous accomplishment followed soon after. By levying a special assessment and putting every bit of extra revenue into the Maxwell Fund, the club was able to pay off its mortgage in full at the earliest opportunity. "The Burning of the Mortgage" took place on the evening of October 1, 1993, at a glorious black-tie dinner dance, when a crowd of two hundred watched with hushed excitement as President Gifford and Wayne Maxwell set fire to that much-thumbed document. It took a few seconds to fan up in flames. A minute later it was a small pile of ashes in a silver bowl. As of that moment, the club was home free, clear of debt, its future forever secure.

The Woman's Athletic Club could now move confidently toward its second century, prepared to accommodate the needs of a diverse membership immersed in all aspects of business, civic, and family life. Back when the WAC and other such clubs were first organized, a ladies magazine noted that "these new clubhouses are now teaching women that relaxation is as important as work." In the 1990s that message would resonate with new meaning. How fortunate that this beautiful and serene island was here, a place to cultivate physical fitness and a comely appearance, entertain in style and comfort, hear leading figures of the day, and share the age-old pleasure of belonging to a company of friends.

A new Health & Fitness Department blossomed under the guidance of Mrs. John P. McGowan. Building on the programs established in the 1980s, Director Dana Peregrine added a winter camp for children, created a newsy "wellness" bulletin which went out every month with the program announcements, and started to assemble a Weight Room with state-of-the-art exercise equipment. With every

WAYNE MAXWELL and President Gifford set fire to the club's mortgage on October 1, 1993, which was paid off in full eight years ahead of schedule.

extra nickel then earmarked for mortgage payments, the club was pleased to receive a Nordic Track machine from Mrs. Eva Grafft Quateman and a cross-aerobics exercise machine from Mrs. Robert S. Lunn. The costs of additional treadmills, a computerized bicycle, weights, and resistance machines were largely covered by donations from members, most notably Mrs. James N. Bay, Sr., who gave generous support over a long period of time.

"Every so often Julie Bay would ask us, 'What do you need?'" Barbara McGowan recalls. "Then she would send our athletic director shopping for the best new equipment. Dana did all the research on the machines. They were chosen to work every muscle in the body and provide a complete aerobic work-out." In the summer of 1992 all this equipment was moved up to the eighth floor, where that open sunny space was transformed yet again into the new Fitness Center.

When Melissa Bachi took over as department director, she put together an athletic contract for members and organized a wide range of classes – aerobics, fencing, yoga, cross training, CPR, ballroom dancing, circuit class, step class, and group swim lessons. Says Mrs. Edward Hayes Daly, who followed Barbara McGowan as Athletic Chair, "Melissa would try anything. If five interested ladies had an idea, she'd get up a class. Even the bridgers were doing Tai Chi before their card games for a while. Melissa brought in two or three personal trainers. She invented a Shaping Up Contest. It wasn't how much you weighed or what dress size you wore. It was how many times you worked out. The winner would get a free massage or a manicure."

One of the most exotic offerings was Tango, taught by Jorge Niedas who danced with his partner Sandra Adrian at the Argentine Christmas Evening in 1995. Their thrilling and sensuous performance still stands out in the annals of WAC

MRS. JAMES N. BAY, SR., a generous
donor to the Health & Fitness Department
over many years. A great equestrienne,
she is pictured here with her son James Jr.
and two champion American foxhounds
at the Longmeadow course in 1954.

THE ATTIC PENTHOUSE, transformed yet
again, as the club's Fitness Center.

entertainments. "They danced the tango that night," Pat Kemper recalls, "and everybody went crazy. The men were leaping to their feet. People were jumping up and down on the balcony, applauding. All of a sudden everybody wanted to take tango lessons."

Mrs. Gary C. Comer, Colette Novich, Mrs. Harvey Struthers, Mrs. Robert S. Study, and Judy York were among Señor Niedas' pupils. "Jorge was originally with the Teatro de Cologne," says another student, Mrs. Gustavo A. Bermudez, "and traveled all over South America. When he came to the States, he started dancing the tango professionally. What he really taught us was exercise ballet. He focused on posture, balance, carriage. How to hold yourself. He was just fantastic, a wonderful person to be around."

Barbara McGowan also brought in many health care specialists to talk about matters like breast cancer, menopause, weight management, cardiac problems, and plastic surgery. A nutrition counselor explained low-fat, low-salt cooking. The club's own kitchen introduced such items as bran muffins, herbal teas, and steamed vegetable platters on the daily menu, though many member remained joined at the hip, so to speak, to their apricot rolls and Lobster Alaska. Covert Bailey, TV star and author of *Fit or Fat*, was invited to speak and drew a packed house. "He stood up there with flip charts," Mrs. McGowan recalls, "and he explained what happens to a pat of butter in your body. 'You might as well eat a teaspoon of Vaseline,' he said, and the crowd just groaned. Then we all went down to one of our beautiful WAC dinners. The waitresses came out with the butter and rolls and the fabulous pastries. People were afraid to touch them. The waitresses couldn't figure out what was wrong."

THE
LIBRARY

THE LIBRARY ON A QUIET summer morning. The painting over the fireplace was a gift in 1929 from Mrs. H. Newton Hudson, Chairman of the Decorating Committee. Her father was Thomas Jeffery, a transplanted Englishman who built "The Rambler" automobile in 1902. He later added an accessory he called "the fifth wheel," a forerunner of today's spare tire. After Jeffery's death his children sold his company to Charles Nash, who rechristened the car "the Nash Rambler" and established its legendary place in automotive history. Florence Hudson lived in a grand house on Hawthorne Place and retained a life-long love of all things English. She was pleased to purchase Sir Peter Lely's *Portrait of a Court Lady* for the club's new library, where it resides to this day.

AN UNUSUAL BIRTHDAY PARTY in the
Presidents' Room. Dr. Catherine L. Choy (left)
hosted a "Terrible Twos" celebration for
her parrot Phinneas. Exceedingly well behaved,
Phinneas squawked at his two aunties,
Mrs. G. Elwood Franche (center) and Faith
Vilas, and sipped tea out of a porcelain cup.

Many members prefer to stay svelte with frequent visits to the Personal Service Department, where a group of skilled technicians made it all so easy. Janina Szlachetko gave an invigorating massage, Cheng Almonte a quick manicure, and Luba Kazimirova specialized in custom facials and waxes. Regina Grach's hot oil treatments brought the shine back to the limpest head of hair. Mrs. Arthur S. Bowes was in Regina's chair every Thursday without fail for a weekly shampoo and set, and Mrs. Vernile Morgan still claims, "She gives me the most beautiful permanent I ever had in my life." Kids like Regina too. Fast with the scissors, she laughs a lot and produces a lollipop when the whole ordeal is over.

During this decade the department was remodeled as a comfortable garden room, with soft colors and a spacious reception area. The redo was celebrated at an open house when ten Bobbi Brown beauticians, all in black, gave free cosmetic make-overs. Linda Salisbury courageously volunteered to be powdered and penciled on stage. After lunch the crew turned its magic on the rest of the crowd. Faces washed, members lined up for transformations in the Audubon Room while waitresses passed champagne and coconut balls. Absentees got a second chance when Marilyn Miglin put on a similar show the following month. Another great success was the Hermes scarf-tying seminar, when two store representatives demonstrated all sorts of knots and revealed the clothes horse's secret of how to turn a scarf into a blouse.

On the subject of clothes, the club's dress code sparked one of the most contentious debates in years. Since the day it was opened the Woman's Athletic Club had deemed dresses or skirted suits the proper attire of a lady. Denims, shorts, jogging outfits, and pants of all kinds – dressy or not – were restricted to the beauty salon, pool area, and exercise rooms of the club. In the late 1980s rules were relaxed slightly to permit casual attire in the dining room on Saturdays, when husbands might typically be on their way to the golf course or families out for a day of errands.

Into the 1990s many members lobbied to wear pants in the dining room on weekdays, citing the wardrobe preferences of young career women, the growing acceptance of "Casual Fridays," and Chicago's rugged winters. "Let's get with the times," they insisted. Ladies in Armani pants suits were getting rather huffy when stopped at the dining room door.

A group of staunch dissenters felt that, like the use of formal family names, skirts had long been a benchmark of WAC identity. Mrs. John A. Daniels was one of these. "There were many of us who said, 'No, don't do it,'" she still remembers. "'It will take something away from the WAC. I can go to any restaurant in the city and sit next to somebody in pants. The WAC is different, unique. And once you change, you can never go back.'"

The question was tabled several times. The Amenities Review Committee came up with the idea of counting the number of panted ladies who arrived and then stashing them in the Pillement Room for lunch. Finally a questionnaire was mailed out, which showed that a majority of members favored allowing trouser suits in the dining room. So in January 1995 the rules were changed. The pants couldn't be jeans or culottes and they needed a matching jacket, but a good-looking pants suit was now acceptable. For those who disagreed, the decision still rankles.

Though it is not so many years since ashtrays were placed at every chair for any meeting in the clubhouse, nobody raised a finger when smoking was limited to a small section of the dining room and cellular phones were firmly prohibited. Civilized manners are still uppermost in the minds of the membership, and to that end the club sponsored a children's etiquette class for several years, conducted by Paula Persons of Children's Spoon. "She had some prior connection to the diplomatic corps," says Barbara McGowan, whose own youngsters were enrolled in the group. "The sessions were held in the Silver Room. The children had to be dressed properly and sit straight, shoulders back. She taught them place settings and what the different pieces of silver were for. How to eat soup and the proper way to cut food. For graduation the children had to go through a receiving line with their parents. Oh, the kids were rolling their eyes. My children still tease me, 'What would Miss Persons say?' But all the mothers loved it, and children do watch. So now when they're out somewhere, they can be comfortable in any situation."

For women with many demands on their time and energies, it was a large relief to be able to turn the details of gracious entertaining over to the club's talented staff (though members still enjoyed preparing some of the old dishes at home and the WAC cookbook was reprinted, by popular demand, under the direction of Barbara Knuckles and her committee in 1992). For a short time a Food & Beverage Committee, headed by Mrs. Stanley E. Huff and then Donna Kuhns, worked with chef Jim McParland to update the menu and bolster the wine list. Mrs. Kuhns, who had ten years' catering experience herself, introduced a weekly gourmet pizza, Soufflé and Salad Month, and lots more clear soups, fresh herbs, and colorful garnishes.

When Lynn Riggs joined the club as manager in 1994, she assembled an in-house team of professionals who took over all the logistics of virtuoso food service and party planning. There were new events on the calendar. The club had never hosted a Sunday brunch. When Mrs. Rodger A. Owen announced the first Mother's Day Brunch in 1995, it was a daring experiment. Within a few days the event was sold out and a new tradition was born. The St. Patrick's Day Brunch met with similar success and also the Easter Brunch, though some of the more starched members were taken aback at the sight of a large goat munching hay in the second-floor card room (site of the children's petting zoo). The board nixed the idea of a Cigar Night, but a series of intimate Winemakers Dinners with guest chefs from Chicago's great restaurants hit the mark. "The first chef was from Trio," says Mrs. Robert A. Beatty, who suggested this innovation. "We had the hot chef of the year from Spruce. Charlie Trotter brought his whole staff. We had 16 people in the kitchen that night. He cooked duck confit and saddle of lamb, and he thought our kitchen was very nice. Of course, by that time, we'd remodeled it."

The little ones were feted too. For several years a circus party was held every spring in the ballroom. There were games with buckets and balls, clowns, face paints, and a large flock of animals. Except for the panther and the white arctic fox, which were never let out of their cages, the children could touch and play with them all. "The monkey was an absolute dear," says Faith Vilas. "He would hop in their laps and oh my! I used to borrow my neighbor's children and bring them down to the party. One year the little girl who always held the snake was sick. 'Poor old snake,' she cried. I told her one of us would hold it. But none of the rest of her family would do it, so that's how I happened to get that boa constrictor around my neck. They called him Julius Squeezer."

The club was a popular venue for private parties of all kinds, with Sandra Burl presiding upstairs and Martha Segura keeping a watchful eye over birthday celebrations at the pool. Husbands were also coming into the club more often on their own, and besides Wayne Maxwell, another one of them, Russell O. Bennett, who has advised the club on legal and insurance matters for years, was elected to membership. Philip S. J. Moriarity likes to walk over from his office for a quiet sandwich. J. Curtis Fee saves his WAC luncheons for out-of-town guests. "City restaurants are starting to look and act very much the same the world over," he points out. "My sophisticated European and Latin clients make quite a fuss about the WAC. The ambiance is decidedly different than any other place they go. They always ask to come back."

The holidays are still the most brilliant time of year at the club, with splendid trimmings, grand entertainments, and a boutique where members enjoy one-stop

Christmas shopping. Children make their own fun at the annual Gingerbread House Workshop. In the mid-1980s Mrs. Lee D. Kellar organized a top-to-bottom decorating plan. "For the first time we had something festive on all seven floors," she recalls. "We had no budget, and my committee put their own money into it. We begged and borrowed trees from everywhere. We got new ornaments and bought little pine cone trees for the dining room. We hung garlands in the ballroom and put lights on the railings. The whole club really glittered."

In the 1990s this job was taken over by Mrs. Robert E. Vanden Bosch, who brought new ideas from her years with a Sloane Street florist in London. "We had a teddy bear tree one year," she says, "and we did one with velvet hearts. My favorite was the Victorian tree with gold, white, and crystal ornaments. I took cranberry-colored ribbons and made bows with long streamers. Maria Harrison did beautiful bows. Paul Trienens gave the roping for the canopy."

One of the club's loveliest traditions is the international Christmas tree on the third floor, established by Pat Kemper in 1981. "I asked the consular members if they would donate ornaments," she remembers, "and we presented the tree at the Christmas buffet. The next year I got a taller tree and put it on a stand outside the dining room. I decorate it every year myself. At 11:00 A.M. Sandra pushes the button, and it slowly rotates so members can see the ornaments. Over the years we have received these ornaments from so many countries — the Philippines, Spain, Sweden, Denmark, Germany, France, Canada. The consular members who came from places where they didn't have a Christmas tradition were very generous with dolls, which we put around the tree. And now many of them have given dolls,

LITERARY LADIES at a spring program "About Books." (Standing left to right) Mrs. Marilyn Cagnoni, About Books Chairman Mrs. Paul J. Miller, Mrs. Morton D. Barker, Jr., Mrs. David C. Hilliard, Mrs. Charles M. Dykema, Ms. Mary Beth Beal, Mrs. R. Thomas Howell, book dramatist Greta Wiley, Mrs. Richard M. Jaffee, Phyllis Chambers, Mrs. John E. Freund, and Mrs. Wayne R. Hannah, Jr. (Seated left to right) Mrs. Susie Forstmann Kealy, Mrs. James E. Taich, Mrs. David L. Conlan, and Ms. Lynn Evans.

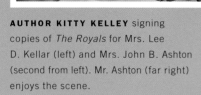

AUTHOR KITTY KELLEY signing copies of *The Royals* for Mrs. Lee D. Kellar (left) and Mrs. John B. Ashton (second from left). Mr. Ashton (far right) enjoys the scene.

MRS. RONALD WOLFF (left to right), Mrs. Bennett Armchambault, and Helen Dillen Miller in rare form at the annual Madhatters Luncheon in 1998.

which a lot of members would like to see on permanent display because they're so gorgeous."

In the last analysis, friendship is still the club's most important currency, fostered at weekly events where newsmakers and experts of all kinds come to instruct, entertain, and divert. No one has worked harder to draw luminous speakers and bring out a large audience of members than Mrs. Helen Dillen Miller, who served as program chair for three years and then president 1996–98. She is a colorful and dramatic presence herself and Secretary-Treasurer of Carter Controls International, a family-owned company that manufactured parts for the Apollo space flights. Mrs. Miller arranged many of the decade's most exciting events. Her friend Georgette Mosbacher drew a large crowd, as did TV stars Carol Marin, comedian Mark Russell, Victor Skrebneski, Michael Killian, Tish Baldridge, and Judith Terra. The Purdue Glee Club from her home state of Indiana sings every year. "Sixty men, all in tuxedos, who have an A grade point average and get their hair cut once a month," she points out with pride. "They're not just a glee club, they're like a Broadway show."

Helen Miller also loves remarkable hats and is at her spirited best presiding over the annual Madhatters Luncheon, where members wear their most exotic headgear for a group of judges which awards prizes in nine categories. The hats seem to get wilder every year. One year Helen Miller wore an authentic medicine man hat with shotgun bullets and foxtails around the crown. Mrs. Helmut Jahn won a prize with a headpiece of lacquered banana palm netting. Another time Mrs. James Henry Hawk's English garden bonnet, complete with green moss, fresh pansies, and a tiny tea service, was voted "Most Beautiful." A real original was Mrs. John B. Buenz's inverted bouquet, with reedy green stems pointing straight to the ceiling, and everybody was dazzled by Siobhan Engle's lacey Jacques Fath creation. It wasn't really a category, but "Most Indigenous" would have been Collier Thompson's millinery rendition of the WAC's famous coconut cake. "It was a Styrofoam cake with tulle and birds and ribbons," she explains. "I frosted it with real white icing and fresh coconut. Being perishable, of course, it's disappeared."

The club's fellowship of readers expanded under the direction of Mrs. Paul J. Miller, who invited a broad spectrum of authors to address the literary group, now renamed "About Books." Among the most renowned guests were Pulitzer Prize–winner Russell Banks, Doris Kearns Goodwin, Anne Perry, Kitty Kelly, Lois Wyse, and Joyce Maynard (a charming young novelist who turned down all questions about her teenage romance with J. D. Salinger). The book forum touched many points of the globe. Gabriella de Ferrari recalled her Peruvian childhood. Jianying Zha dissected Chinese popular culture. Four Gorbachev-era literati from the Soviet Union held forth on Russian culture. Yet no one ever outdrew that mistress of gracious entertaining, Martha Stewart. For the day of her visit the dining room was reset with rectangular tables and small rented chairs to squeeze in as many members as possible. "We chose our luncheon menu right out of her book," Michal Miller remembers. "She came in hungry and we brought her a basket of rolls, which she said were almost as good as hers. Everybody was delighted with her. We set up the Pillement Room with copies of every book she had ever written, and after lunch people bought as many as a dozen each. She signed every one of them."

The book program was expedited by a pleasant relationship with Kroch's & Brentano's after Mrs. James R. De Stefano introduced the club to the store's cordial president, William Rickman, who attended many of the programs himself. A similar partnership was arranged with Roberta Rubin of the Book Stall at Chestnut Court. The literary group also hosted various scholars and Chicago notables like John Callaway, Terry Savage, Sara Paretsky, Jane Byrne, and Shakespeare Repertory founder Barbara Gaines, who carted the group off in a bus to watch a performance of *Troilus and Cressida.* Many years the season was opened with an appearance by popular book dramatist Barbara Rinella and closed by the enchanting Greta Wiley. ("Listening to Greta," says Mrs. Russell O. Bennett, one of her longtime fans, "is like an evening at the theater.") Members still did some of the reviewing themselves on occasion. Michal Miller presented several biographies, including a fascinating glimpse of Nora Joyce, and Jane Hunt laid out the case for and against Lizzie Borden. (That program closed with a vote, which was unanimous. Guilty.)

Overlapping circles of readers, swimmers, bridgers, and exercisers nurtured a web of friendships, and the "Networkers" were as strong as ever, presenting varied programs of interest for the working woman. Many successful professionals spoke, and it was a comment on the times that Jean Allard's talk about what it was like to be one of the first women lawyers in Chicago was presented as a piece of nostalgia. Aside from sessions on investing, computers, and career management, the open-minded group was eager to hear from plastic surgeons, fashion designers, and (without apology) an astrologer. "We had a workshop to explore entrepreneurship," says Network Chairman Karen Zupko Stuart. "We have all these members now who own their own companies. With all due respect to the founding mothers, we have become the men they were married to."

As the club moved closer to its 100th anniversary, plans were hatched to celebrate in style. During her presidency Mrs. Robert A. Beatty worked with Mrs. Richard D. Gifford to map out not only a year of special events and this book of history, but a complete refurbishment of the clubhouse. "Paying off the mortgage had been a hardship for us," Fran Beatty recalls. "Everything else fell by the wayside. Now we wanted to do something smashing to bring the clubhouse back. It was Joan Gifford who said it best. 'The Queen of the Magnificent Mile needs a new dress.'"

A onetime centennial assessment was levied to cover the costs of these projects, with Corporate Members contributing twice the sum of Residents. The exterior was tuckpointed and seventy years' worth of grime washed off its limestone facade. The Michigan Avenue gardens were replanted, for which the club received its first

Beautification Award from the Greater North Michigan Avenue Association. Much of the interior was redecorated under the direction of Nancy Vert, who worked closely with Decorating Chairs Mrs. Robert W. Galvin and Mrs. Don J. Hindman. Furniture on the first and second floors was reupholstered, the glorious Georgian windows were restored, and the tall columns in the gallery marbled in black and glazed in gold leaf. The cloak room was redesigned and the powder room refurnished in tones of raspberry and gold, a gift of Ms. Vert and her colleague Nancy Sublette. Displayed there to the great delight of the membership was a group of Thorne Rooms donated by the estate of Mrs. James S. Kemper. These shadow boxes (and two others of ducks over the marshes, which were hung near the sixth-floor men's room) were cleaned and restored by Mrs. Thorne's longtime collaborator, Eugene Kupjack, and his sons. All of the club's fine objects were appraised during this decade by Curators Pamela Bardo and Leslie Hindman.

The Silver Room was resplendent again, entirely refurbished "behind the walls" and papered with a glowing new rendition of the original pattern. As a fabulous birthday surprise, Mrs. Florence D. Sewell made a gift of $25,000 for the renewal of the Mirror Room, which has now recovered its Twenties' sparkle. The dining room had been recarpeted back in 1991 and its hopelessly tattered window hangings replaced with new draperies and sheers. With virtually no money in the decorating budget at that time, the ladies who covered the large bills for those third-floor curtains merit mention. They were Mesdames Walter G. Baryl, Russell O.

MEMBERS OF THE WAC STAFF. (Front row left to right) Anna Dominguez, Ana Lopez, Ingrid Martiniz, Veronica Canela, Martha Segura, Bertha Perez, Maria Fuentes, and Martha Lopez; (second row seated) Larry Ferguson, Donna Dempsey, Sandra Robeznieks, Mary Barrow, Sandra Burl, Manager Jan Ahern, Doris Norman, Hattie Egan, and Kay Razor; (back row standing) Wilbert Williams, Sergio Miranda, John Cusack, Jerry Grotthus, Mary Watkins, Maura Hoey, Valerie Burl, Willie Folwiley, Michael Krabbe, Marcelina Fuertes, Brian Sabbs, Martha Jiminiz, Shahen Safarian, Kimble Knox, Estelle Cesokas, Efren Rosas, Rosalva Hernandez, Alberto Vasguez, Juan Aybar, Jaime Campu Verde, Hector Quezada, Gabrial Arroyo, Grimaldo Aybar, Anastacio Munoz, and Gus Rojas.

THE DRAWING ROOM, redecorated
for the club's centennial.

Bennett, Arthur S. Bowes, Dawn Mitchell Chutkow, David L. Conlan, John O. Foy, Charles F. Grey, John L. Haverkampf, III, William R. Jentes, Carter H. Manny, Jr., D. Williams Parker, Alva W. Phelps, Frederick Roe, Ellis B. Rosenzweig, Harry E. Simpson, Thomas L. Williams, Jr., and Miss Elizabeth Hoffman, in honor of the 100th birthday of her sister, Mrs. Henry S. Faust.

Much of the furniture restoration in the course of this project was done by the club's own Grimaldo Aybar, a native of Peru who learned his trade in Washington, D.C. His first job was caning chairs for the White House, and he spent several years refinishing antiques for the likes of Jacqueline Kennedy, Averill Harriman, Katherine Graham, and Robert Kennedy. He worked in the Watergate complex too, before it was famous, and did much of his sanding and painting in the basement there. ("When the big story broke," he recalls, "I understood the whole thing right away.") Some time after he moved to Chicago, Grimaldo was introduced to the WAC by his cousins Marcellina Fuertes and her mother Louise. The old bishop's chair used by club Santas for years was in pieces, minus an arm and one of its carved faces, and Mrs. John T. Moore had offered to pay for its repair. "I can do that," Grimaldo told them. Thus the club acquired the services of a master craftsman, who has spent ten years bringing the club's antiques and original furnishings back to their old luster.

The centennial enterprise included the purchase of a new china pattern, an advanced phone system, and air conditioning for the lobby. Many back-of-the-house projects which could no longer be postponed were also tackled with the expert supervision of Chief Engineer Larry Ferguson, who knows and loves every square foot of this aging dowager of a building. "Shutdown," the closing of the club for three weeks in the latter part of the summer and an old custom in place since August of 1943, was eliminated in 1996. With the advent of air conditioning and members who liked to spend summers in the city, it was better business to stay open all year round.

The employee quarters were also refurbished with a generous gift from Mesdames Beatty and Gifford, but it could be said that the staff received its biggest anniversary present a decade ahead of time. In 1989 the WAC was notified by the estate of Mrs. Eben W. Erikson of a magnanimous bequest, left not to the club but directly to the employees who had made her life so pleasant during her thirty years' membership. The sum of $37,354 was distributed according to an ingenious formula worked out by Faith Vilas and reached even those who had retired years before or moved to distant parts. "We even found Astrid Bidne," says Faith Vilas, "our former cook, who was living in Norway." The bequest was a great tribute to a well-loved staff and seemed to sum up a century of service. Ms. Jan Ahern, who joined the club as manager in 1997, has added expertise and her own elegant sense of hospitality to this record of proficient and devoted service.

On the eve of its second century, a new president, Mary Burrus Babson, stands at the WAC helm. A certified public accountant with an impressive resume, she brings a fresh outlook to the club's present tasks and future possibilities. She has devoted much of her time to women's groups and causes and fervently believes that when committed women set their minds to accomplishing a worthy goal, they are virtually unstoppable. At the Woman's Athletic Club, this has a somehow familiar ring. It is an echo of the faith and determination of the founders and all those who followed, of their perseverance in the face of changing times and shifting perspectives. The tradition continues.

Through an anniversary year of gala occasions, a sense of celebration reigns. It is clear that the Woman's Athletic Club of Chicago remains true to its beginnings, an oasis of civility and charm with a matchless program of service and events. Its strongest asset is still its members and their will to carry the vision forward. It is not hard to conjure up the ghost of Paulina Lyon striding about in her bloomers, reveling in the vigorous company of today's young women, returning the toast that was given on the eve of the club's official opening in 1899:

TO THE WOMEN OF CHICAGO!

TO THE FUTURE OF THE CLUB!

Bonnets Off!

A SAKS FIFTH AVENUE MODEL strides the runway in a vintage WAC bathing costume at the Centennial Fashion Show. The wool knit suit bears the club's logo and a member's label on the hem: "J. Mitchell. No. 105."

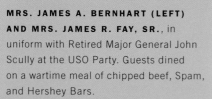

MRS. JAMES A. BERNHART (LEFT) AND MRS. JAMES R. FAY, SR., in uniform with Retired Major General John Scully at the USO Party. Guests dined on a wartime meal of chipped beef, Spam, and Hershey Bars.

THE 1998–99 BOARD OF DIRECTORS. (Front row) Mrs. O. J. Heestand, Jr., Mrs. John Scales, Mrs. John A. Daniels, Mrs. James G. Stuart, Jr., Mrs. James E. Taich, Mrs. Robert W. Thomas, and Mrs. Jeffry J. Knuckles; (Back row) Mrs. J. Douglas Gray, Courtenay Robinson Wood, Mrs. Robert E. Vanden Bosch, Mrs. George A. Bay, Helen Dillen Miller (Immediate Past President), Mary Burrus Babson (President), Mrs. Edward Hayes Daly, Linda E. Salisbury, Mrs. Rodger A. Owen, Margaret Snorf, and Mrs. David C. Hilliard. Not pictured are Mrs. Robert A. Beatty, Mrs. Gustavo Bermudez, Mrs. Robert W. Galvin, Mrs. Michael J. McGuinnis, and Mrs. William C. Vance.

the *Centennial Year*

**MRS. O. J. HEESTAND, JR., (LEFT)
AND MRS. HELEN DILLEN MILLER**
with centennial headliner Mark Russell
after his comedy performance in the
WAC ballroom. The audience laughed till
they cried. "I have been to the
Woman's Athletic Club," Russell concluded. "Therefore, I am." He received
a standing ovation.

CLUB HISTORIAN CELIA HILLIARD,
author of the centennial history.

MEMBERS OF THE CENTENNIAL BALL AND PUBLICATIONS ADVISORY COMMITTEES preview the new Silver Room. (Seated left to right) Mrs. Paul J. Miller, Mary Beth Beal, Helen Dillen Miller, Mrs. Lee W. Jennings, Mrs. Joseph Andrew Hays, Mrs. Charles M. Dykema, and Mrs. John C. Telander; (Standing) Mrs. Don J. Hindman, Leslie S. Hindman, Mary Burrus Babson, Mrs. Robert A. Beatty, Linda E. Salisbury, Karen Zupko Stuart, Joan Elizabeth Steel, Mrs. Lawrence J. Lawson, Jr., Mrs. David C. Hilliard, Mrs. Gregory R. Swenson, Mrs. Richard D. Gifford, and Mrs. Kenneth P. Kinney.

KAREN ZUPKO STUART AND HER
HUSBAND JAMIE studied turn-of-
the-century culinary records to select a
menu of food and wines which might
have been set before the gourmands of
old Chicago.

CENTENNIAL BALL MENU

1996 Louis Latour Grand Ardéche Chardonnay

SOUPE
Potage Crème d'Asperges
Bâtonnets au Fromage

POISSON
Salade de Homard et Crevettes
Vinaigrette au Champagne

1996 M. Chapoutier Crozes-Hermitage Petite Ruche

GIBIER
Cailles Roties
Farce Riz Sauvage avec Fruits Secs
Sauce au Porto
Haricots Verts et Petites Carottes

TRIO DE DESSERT
Petits-fours Truffes au Chocolat
Tartelettes aux Fruits Frais
Eclairs au Cappuccino

In celebration of our centennial

The Board of Directors

of the

Woman's Athletic Club of Chicago

requests the pleasure of your company

for dinner and dancing at

The Centennial Ball

at seven o'clock

Friday, the eleventh of September

Nineteen hundred and ninety-eight

Woman's Athletic Club of Chicago

626 North Michigan Avenue

Chicago, Illinois

Black Tie

INVITATION to the club's red-carpet
Centennial Ball.

the
Centennial Ball

MRS. DON J. HINDMAN (LEFT) AND HER DAUGHTER LESLIE, co-chairmen of the Centennial Ball.

THE NEW SILVER ROOM set for its debut at the Centennial Ball.

PRESIDENT MARY BURRUS BABSON dancing with her husband, Nicholas Babson. It's all in the family. Nick's grandmother was a Life Member of the WAC.

MRS. JOHN C. TELANDER placing the names of everyone who attended the party into the Centennial Time Capsule – a salute to the future from the members of today.

DANCERS swaying to the strains of Stanley Paul's "Centennial Waltz," a melody he composed just for this gala occasion.

HEALTH & FITNESS
McGuinnis, Mrs. John P.,
   Co-Chairman
Salisbury, Ms. Linda E.,
   Co-Chairman
Adams, Mrs. William, IV
Babson, Mrs. Mary Burrus
Beatty, Mrs. Robert A.
Bermudez, Mrs. Gustavo A.
Bomier, Mrs. David W.
Daly, Mrs. Edward Hayes
Ekdahl, Mrs. Jon N.
Heestand, Jr., Mrs. O. J.
Hurley, Mrs. Elizabeth Arnold
   Sheppard
Novich, Mrs. Colette
Vanden Bosch, Mrs. Robert E.
Wanders, Mrs. David G.

HISTORY/ARCHIVES
Hilliard, Mrs. David C.,
   Chairman
Beal, Ms. Mary Beth
Beatty, Mrs. Robert A.
Conlan, Mrs. David L.
Dykema, Mrs. Charles M.
Gifford, Mrs. Richard D.
Hunt, Mrs. Jane C.
Lawson, Jr., Mrs. Lawrence J.
Miller, Mrs. Helen Dillen
Miller, Mrs. Paul J.
Salisbury, Ms. Linda E.
Swenson, Mrs. Gregory R.
Vilas, Mrs. Faith Lehman
Wright, Mrs. John B.

HOUSE
Daniels, Mrs. John A.,
   Chairman
Beatty, Mrs. Robert A.
Galvin, Mrs. Robert W.
Knuckles, Mrs. Jeffry J.
Miller, Mrs. Helen Dillen
Vanden Bosch, Mrs. Robert E.

INSURANCE
Kellar, Mrs. Lee D., *Chairman*
Daniels, Mrs. John A.
Thomas, Mrs. Robert W.
Wood, Ms. Courtenay Robinson

INVESTMENT
Thomas, Mrs. Robert W.,
   Chairman
Beatty, Mrs. Robert A.
Knuckles, Mrs. Jeffry J.
McGuinnis, Mrs. Michael J.
Salisbury, Ms. Linda E.
Wood, Ms. Courtenay Robinson

LONG RANGE PLANNING
Daniels, Mrs. John A.,
   Chairman
Bay, Mrs. George A.
Beatty, Mrs. Robert A.
Bermudez, Mrs. Gustavo A.
Daly, Mrs. Edward Hayes
Knuckles, Mrs. Jeffry J.
Miller, Mrs. Helen Dillen
Salisbury, Ms. Linda E.
Thomas, Mrs. Robert W.

MEMBERSHIP
Bay, Mrs. George A., *Chairman*
Wood, Mrs. Courtenay Robinson,
   Co-Chairman

PERSONAL SERVICE
McGuinnis, Mrs. John P.,
   Co-Chairman
Salisbury, Ms. Linda E.,
   Co-Chairman
Campion, Mrs. Russell R.
Owen, Mrs. Rodger A.
Stuart, Jr., Mrs. James G.

PRINTING
Gray, Mrs. J. Douglas,
   Co-Chairman
Bolanowski, Mrs. Stephen A.,
   Co-Chairman
Hall, Mrs. Brian Ellis
Ogilvie, Mrs. Richard B.
Sweeney, Miss Sharon
Walter, Mrs. John R.

REAL ESTATE
Owen, Mrs. Rodger A.,
   Co-Chairman
Cronin, Mrs. Thomas E.,
   Co-Chairman

RECIPROCITY
Kern, Mrs. John C., *Chairman*

WAC NETWORK
Stuart, Jr., Mrs. James G.,
   Chairman
Evans, Ms. Lynn
Hindman, Ms. Leslie S.
Kuhns, Mrs. Donna
Logsdon, Ms. Leslie Ann
Tampas, Ms. Jessica

PAST PRESIDENTS ADVISORY
Beatty, Mrs. Robert A.
Christensen, Mrs. Earnest E.
Cochran, Mrs. Philip L.
Gifford, Mrs. Richard D.
Hays, Mrs. Joseph Andrew
Jennings, Mrs. Lee W.
Maxwell, Mrs. Wayne
Miller, Mrs. Helen Dillen
Vilas, Mrs. Faith Lehman

*The president serves as an ex-officio
member of all committees except
the Nominating Committee.*

SPECIAL COMMITTEES 1998

CENTENNIAL COMMITTEE
Beatty, Mrs. Robert A.,
   Co-Chairman
Gifford, Mrs. Richard D.,
   Co-Chairman

CENTENNIAL EVENT CHAIRMEN
"Forever Plaid"
   Mrs. Lee D. Kellar
Fashion Through the Years
   Mrs. James Crown
   Mrs. Marc E. Thompson
An Evening with Mark Russell
   Mrs. O. J. Heestand, Jr.
USO Night
   Mrs. James A. Bernhart
   Mrs. James R. Fay, Sr.
A Date with Tom Dreesen
   Mrs. Wayne R. Hannah, Jr.
Rubber Bridge Tournament
   Mrs. Cynthia W. Rummel
History of the WAC Luncheon
   Mrs. Paul J. Miller

CENTENNIAL BALL COMMITTEE
Mrs. Don J. Hindman
   Co-Chairman
Ms. Leslie S. Hindman
   Co-Chairman
Mrs. Donald L. Asher
Mrs. Mary Burrus Babson
Mrs. Robert A. Beatty
Mrs. Philip D. Block, III
Mrs. Douglas H. Cameron, Sr.
Mrs. Gary C. Comer
Mrs. Howard M. Dean, Jr.
Mrs. Owen H. Deutsch
Mrs. Jon N. Ekdahl
Mrs. Richard D. Gifford
Mrs. J. Douglas Gray
Mrs. Joseph Andrew Hays
Mrs. David C. Hilliard
Mrs. Lee W. Jennings
Mrs. Eugene J. Kiley
Mrs. Kenneth P. Kinney
Mrs. Walter R. Lovejoy
Mrs. Helen Dillen Miller
Mrs. Neil K. Quinn
Ms. Joan Elizabeth Steel
Mrs. James G. Stuart, Jr.
Mrs. James E. Taich
Mrs. John C. Telander
Mrs. Dana R. Temple
Mrs. Marc E. Thompson
Mrs. Alexander J. Vogl
Mrs. Edward R. Weed
Mrs. Clayton Edward Whiting, Jr.
Mrs. Ronald Wolff
Mrs. Judith C. York

CENTENNIAL PUBLICATION ADVISORY COMMITTEE
Hilliard, Mrs. David C.,
   Chairman
Babson, Mrs. Mary Burrus
Beal, Ms. Mary Beth
Beatty, Mrs. Robert A.
Conlan, Mrs. David L.
Dykema, Mrs. Charles M.
Gifford, Mrs. Richard D.
Hunt, Mrs. Jane C.
Lawson, Jr., Mrs. Lawrence J.
Miller, Mrs. Helen Dillen
Miller, Mrs. Paul J.
Salisbury, Ms. Linda E.
Swenson, Mrs. Gregory R.
Vilas, Mrs. Faith Lehman
Wright, Mrs. John B.

EXECUTIVE STAFF
Jan Ahern, *General Manager*
Claudia Pernal, *Executive Assistant*
Diana Sherry, *Controller*
Sandra Robeznieks, *Accounting
   Assistant*
Michael Krabbe, *Food & Beverage
   Director*
Lawrence Asher, *Executive Chef*
Sandra Burl, *Dining Room
   Manager*
Sheila Calvin, *Assistant Dining
   Room Supervisor*
Gina Rizzo, *Personal Service
   Director*
Lisa Geraci, *Athletic Director*
Ingrid Berg, *Aquatic Director*
Larry Ferguson, *Chief Engineer*
Enrique Melado, *Houseman
   Supervisor*
Bertha Perez, *Houskeeping
   Supervisor*

Membership roster

LIFE MEMBERS

Allen, Mrs. Ronald L.
(Ruth Agnes Koch)
Ashcraft, Mrs. Dale
(Laurie Cragg)
Beck Von Peccoz, Miss Martha
Morse
Cannon, Ms. Elsa
(Elsa Adelaide Kochs)
Carne, Mrs. Rew P.
(Rew Price)
Chamales, Mrs. Christopher J.
(Margaret M. Goehst)
Cochran, Mrs. Philip Lee
(Grace Clement Newcomb)
Fallon, Mrs. Bernard J.
(Mary Ann Bennan)
Garvy, Mrs. William J.
(Mildred Gloria Starck)
Jamieson, Mrs. James P.
(Mary Randolph Matteson)
Johnston, Mrs. Richard C.
(Alison Hunter)
Lagorio, Mrs. Francis A.
(Eleanor Genevieve Tevander)
Lawson, Jr., Mrs. Lawrence J.
(Barbara Ann Busse)
Maynard, III, Mrs. James G.
(Joan Kerrwin Barry)
McKinlay, Mrs. John
(Elnora Carolyn Davis)
Milnor, Mrs. Frank R.
(Barbara Wakeley)
Mitchell, Mrs. John M.
(Elizabeth L. Seabury)
Pruyn, Mrs. John A.
(Laverne Louer)
Seabury-Houser, Mrs. Charlene B.
(Charlene Adrienne Brown)
Showtis, Mrs. Edward P.
(Melanie Reilly)

CORPORATE MEMBERS

Anderson, Mrs. Davis Given
(Jackie Eleanor Simpson)
Applegate, Jr., Mrs. Ralph W.
(Helen Elisa Alonso)
Atchison, Mrs. John R.
(Jean Suzanne Zakas)
Babb, Mrs. Patricia M.
(Patricia Ann McClaren)
Babson, Mrs. Mary Burrus
(Mrs. Nicholas C. Babson)
Bay, Mrs. George A.
(Sally McKenzie Coe)
Beal, Ms. Mary Beth
Beatty, Mrs. Robert A.
(Frances Jean Calomeni)

Bennett, Mrs. Russell O.
(Patricia Birch)
Bermudez, Mrs. Gustavo A.
(Barbara Schumacher)
Bernhart, Mrs. James A.
(Jean Hurley)
Blatchford, III, Mrs. Frank W.
(Irma Leignadier)
Bodeen, Mrs. George H.
(Nancy Jane Lindberg)
Bolanowski, Jr., Mrs. Stephen A.
(Elinor M. Wilke)
Bomier, Mrs. David W.
(Carolyn Anne Cheetham)
Borland, Jr., Mrs. John J.
(Suzanne Sivage)
Bowes, Mrs. Arthur S.
(Patricia Forsyth Kelly)
Brown, Mrs. Louis M.
(Sarah McNeely Rummel)
Buenz, Mrs. John B.
(Olga Marie Lindfors)
Cameron, Sr., Mrs. Douglas H.
(M. Lenore Pollard)
Chalmers, Mrs. Douglas M.
(Elizabeth Anne Kern)
Christy, Mrs. Lawrence
(Mary Ellen Brooks)
Comer, Mrs. Gary C.
(Frances Ceraulo)
Connellan, Mrs. Kevin A.
(Mary Ellen Kelliher)
Cronin, Mrs. Pamela Bruce
(Mrs. Thomas E. Cronin)
Crowe, Mrs. John V.
(Margaret Ann Toohey)
Crown, Mrs. Paula Hannaway
(Mrs. James Crown)
Daly, Mrs. Edward Hayes
(Georg'Ann Glaeser)
Daniels, Mrs. John A.
(Barbara Tilly)
Dean, Jr., Mrs. Howard M.
(Fay Diane Nicholson)
Dunea, Mrs. M. Suzanne
(Mary Suzanne Mills)
Dykema, Mrs. Charles M.
(Clarice Bryant)
Ekdahl, Mrs. Jon N.
(Marcia Jean Opp)
Emmert, Mrs. Michael P.
(Janice Kay Conroy)
Ewing, Mrs. Robert P.
(Nancy Best)
Fay, Sr., Mrs. James R.
(Margaret Cunningham)

Galvin, Mrs. Robert W.
(Mary Barnes)
Gebelein, Mrs. Christopher A.
(Dr. Catherine L. Choy)
Gignilliat, Mrs. Paul C.
(Ellen Cash)
Goebel, Mrs. Matthew J.
(Roxanna Frances Beatty)
Gray, Mrs. J. Douglas
(Karen Zateslo)
Griffin, Jr., Mrs. William J.
(Rosemary McCarron)
Grube, Mrs. John P.
(Ann Elliott)
Hannah, Jr., Mrs. Wayne R.
(Patricia Anne Matthews)
Hays, Mrs. Joseph Andrew
(Carol Florence Schildgen)
Heestand, Jr., Mrs. O. J.
(Patricia Lu Herrmann)
Heise, Mrs. Richard A.
(Clair Fogarty)
Herget, Ms. Victoria J.
(Mrs. Robert K. Parsons)
Heroy, Mrs. David
(Donna Tuke)
Hilliard, Mrs. David C.
(Celia Valerie Schmid)
Hindman, Mrs. Don J.
(Patricia Joan De Forest)
Hindman, Ms. Leslie S.
Hokin, Mrs. William J.
(Anne Powalowski)
Holinger, Mrs. Susan
(Susan Ann Wherry)
Howell, Jr., Mrs. R. Thomas
(Karen Wallace Corbett)
Hoyt, Mrs. Barry G.
(Cynthia Dellard)
Hughes, Mrs. Richard A.
(Jean DeSotell)
Hunt, Mrs. Jane C.
(Mrs. Donald S. Hunt)
Hurckes, Mrs. Richard W.
(Mary Louise Werner)
Hurley, Mrs. Mark N.
(Elizabeth Arnold Sheppard)
Hurtgen, Sr., Mrs. P. Nicholas
(Catherine Witter Prange)
Jeffreys, Mrs. Lyman Wood
(Elizabeth Stuart Rodgers)
Jennings, Mrs. Lee W.
(Billye Ruth Barnes)
Jentes, Mrs. William R.
(Jan Oberg)
Keiser, Mrs. Michael L.
(Rosalind Garrett Curme)
Kellar, Mrs. Lee D.
(Denise Gail Malizia)

Kemper, Mrs. Philip H.
(Patricia Lewin)
Kern, Mrs. John C.
(Anne Rumsey Moreland)
Klimley, Mrs. Francis J.
(Nancy Lee Enzweiler)
Knox, Mrs. John G.
(Betty Schultz)
Knuckles, Mrs. Jeffry J.
(Barbara Anne Miller)
Kolar, Mrs. Robert D.
(Brooke Stengel)
Krehbiel, Mrs. Fred A.
(Kathleen Cecilia Kirby)
Kuhns, Mrs. Donna
(Donna Sue McGrath)
Lawson, Jr., Mrs. Lawrence J.
(Barbara Ann Busse)
Lind, Mrs. Stanley L.
(Edna Bundegard)
Lovejoy, Mrs. Walter R.
(Susan Blair Pike)
Marks, Jr., Mrs. Scott P.
(Pamela Riser)
Martin, Mrs. Harold T.
(Eloise Virginia Wright)
Mathewson, Mrs. Joseph D.
(Mary Lorene Ingalls)
Maxwell, Mrs. Wayne
(Nancy Eugenia Weece)
Maynard, III, Mrs. James G.
(Joan Kerrwin Barry)
McDermott, Mrs. Edward H.
(Mildred B. Wetten)
McGowan, Mrs. John P.
(Barbara S. Call)
McGuinnis, Mrs. John P.
(Nancy J. Crossman)
McGuinnis, Mrs. Michael J.
(Ruth Ann Mary Gillis)
Meiners, Mrs. Dawn G.
(Dawn Celeste Galvin)
Miller, Mrs. Helen Dillen
Miller, Mrs. Paul J.
(Michal Karan Davis)
Miller, Mrs. William A.
(Rhoda Ann Szudzinski)
Milnor, Mrs. Frank R.
(Barbara Wakeley)
Moore, Mrs. John Thomas
(Katherine Elma Jaqua)
Mosher, Mrs. David F.
(Yoko Kusama)
Notz, Jr., Mrs. John K.
(Janis Lee Wellin)

Novak, Mrs. Theodore J.
 (Carol Ann Egdorf)
O'Malley, Mrs. Michael
 (Catherine Greer)
Ogilvie, Mrs. Richard B.
 (Dorothy Louise Shriver)
Osment, Mrs. Frank C.
 (Josephine Kathryn Finke)
Owen, Mrs. Rodger A.
 (Janet Karen Schultz)
Pattishall, Mrs. Beverly W.
 (Dorothy Daniels Mashek)
Phillips, Mrs. David M.
 (Ruth Ann Huffman)
Pitz, Ms. Mary Elisabeth
Prendergast, Mrs. Robert
 (Barbara Ellen Kerrigan)
Quinn, Mrs. Neil K.
 (Ruth Ann Baker)
Rasin, Mrs. Rudolph S.
 (Joy Peterkin)
Rosenzweig, Mrs. Ellis B.
 (Linda Joan Fahrbach)
Rummel, Ms. Cynthia W.
 (Cynthia Ann Walker)
Salisbury, Ms. Linda E.
Scales, Mrs. John
 (Karen Waldeck)
Seabury-Houser, Mrs. Charlene B.
 (Charlene Adrienne Brown)
Senior, Mrs. Richard J. L.
 (Diana Thatcher Morgan)
Sharp, Mrs. Jeffrey S.
 (Elizabeth Gleason Dillon)
Sheffield, Jr., Mrs. Thomas C.
 (Pamela Starry)
Smith, Mrs. Steven
 (Lisa Ann Moore)
Snorf, Ms. Margaret
Starshak, Mrs. Joseph B.
 (Mary Clare Spencer)
Stovall, Mrs. Robert L.
 (Verna Callahan)
Stuart, Jr., Mrs. James G.
 (Karen Zupko)
Study, Mrs. Robert S.
 (Patricia Ann Connor)
Taich, Mrs. James E.
 (Sarah Rodgers Lile)
Telander, Mrs. John C.
 (Gloria Brown-Miller)
Temple, Mrs. Dana R.
Thomas, Mrs. Robert W.
 (Sandra Kay Henderson)
Thompson, Mrs. Collier Y.
 (Collier Sheridan Young)
Trienens, Mrs. Howard J.
 (Paula R. Miller)
Trump, Mrs. Robert M.
 (Rosemary De Lee Utterback)
Vance, Mrs. William C.
 (Valerie Laurusonis)
Vanden Bosch, Mrs. Robert E.
 (Ann McCarthy)
Vilas, Mrs. Faith Lehman
Vogl, Mrs. Alexander J.
 (Barbara Joanne Bradford)
Wanders, Mrs. David G.
 (Kristin C. Brinkman)

Weed, Mrs. Edward R.
 (Lawrie Irving Bowes)
Whiting, Jr., Mrs. Clayton Edward
 (Kathleen Lydia Mouzakeotis)
Wolff, Mrs. Ronald
 (Virginia Louise Schreiber)
Wood, Ms. Courtenay Robinson
 (Mrs. H. Noel Jackson, Jr.)
York, Mrs. Judith C.
 (Judith Anne Carmack)

GENERAL MEMBERSHIP

Abbott, Mrs. Geoffrey
 (Pamela J. Cash)
Adams, IV, Mrs. William
 (Elisabeth A. Lewis)
Adamson, Mrs. Gordon
 (Emily Dyas Norcross)
Ahern, Mrs. Mark T.
 (Charlotte M. Flanagan)
Aktas, Mrs. Yavuz
 (Fatma Kiran)
Aladjem, Mrs. Sonia
 (Sonia Goldberg)
Alden, Mrs. Geraldine Scannell
 (Mrs. Shakeab Alshabkhoun)
Alden, Miss Lara Lynn
Aldrich, Mrs. James W.
 (Irene C. Mellion)
Allen, Mrs. Robert Wellington
 (Mary Coleman Crowell)
Allen, Mrs. Ronald J.
 (Julie O'Donnell)
Almeida, Mrs. Richard J.
 (Jill E. Farris)
Alport, Mrs. Stephen A.
 (Catharine E. McAdams)
Anagnost, Mrs. Alexander T.
 (Karen Mortensen)
Andersen, Jr., Mrs. Robert M.
 (Claudia Jean Latoria)
Anderson, Mrs. Allen S.
 (Priscilla Ransom Macdougall)
Anderson, Mrs. Carol N.
 (Carol Ann Nordvall)
Anderson, Mrs. James L.
 (Angela Ambrosia)
Anderson, Miss Judith W.
Anderson, Mrs. Robert E.
 (Ann Louise Stafford)
Anderson, Jr., Mrs. Robert M.
 (Claudia Jean Latoria)
Anderson, Ms. Susan
 (Mrs. Donald L. Metzger)
Andrews, Mrs. William D.
 (Laurie Hand)
Appenbrink, Mrs. Ronald
 (Maxine Westerheide)
Archambault, Mrs. Bennett
 (Margaret Henrietta Morgan)
Ascher, Mrs. Maria
 (Maria Salem)
Asher, Mrs. Donald L.
 (Carol Jean Weiss)

Ashley, Mrs. Richard W.
 (Helen Mawicke)
Ashton, Mrs. John B.
 (June Evelyn Goodale)
Atkinson, Mrs. James
 (Pamela Claire Pavilck)
Avedisian, Mrs. Dorothy D.
 (Dorothy Donian)
Bacaintan, Mrs. Nicolas N.
 (Constance Gregory)
Bacon, Ms. Andrea
Baird, Mrs. Stephen W.
 (Susan Elizabeth Merritt)
Baldwin, Mrs. Thomas G., Jr.
 (Eleanor Fisher)
Bankard, Mrs. James H.
 (Susan Jane Turner)
Baran, Mrs. Edward J.
 (Kathleen M. Foley)
Bardo, Mrs. Pamela Pierrepont
Barenberg, Mrs. Sumner A.
 (Sally Franc Viden)
Barker, Jr., Mrs. Morton Darrell
 (R-Lou Porter)
Barlow, Mrs. Aaron
 (Priscilla Stearns Baybutt)
Barnum, Mrs. David R.
 (Marjory W. Church)
Barr, Mrs. William A.
 (E. Anne Quick)
Barrett, Mrs. Roger S.
 (Barbara Reed Barry)
Barron, Mrs. Harold S.
 (Roberta Yellin)
Bartels, Mrs. Gordon H.
 (Francine Cynthia Buhl Clarke)
Barton, Miss Patricia Anne
Basler, Jr., Mrs. Douglas S.
 (Mary Jo)
Bateman, Mrs. James
 (Betsy Kearns)
Bauer, Ms. Tracy
Baumgartner, Mrs. William
 (Andrea J. Coath)
Bax, Mrs. William L.
 (Kim Hackett)
Bay, Jr., Mrs. James N.
 (Laurie L. Veda)
Beam, Mrs. John D.
 (Ruthie Reid)
Beemer, Mr. Gordon G.
Begel, Mrs. Thomas M.
 (Sarah Beilke)
Beitler, Jr., Mrs. Paul J.
 (Penny Jo Powers)
Bellows, Mrs. Joel J.
 (Laurel Gordon)
Belmore, Mrs. F. Martin
 (Suzanne Corkedale)
Bendy, Mrs. C. Joseph
 (Celine Setsuko Matsumoto)
Benish, Miss Nell McNally
Bennett, Mr. Russell O.
Bent, Mrs. Stephen P.
 (Anne F. Searle)
Bercher, Mrs. Harry
 (Patricia Ann Cornell)
Berger, Mrs. Richard S.
 (Linda Shaughnessy)

Bernhart, Mrs. Daniel J.
 (Elizabeth H. Fields)
Bestler, Mrs. Timothy W.
 (Marianne Kiefer)
Biel-Cohen, Mrs. Mimis
 (Andrea Biel)
Birkos, Mrs. Russell J.
 (Barbara Hall Taylor)
Birnkrant, Jr., Mrs. Michael C.
 (Susan Francoise Delaney)
Bivins, Mrs. Terry
 (Lyn Morhardt)
Blatt, Mrs. Richard L.
 (Carolyn E. LeBlanc)
Blazer, Ms. Judith Elizabeth
Block, III, Mrs. Philip D.
 (Judith Lynn Stofer)
Bobrinskoy, Mrs. Charles K.
 (Mary Anne Kane)
Boe, Mrs. Archie R.
 (Elaine Beverly Jansson)
Boemi, Mrs. A. Andrew
 (Flora Dorothy De Muro)
Bogert, Mrs. George T.
 (Rosemary Kaiser)
Boice, Ms. Jacklyn P.
Bolz, Mrs. John A.
 (Marian Erma Richter)
Bolz, Mrs. Robert M.
 (Anne Wilkins)
Bon Durant, Mrs. Robert E.
 (Isabelle Hadley)
Bonnell, Mrs. Howard William
 (Marie Elizabeth Adams York)
Borwell, Mrs. Robert C.
 (Naomi Tudor)
Bowen, Mrs. William
 (Betsy Bass)
Bowes, Mrs. Henry E.
 (Lauretta Helen Schultz)
Bradley, Mrs. David
 (Betsy Huizenga)
Bransfield, Jr., Mrs. John J.
 (Myriam Ensenat Ledo)
Brault, Mrs. Jerome J.
 (Mary Landrigan)
Braver, Mrs. Anita
 (Anita Vander Meer)
Brennan, Mrs. James J.
 (Sarah Anne Cahill)
Brennan, Mrs. Nancy H.
 (Nancy Hough)
Bricker, Ms. Deborah A.
Brinson, Mrs. Gary P.
 (Suzann Hawkins)
Bristol, Mrs. Douglas W.
 (Maureen E. Moore)
Brooker, Mrs. T. Kimball
 (Nancy Belle Neumann)

Brooksher, Mrs. K. Dane
  (Carter Jean Stafford)
Brown III, Mrs. Charles F.
  (Angeline Johnson Galbraith)
Brown, Mrs. Christopher C.
  (Joyce Elizabeth Martin)
Brumback, Mrs. Charles T.
  (Mary Louise Howe)
Buettner, Jr., Mrs. Alfred P.
  (Leigh Elliott Schweppe)
Bulger, Mrs. Richard
  (Judith Diane Harms)
Buntrock, Mrs. Dean L.
  (Rosemarie Nuzzo)
Burditt, Mrs. George M.
  (Barbara Stenger)
Burgess, Mrs. Harlan H.
  (Suzanne Culbertson)
Burgess, Mrs. Richard B.
  (Diane Letchworth)
Burgess, Mrs. Warren C.
  (Susan A. Gebhardt)
Burke, Mrs. Richard W.
  (Maryjeanne Ryan)
Byun, Mrs. Jong Kyou
  (Young Hee Park)
Cagney, Ms. Mary Ellen
  (Mrs. Lee J. Schoen)
Cagnoni, Mrs. Marilyn Mason
  (Marilyn Eck Mason)
Calihan, III, Mrs. E. John
  (Mary Lee Stacy)
Callahan, Jr., Mrs. Patrick J.
  (Patricia Ann Henebry)
Campbell, Jr., Mrs. William J.
  (Victoria M. Mansfield)
Campion, Ms. Karim Jacobus
  (Mrs. Russell R. Campion)
Carlson, Mrs. Roger L.
  (Virginia B. Glass)
Carroll, Mrs. Barry J.
  (Barbara Pehrson)
Carroll, Mrs. Cornelius X.
  (Sally Anne Jewell)
Carroll, Miss Dierdre Holden
Carroll, Dr. Donna M.
Carson, Mrs. E. Bruce
  (Elizabeth Essington)
Caufield, Mrs. Farlin
  (Clarice M. Decker)
Cerullo, Mrs. Leonard J.
  (Cheryl Weir)
Chace, Ms. Beverly J.
Challenger, Mrs. James E.
  (Ruth Rozier)
Chambers, Mrs. William
  (Phyllis Greene)
Chapman, Jr., Mrs. Alger B.
  (Beatrice Bishop)
Childress, Mrs. Kevin C.
  (Lory Davis)
Chilla, III, Mrs. Charles
  (Elizabeth Sims)

Christensen, Mrs. Earnest E.
  (Phyllis Nash)
Christopherson, Mrs. Weston R.
  (Myrna Louisa Christensen)
Chun, Mrs. Gregory H.
  (Flicia S. Kim)
Church, Jr., Mrs. Ralph E.
  (Marion P. Phillips)
Chutkow, Ms. Dawn Michelle
Cicchinelli, Mrs. David
  (Gerri Heitzman)
Clark, Mrs. Thomas C.
  (Winifred Chambers)
Cleavenger, Mrs. Timothy Q.
  (Margaret R. Anderson)
Cleveland, Mrs. Dwight M.
  (Gabriela Franco-Abarca)
Clifford, Mrs. John S.
  (Mary R. Warner)
Cline, Miss Virginia Mae
Cochran, Mrs. George N.
  (Barbara King Doepke)
Cole, Ms. Lucy Darby
Coleman, Mrs. Henry Neal
  (Imogene Courington)
Coley, Mrs. Stephen C.
  (Jane Victoria Graham)
Collens, Mrs. Lewis W.
  (Marge Tepper)
Comiskey, II, Mrs. Charles Albert
  (Donna Jo Curran)
Conger, Mrs. Robert Alan
  (Dorothy Louise Gallagher)
Conkey, II, Mrs. Harry D.
  (Lynn Sitterly)
Conlan, Mrs. David L.
  (Jane Mills)
Conley, Mrs. John G.
  (Margaret Mary Barry-O'Neill)
Connolly, Jr., Mrs. Frank A.
  (Mary McDonough)
Connolly, Ms. Trudye
Considine, Mrs. Frank W.
  (Nancy Scott)
Cook, Mrs. John A.
  (Barbara Ann Humes)
Cook, Mrs. John Q.
  (Kathleen Kampp)
Coolidge, III, Mrs. E. David
  (Constance L. Bennett)
Cooney, Sr., Mrs. Robert J.
  (Linda Anne Williams)
Cooper, Mrs. Douglass A.
  (Eugenie Letourneau)
Cooper, Mrs. Richard C.
  (Sharon Wootten Stafford)
Cooper, Mrs. Richard H.
  (Lana Sue Traeger)
Cooper, Mrs. Thomas E.
  (Janie Widman Leader)
Cozad, Mrs. James W.
  (Virginia Earline Alley)
Craft, Mrs. Alfred T.
  (Thelma Ley)
Craig, Mrs. Scott
  (Mary Evelyn Earle)
Cramer, Mrs. Ronald E.
  (Corlita Woodward Reich)

Crane, Mrs. Michael E.
  (Nancy Timberlake)
Crane, Mrs. William A.
  (Margaret A. Kerwin)
Craven, Mrs. Christopher C.
  (Mari Hatzenbuehler)
Crawford, Mrs. William Fowle
  (Ruth M. Fellinger)
Cregan, Mrs. John D.
  (Lisa Dannucci)
Cremin, Miss Susan E.
Crocker, Mrs. Samuel Sackett
  (Dorothy Hatch Macdonald)
Crowe, Mrs. Peter Toohey
  (Lesley Spencer Staley)
Crown, Mrs. Robert
  (Joanne Strauss)
Cuneo, Jr., Mrs. John F.
  (Herta Klauser)
D'Avino, Mrs. Pasquale
  (Maria Teresa Pastore)
Daleiden, Mrs. Dianne
  (Dianne Gettings)
von Dallwitz-Wegner, Mrs. Helen
  (Helen E. Berry)
Dammeyer, Mrs. Diane
Danforth, Jr., Mrs. David N.
  (Anne Walker Nickson)
Darnall, Mrs. Robert
  (Linda Marletta Farrier)
Dassios, Mrs. John
  (Alexis Youtsos)
Davies, Mrs. Lee
  (Barbara Lee LaRochelle)
Davies, Mrs. Mary M.
  (Mary Walden Murphy)
De La Torre, Mrs. Franklin
  (Luciana Caparrini)
DeAngelis, Mrs. Donald Lee
  (Madeline Reilly)
De Froideville, Mrs. Gilbert
  (Monod Reigersman)
DeStefano, Mrs. James R.
  (Judith Nelson)
Deutsch, Mrs. Owen H.
  (Bonnie Kausal)
DeYoung, Mrs. James W.
  (Penelope Wick)
Dicke, Mrs. James F.
  (Eilleen Webster)
Dicke, II, Mrs. James F.
  (Janet St. Clair)
Dickes, Mrs. Byram E.
  (Suzanne M. Hadley)
Dickson, Mrs. Charles Foote
  (Mirra L. Prendergast)
Diederichs, Mrs. John K.
  (Janet Wood)
Diermeier, Mrs. Jeffrey J.
  (Julie M. Evans)
Dille, Mrs. Robert C.
  (Virginia L. Nichols)
Doan, Mrs. Herbert D.
  (Junia Cassell)

Doherty, Mrs. Charles V.
  (Marilyn Bongiorno)
Dolan, Jr., Mrs. Daniel D.
  (Mary Elizabeth McCoy)
Dombek, Jr., Mrs. John J.
  (Priscilla Anne Wright)
Donoghue, Miss Sue A.
Dooley, Mrs. James A.
  (Virginia Proesel)
Douglas, Mrs. Kenneth J.
  (Ann Schweizer)
Dowdle, Mrs. James C.
  (Sally Sayers)
Drake, Jr., Mrs. Lyman M.
  (Margaretta Spence)
DuBoe, Miss Wendy Lynn
Duchossois, Ms. Kimberly
Dugan, Mrs. John J.
  (Maureen A. Moran)
Dunea, Miss Melanie Serena
  Alexandra
Dunn, Mrs. B. F.
  (Kay Kennedy)
Dunn, Mrs. E. Bruce
  (Nancie Turner-Smith)
Dunn, Mrs. John
  (Kathleen Shreibak)
Durkin, Mrs. Patrick J.
  (Tamra L. Semmer)
Dykema, Miss Julie
Early, Mrs. Robert C.
  (Barbara Guelfi)
Eberhardt, Mrs. Jerrold L.
  (Margaret Decker)
Echols, Mrs. David H.
  (Evelyn Bassett)
Edwards, Mrs. Alfred H.
  (Virginia Ruth Farmiloe)
Edwards, Ms. Taryn Baldwin
Edwards, Mrs. Robert C.
  (Elizabeth Rinehimer)
Eggers, Mrs. Catherine B.
  (Catherine O'Connell)
Eidell, Mrs. Ronald
  (Nina L. Barnes)
Eldridge, Mrs. Huntington
  (Barbara Anne Buchanan)
Eldridge, Jr., Mrs. Huntington
  (Deborah Marie West)
Elmquist, Ms. Marion Loraine
Engelhard, Mrs. Michael
  (Ute Mana Hoffman)
Enright, Miss Susan Anne
Evans, Ms. Lynn
Eyerman, Mrs. Thomas J.
  (Mary Kathryn Evans)
Farley, Mrs. Shelley MacArthur
  (Shelley Suzanne Michels)
Farr, Mrs. Harriet W.
  (Harriet Amelia Westover)
Fazzano, Miss Mary Louise
Fee, Ms. Mary Carol
  (Mrs. J. Curtis Fee)
Feeley, Mrs. Henry J.
  (Diane Dudenhoefer)
Feldman, Mrs. William M.
  (Barbara Ann Staren)
Ferguson, Mrs. Howard
  (Ann Duffy)

200

Ferguson, Mrs. Mark E.
(Elizabeth B. Yntema)
Field, Ms. Jane
(Jane Margaret Seaborg)
Fields, Miss Allison
Fields, Mrs. Charles J.
(Mary Elizabeth Alverson)
Finley, Mrs. Kathryn Ann
Fisher, Mrs. Robert L.
(Marilyn June Peterson)
Fitzgerald, Miss Lee
Fitzgerald, Mrs. S. Peterson
(Suzanne Arnet)
Fitzgerald, Mrs. Thomas Gosselin
(Joyce Ann Mancari)
Florence-Smith, Mrs. Susan
Florsheim, Mrs. Harold
(Sarabel Windt)
Flury, Mrs. L. Richard
(Elizabeth Edgelow)
Fondrevay, Ms. Jennifer Jayne
Foran, Mrs. Thomas A.
(Jean Marie Burke)
Foufas, Mrs. Teddy Mouzakeotis
Franche, Mrs. G. Elwood
(Virginia Carson Elwood)
Frazier, Jr., Mrs. William J.
(Jane Grathwohl)
Freeman, Mrs. Brena D.
(Brena Dietz)
Freidheim, Jr., Mrs. Cyrus F.
(Marguerite Vanden Bosch)
Freund, Mrs. John E.
(Penny Goldstein)
Frey, Ms. M. E.
(Mary E. Glynn)
Frick, Mrs. Raymond
(Elizabeth Murray)
Fridrich, Miss Jacquelin M.
Friedeman, Jr., Mrs. Richard F.
(Kathleen Joanne Hall)
Front, Mrs. Marshall B.
(Laura De Ferrari)
Fuller, Mrs. H. Laurance
(Nancy Louise Lawrence)
Fultz, Mrs. Susan
(Susan Greenleaf Flynn)
Funk, Mrs. Donald E.
(Aline O'Connor)
Furrer, Mrs. John R.
(Annie Louise Waldo)
Gage, Mrs. William Bolton
(Mary Agnes Burns)
Galbraith, III, Mrs. John D.
(Victoria Leigh Brauckman)
Gallagher, Mrs. Charles J.
(Veronica Anne Palandech)
Gallas, Mrs. Jack A.
(Barbara Anne Barringer)
Galvin, Mrs. Christopher B.
(Cynthia Elizabeth Bardes)
Galvin, Mrs. Michael
(Elizabeth Anne Wylie)
Gardner, Miss Anne Ashforth

Gardner, Mrs. John Robert
(Dorothy S. Hannon)
Gardner, Mrs William E.
(Helene Jacqueline Salamon)
Gately, Mrs. John
(Shirley Hanway Fitzgerald)
Gebhard, Mrs. Paul G.
(Maria George Svolos)
Gehan, Mrs. Rene-Jean
(Sophie Taubert)
Genet, Miss Mary Eliza
Gent, Mrs. Donald A.
(Ann Marie Koons)
Gerst, Mrs. C. Gary
(Virginia Clarke Caspari)
Getz, Mrs. Sandra L.
(Sandra L. Maclean)
Giannoulias, Mrs. Alexis
(Anna Xirouhaki)
Gibson, Mrs. Robert C.
(Gail Skiles Conder)
Gidwitz, Mrs. James G.
(Kathryn Westfall)
Giesen, Mrs. Richard A.
(Jeannine Lee St. Bernard)
Gifford, Mrs. Richard D.
(Joan Clare Oswald)
Glass, Mrs. George Holt
(Myra Elizabeth Best)
Golan, Mrs. Leonard W.
(Eileen V. McDonough)
Goodman, Mrs. Gary A.
(Dr. Teresa Elaine Berry)
Goodyear, Jr., Mrs. William M.
(Karen Elaine Schultz)
Gordon, Mrs. Alan D.
(Lynn Griffin)
Gordon, II, Mrs. Jerome J.
(Patricia Sanger Kaufman)
Gosselin, Mrs. John W.
(Carol Jessup Hall)
Gottlieb, Mrs. Richard H.
(Gloria Gasul)
Grady-Cornell, Mrs. D. Lynne
Graettinger, Mrs. John Sells
(Elizabeth D. Shorey)
Grainger, Mrs. David W.
(Juli Plant)
Grant, Miss Barbara Nelson
Grant, Mrs. Tone N.
(Kathi S. Schmid)
Granville, III, Mrs. Charles N.
(Elizabeth Lennox)
Greene, Mrs. John
(Joan Elizabeth Frazier)
Greig, Mrs. W. George
(Margaret A. Banonis)
Grenzebach, Ms. Elizabeth
Blanchard
(Mrs. Frederick C. Broda)
Griffin, Mrs. Hollis J.
(Ginger Sweet)
Griffin, Mrs. Roger S.
(Sherryl Louise Ware)
Griffiths, Mrs. Julian M.
(Nan Armstrong Pollock)
Grimes, Mrs. Joseph F.
(Barbara Sweet)

Groen, Jr., Mrs. Fred H.
(Jean Gardner)
Gross, Mrs. W. B. Martin
(Lavina Sack)
Grosse, Mrs. O. Howard
(Rose Buehler)
Gustaitis, Mrs. Nancy
(Nancy Udowski)
Guthrie, Mrs. William N.
(Kathryn Lide)
Haarlow, Mrs. William
(Lynne Rupp)
Haberli, Mrs. Ernst A.
(Ute Clemens)
Habermann, Mrs. Marjorie
(Marjorie J. Edmondson)
Haffner, Mrs. Charles C.
(Anne Peronneau Clark)
Hagenah, Mrs. John A.
(Dana Perry Welsh)
Hagenah, Jr., Mrs. William J.
(Marjorie Elizabeth Clark)
Hahn, Mrs. Rainer
(Marianne Brunzlow)
Hakola, Mrs. Vern E.
(Mary Crowe)
Hall, Mrs. Brian Ellis
(Rosemary Fandel)
Hall, Mrs. Thomas Thonet
(Diane Lee Rodi)
Halpern, Mrs. Richard C.
(Madeline Elaine Jackolin)
Hambleton, Jr., Mrs. Chalkley J.
(Genevieve Amberg Cremin)
Hambleton, Mrs. Douglas M.
(Barbara Ellen Nielsen)
Hamilton, Mrs. David R.
(Catharine Cline)
Hammond, Ms. Suzanne
Hand, Mrs. Jack C.
(Jane Christensen Kuoni)
Hanna, Mrs. Albert C.
(R. Christie)
Hansen, Mrs. Loren A.
(Monica Marie McCue)
Hansen, Mrs. Samuel C.
(Julia Knight Patterson)
Hanson, Mrs. David
(Terri Dangerfield)
Hanzlik, Mrs. Paul Frank
(Marcia Lynn Mayberry)
Hark, Mrs. William A.
(Marguerite DeLany)
Harrington, Ms. Elizabeth D.
(Mrs. William F. Lynch)
Harrington, Ms. Francia E.
Harris, Mrs. Joel T.
(Judy Kantowick)
Harris, Miss Margaret
Harvey, Mrs. Paul
(Lynne Cooper)
Haser, Jr., Mrs. Harry William
(Clara Morris McGuire)

Haskin, Mrs. Warren
(Clare-Ru Mueller)
Hatzenbuehler, Mrs. Camille C.
(Camille D. Chaddick)
Hauptfuhrer, Miss Elizabeth Leigh
Haverkampf, Mrs. Gordon D.
(Frances Ellen Durr)
Hawk, Mrs. James Henry
(Charlcye J. Smith)
Hawley, Mrs. David C.
(Dorothy Devereaux)
Hayden, Mrs. Mark
(Diana Niedermaier)
Hayes, Jr., Mrs. C. Kirtland
(Winifred H. Date)
Hayes, Mrs. James E.
(M. Marie Mitchell)
Haynes, III, Mrs. Patrick J.
(Lorill Ann Moe)
Hayward, Jr., Mrs. Thomas Z.
(Sally Ann Madden)
Healy, Mrs. Denis J.
(Sondra A. Hirsch)
Healy, Dr. Nancy
Hedlund, Mrs. Reuben L.
(Cynthia Loar Hill)
Heenan, Mrs. Thomas W.
(Jane E. Budelman)
Heimark, Mrs. Craig
(Libby Ann Hirsh)
Hennessy, Jr., Mrs. John F.
(Elizabeth Ann Munroe)
Hennessy, Miss Mary Ellen
Henry, Mrs. Patrick
(Heather Therese Campbell)
Hermann, Mrs. James R.
(Susan Mullane)
Hershenhorn, Mrs. Robert G.
(Judith Marie Holmberg)
Hickey, Mrs. Jerome E.
(Denise Coakley)
Hickey, Ms. M. Lynne
Higinbotham, Mrs. Harlow N.
(Susan Ellen Spika)
Hinchion, Mrs. Richard
(Ann T. Scannell)
Hines, Miss Barbara Notz
Hines, III, Mrs. Charles Leonard
(Bernadine Gene Tosetti)
Hines, Mrs. Edward
(Marcia Dicks McMillan)
Hochfelder, Mrs. Allen R.
(Stephanie Alice LeVee)
Hoffmann, Mrs. David H.
(Jerrilyn M. Noelke)
Hoffman, Mrs. Janet
(Janet Laningham Rowe)
Hoffman, Mrs. Robert B.
(Janet Alissa O'Brien)
Holland, Mrs. Jeffrey J.
(Liliane Diana Kayloe)
Holland, Mrs. Leslie
(Leslie Scardino)
Holland, Mrs. Robert J.
(Barbara Jane Drake)
Hooper, Mrs. George R.
(Ruth Reichmann)
Hoover, Mrs. H. Earl
(Miriam F. Ulvinen)

Horne, Mrs. Ronald
(Peyton Stewart Chapman)
Horween, Jr., Mrs. Arnold
(Ellen A. Rand)
Houck, Mrs. Irvin E.
(Margaret Lucille Ratledge)
Huizenga, Mrs. Peter
(Heidi Schultz)
Hummer, Mrs. William B.
(Melanie Susan Sayles)
Hunt, Ms. Janice S.
(Janice Elizabeth Sutter)
Hunt, Ms. Valerie C. Smith
Hunter, III, Mrs. Thomas Benton
(Maxine Mae Morrison)
Hurley, Mrs. Jason
(Virginia O'Brien)
Huscher, Mrs. Justin S.
(Hilarie Viator)
Husman, Mrs. David L.
(Kathleen Walsh)
Igoe, Mrs. Michael L.
(Helen Douaire)
Ingersoll, Mrs. William C.
(Marilyn Helen Jones)
Isselhard, Mrs. Terrell J.
(Jill Marie Slone)
Istock, Mrs. Verne G.
(Judith Warnke)
Ittelson, Ms. Mary Elizabeth
(Mrs. Richard C. Tuttle)
Ivon, Miss Nena
Jackson, Jr., Mrs. Allen Shannon
(Marcia Lynn Kogan)
Jacobs, Sr., Mrs. William Thad
(Jeanne R. Ferrell)
Jaffee, Mrs. Richard M.
(Shirley Elaine Handmaker)
Jahn, Mrs. Helmut
(Deborah Lampe)
Jaicks, Ms. Sarah Pendleton
(Mrs. Robert B. McDermott)
Jenkins, Mrs. Robert C.
(Sarah Ann Van Ornum)
Jensen, Mrs. James L.
(Caroline Ann Schillinger)
Jessopp, Mrs. Charles E. B.
(Victoria Ware)
Johnson, Mrs. Harry W.
(Marilyn Keeley)
Johnson, Mrs. Steven E.
(Blaine Kinney)
Johnson, Mrs. William Wescott
(Nan Rogers Leonard)
Johnston, IV, Mrs. Harrison
(Luetta Coumbe Robertson)
Johnstone, Mrs. R. Stuart
(Michelle Johnson)
Jones, Ms. Barbara
Jones, Mrs. Robert N.
(Mica L. Moruzzi)
Jordan, Jr., Mrs. George Cook
(Alden Farr King)
Jordan, Jr., Mrs. George T.
(Earline Ray)
Jorgensen, Mrs. Nancy
(Nancy Eugenia Lyon)
Joyce, Mrs. David J.
(Mandy Kelly)

Joyce, Mrs. Edward T.
(Mary Kay Sullivan)
Joyce, Mrs. Thomas P.
(Mary Margaret McConville)
Kahler, Mrs. Richard I.
(Jan Ann Knight)
Kampf, Jr., Mrs. Philip L.
(Cynthia Katherine Tripp)
Karzas, Mrs. Byron C.
(Diane Stathas)
Karzas, Ms. Mary Kay
(Dr. Warren K. Reiss)
Kealy, Mrs. Anna F.
(Anna Louise Forstmann)
Kearns, Mrs. Lewis Gamble
(Elizabeth Lee)
Keats, Mrs. Glenn A.
(Olga Maria Loor)
Kelly, Mrs. John E.
(Janet R. Langford)
Kelly, Mrs. John T.
(Jeane Ness)
Kelly, Miss Marilyn E.
Kelly, Mrs. Thomas A.
(Janet Carle Ingram)
Kelly, Mrs. Thomas B.
(Deborah Ellen Gooch)
Kempf, Jr., Mrs. Donald G.
(Nancy P. Baby)
Kennedy, Mrs. Taylor I.
(Jane Cloud)
Kennedy, Mrs. Thomas M.
(Leslie Mary Pollock)
Kern, Miss Louise Moreland
Kerr, Mrs. Gordon S.
(Kalli Rimikis)
Keseric, Mrs. Peter
(Beverly Jean Gilmore)
Kestnbaum, Mrs. Robert Dana
(Kate Lenore Trynin)
Kiefer, Mrs. James P.
(Paula Jean Behrendt)
Kiilerich, Mrs. Bent
(Ses Inan)
Kiley, Mrs. Eugene J.
(Helen Jessie Hadley)
Kimball, Ms. Alicia Wilson
Kincannon, Mrs. Jack F.
(Mildred Neely)
King, Mrs. Charles W.
(Mary Caroline Dunbar)
King, Jr., Mrs. Donald A.
(Janemarie Dionne)
Kinney, Mrs. Kenneth P.
(Terese Ann Bargen)
Kinsella, Mrs. John
(Jeanette Cullinane)
Kinsella, Mrs. Phillips
(Katherine Bauch)
Kissel, Mrs. Richard J.
(Donna Lou Heidersbach)

Kline, Jr., Mrs. Oliver Perry
(Mary Lew Pope)
Knoelke, Mrs. Katherine
(Katherine Benish)
Knox, Mrs. Philip M.
(Joan Jinnett Sutton)
Knuth, Mrs. Roger A.
(Kathy Sue Orr)
Koch, Ms. Anne Donnelly
Koeneman, Mrs. Keith
(Claire A. Baldikoski)
Koepfgen, Mrs. Bruce L.
(Kristin Nielsen)
Kopp, Mrs. Carl R.
(Jenna Lou Katherine Brown)
Kostbade, Mrs. Howard W.
(Christine Koenig)
Kozak, Mrs. John W.
(Elizabeth Mathias)
Kramer, Mrs. Robert E.
(Susanne M. Meany)
Kreer, Mrs. Henry Blackstone
(Irene Overman)
Krepela, Mrs. Christian
(Irmgard Halosar)
Krez, Mrs. Daniel L.
(Denice Anne Rassas)
Kroeger, Ms. Susan
(Susan Hodel)
Krupka, Mrs. Paula Kelly
(Paula Leist)
Kuhn, Jr., Mr. Paul H.
Kunkler, Mrs. William C.
(Susan M. Crown)
Laaperi, Dr. Cherie
(Mrs. Rod R. McMahan)
Lacaillade, Mrs. Laurence L.
(Vaughan Knox)
Laffey, Mrs. Daniel F.
(Joan Muldoon)
Lagrange, Mrs. Lucien J.
(Jessica Westin Dunne)
Laing, Mrs. James Stuart
(Alison Cornell Blair)
Lamphere, Mrs. Charles R.
(Sarah Gordon Kelley)
Landon, Mrs. Wayne L.
(Janel Davis)
Lang, Mrs. Gordon
(Clara Bates Van Derzee)
Lang, Mrs. Henry Spencer
(Carolyn Marie Haddad)
Langdon, Mrs. Howard S.
(Mary Kathleen Alice Kipping)
Langendorff, Mrs. Judith Louise
Schwartz
Langtry, Mrs. Alfred Leigh
(Mary Ann Peacock)
Largay, Mrs. Robert E.
(Julianne Dempsey)
Lauber, Ms. Patricia R.
(Mrs. Kerry T. Shintani)
Laurain, Mrs. Gerald W.
(Marlene Saint-George)
Lavender, Jr., Mrs. Harold W.
(Judith Ann Kennedy)
Lawson, III, Mrs. Lawrence J.
(Wende Fox)
Ledvina, Ms. Kay Marie

Leffel, Mrs. Charles P.
(Grace Ann Hartnett)
Lehr, Jr., Mrs. Louis A.
(Sherry Mann)
Lelyveld, Mrs. Steven
(Betsy Catherine McCormick)
Lengfelder, Mrs. Terry
(Joyce Jean Sauerwein)
Lerner, Mrs. Alexander R.
(Marianne Ryan)
Leszinske, Mrs. William O.
(Carol Ann Ortlund)
Lever, Mrs. Allan N.
(Nora Starr Hazlewood)
Levine, Mrs. Lou K.
(Lou Kotler)
Lewis, Jr., Mrs. Victor L.
(Jayne Ward Martin)
Lifvendahl, Mrs. Harold
(Joan Mulroy)
Lillie, Jr., Mrs. Richard H.
(Mary Ann Walters)
Lindland, Mrs. Melissa George
(Mrs. Matthew K. Lindland)
Lindner, Mrs. Robert
(Nancy Kuhn)
Linn, Mrs. Alexandra Palmer
(Mrs. Robert L. Linn)
Lockwood, Mrs. Wayne P.
(Carol Ann Condon)
Loewenberg, Mrs. James R.
(Nancy Faith Rosenstein)
Lofgren, Mrs. Lewis C.
(Mary Lehwald)
Logsdon, Ms. Leslie Ann
(Mrs. Duncan Bourne)
Looney, Mrs. James K.
(Claudia A. Schneider)
Luning, Mrs. Henry H.
(Mary Mabel Howson)
Lunn, Mrs. Robert S.
(Laura Ann Scott)
Lynch, Jr., Mrs. John J.
(Stephanie Loftin)
Lyons, Miss Linda Louise
MacArthur, Mrs. Cynthia Wirtz
MacArthur, Mrs. Shawndra A.
(Shawndra Asseff)
MacKenzie, Mrs. Donald D.
(Suzanne P. Grant)
Maddox, Ms. Anne H.
Madigan, Mrs. John W.
(Holly Williams)
Madigan, Jr., Mrs. Joseph D.
(Carol Ann Malloy)
Madigan, Miss Maria C.
Madlener, Ms. Deborah Lowden
Magner, Jr., Mrs. T. Gerald
(Patricia Ann Doering)
Malkin, Mrs. Cary J.
(Lisa Ann Klimley)
Maltman, Mrs. James S.
(Marianne Lyn Ware)

Manderfeld-Furnari, Mrs. Linda
   (Linda Lee Manderfeld)
Mangel, II, Mrs. John
   (Hilda Brumbaugh)
Marchetti, Mrs. Joseph P.
   (Mary Jane Becker)
Markham, Mrs. John Jay
   (Alice Runnells Utley)
Marshall, Miss Megan C.
Marsland, Mrs. Susan L.
   (Susan Ann Little)
Martin, Mrs. Patrick A.
   (Sandra Marie Staskon)
Martin, Mrs. Richard A.
   (Margaret Elizabeth Johnson)
Marzano, Mrs. Arlene M.
   (Arlene Scarpelli)
Matheny, Mrs. James
   (Judith Clark)
Mathias, Ms. Margaret G.
   (Margaret Ann Grossman)
Maton, Ms. Cicily C.
   (Sheldon Lee)
Matteson, Mrs. Stacey Porter
   (Mrs. David Matteson)
Maxwell, Ms. Connie Eugenia
Maxwell, Ms. Julie
Maxwell, Mr. Wayne
McAdams, Mrs. Edward J.
   (Joanne Gail Crowley)
McAdams, Mrs. John
   (Patricia A. Alfernic)
McCabe, Mrs. George L.
   (Jane E. Coleman)
McCann, Mrs. Donald V.
   (Sheila Ann Curley)
McCarter, Jr., Mrs. John W.
   (Judith Field West)
McCarthy, Mrs. James P.
   (Mary Ann Schwartz)
McCarthy, Mrs. Michael S.
   (Jane F. Alberding)
McClayton, Mrs. William R.
   (Melissa Ann Mosbaugh)
McClintic, Mrs. William E.
   (Corrine Lee)
McClung, Mrs. James A.
   (Jean Schubel)
McCormick, Mrs. James
   (Suzanne Cozzini)
McCurry, Ms. Margaret I.
   (Mrs. Stanley Tigerman)
McDermott, Mrs. John H.
   (Ann Pickard)
McDonnell, Mrs. David W.
   (Ashlie Anne MacLaverty)
McDonough, Mrs. James J.
   (Jacqualine Moynihan)
McGrath, Mrs. J. Paul
   (Eileen P. Robinson)
McGuinness, Mrs. J. Luke
   (Gail Donovan)
McKean, III, Mrs. George E.
   (Joan M. DeWitt)
McKechneay, Mrs. Douglas M.
   (Ann C. Hayza)
McKenna, Mrs. Andrew J.
   (Mary Joan Pickett)
McKinney, Miss Ashley Elizabeth

McKinney, Mrs. Peter
   (Donna Maria Poshek)
McKinnon, Mrs. John B.
   (Grace Marie Danhoff)
McLean, Mrs. Robert D.
   (Leslie Taft Breed)
McLean, Mrs. Rosemary P.
McNeill, Mrs. Thomas W.
   (Anne Swain)
McRobie, Mrs. David S.
   (Kyle Thais Hallsteen)
Meade, Mrs. James P.
   (Hildegarde Elizabeth Joosten)
Meehan, Mrs. Joseph G.
   (Anne Mary McCue)
Melcher, Mrs. Richard
   (Barbara Bookey)
Melchior, Mrs. Charles C.
   (Helen Lee Hall)
Meltzer, Ms. Francoise
   (Mrs. Bernard Rubin)
Merritt, Ms. Ann S.
Merritt, Ms. Cynthia Ann
Merritt, Mrs. John B.
   (Madonna Shields)
Merritt, Jr., Mrs. Thomas W.
   (Nancy Shurtleff)
Method, Mrs. Harold L.
   (Margaret N. Nelson)
Meyer, Mrs. Frank C.
   (Rebecca Ann Callanan)
Meyer, III, Mrs. F. Richard
   (Geraldine Schloerb)
Micali, Mrs. Thomas A.
   (Mary Alice Von Zielinski)
Michael, Ms. Sandra Lorde
Migely, Mrs. James E.
   (Jane Ahalt)
Miglin, Mrs. Marilyn
   (Marilyn Janice Klecka)
Miller, Mrs. Bernard J.
   (Brita Naujok)
Mills, Mrs. Edward S.
   (Barbara Lee Martin)
Mitchel, Mrs. James F.
   (Jane A. Colnon)
Mitchell, Mrs. Marvin G.
   (Margaret Lovelady)
Mitchell, Mrs. Matthew J.
   (Helen Jessie Hadley)
Mitchell, Mrs. Todd D.
   (Margaret Ann Crowe)
Moffat, Miss Juliet E.
Mohr, Mrs. Alberding
   (Beth Ann Alberding)
Mohr, Mrs. Scott W.
   (Sally Lockhart)
Molumby, Mrs. Robert E.
   (Edith Nina Taylor)

Montana, Jr., Mrs. James S.
   (Lori Spear)
Montgomery, Mrs. C. Barry
   (Shauna Maureen Michels)
Moore, IV, Mrs. William H.
   (Robin R. Ratch)
Moran, Mrs. George G.
   (Virginia Dundon)
Moran, Ms. Susan J.
   (John M. McDonough)
Morgan, Mrs. Vernile M.
   (Vernile Ann Murrin)
Moriarty, Mrs. Philip S. J.
   (Meredith Gayle Keras)
Morris, Ms. Courtney M.
   (Mrs. Paul W. Schmidt)
Morris, Mrs. Margaret M.
   (Peggy Murphy)
Morro, III, Mrs. William C.
   (Amy Fairbanks)
Morrow, Mrs. Joseph T.
   (Sandra M. Murray)
Mosiman, Miss Dorothy
Moskowitz, Mrs. Erik
   (Paula Beck)
Moss, Mrs. Joseph
   (Gail Carol Sutliff)
Mullins, Miss Kathryn Ruth
Mumford, Jr., Mrs. Edwin Bruce
   (Robin Wylly McCown)
Murphy, Mrs. Daniel J.
   (Catherine Baker Eardley)
Murphy, Miss Margaret Edith
Murphy, Mrs. Michael E.
   (Adele A. Kasupski)
Murphy, Mrs. Robert E.
   (Elizabeth Margaret Shedd)
Murray, Mrs. Michael J.
   (Christine Ann Scribner)
Myers, Mrs. Calvin R.
   (Jill L. Ogden)
Nathan, Mrs. Joseph E.
   (Elizabeth Loeb)
Nelsen, Mrs. Clifford D.
   (Cleon Delores Fulle)
Nelson, Mrs. Thomas C.
   (L. Brooke Morrison)
Neumann, Mrs. Otto Christoph
   (Barbara Isobel Shaffer)
Nevin, Mrs. John J.
   (Anne Filice)
Newton, Mrs. David C.
   (Athena Geron)
Newton, Jr., Mrs. Ray E.
   (Judith O'Donnell)
Noland, Mrs. James E.
   (Marjorie Marie Schuberth)
Nora, Mrs. Paul F.
   (Valerie Norton)
Nordmann, Mrs. Nancy Olivia
Notebaert, Mrs. Richard C.
   (Margaret Schaal)
Novich, Mrs. Colette
   (Colette Carlucci)
O'Connell, Mrs. Richard
   (Ann Marie Fitzgerald)
O'Connor, Mrs. James J.
   (Ellen Lawlor)

O'Doherty, Mrs. Bernard M.
   (Kay Marie Emling)
O'Donnell, Mrs. Thomas P.
   (Patricia Ann Corrigan)
O'Laughlin, Jr., Mrs. John
   (Susan Capp Petty)
O'Leary, Miss Martha Marie
O'Neill, Mrs. Roger L.
   (Sally Ann Forster)
O'Neill, Miss Whitney Elizabeth
O'Shea, Dr. Lynne Edeen
O'Sullivan, Mrs. Margaret
   (Margaret Benish)
Oakes, Mrs. Michael
   (Joanne H. Peters)
Oates, Mrs. Harland W.
   (Norma Nordgren)
Oelerich, Mrs. Francis J.
   (Mary Elizabeth Stoll)
Ogden, Mrs. William S.
   (Marian Elena Dymsa)
Orput, Mrs. Alden E.
   (Joanne Adamson)
Orput, Ms. Kimberly
   (Mrs. Steven van der Zanden)
Padberg, Mrs. Frank T.
   (Helen Louise Swan)
Palmer, Mrs. Diane
   (Diane Yates Scobie)
Palmer, Mrs. Robert
   (Ann Therese Darin)
Papanek, Mrs. Thomas F.
   (Meryl Lee Maxwell)
Pappas, Mrs. Todd J.
   (Iliana Saunders)
Parsons, Ms. Caro L.
Parsons, Mrs. Margaret
   (Margaret Largay)
Pasek, Ms. Laura
Patten, Jr., Mrs. Charles Robertson
   (Susan Irene Roy)
Patterson, Jr., Mrs. Carl Milton
   (Marilyn Virginia Kordick)
Pearl, Mrs. Carleton D.
   (Judi Weatherston)
Pearlman, Mrs. Jerry K.
   (Barbara Katz)
Pegler, Mrs. Westbrook
   (Margaret Terrel)
Pennington, Mrs. James S.
   (Eleanor Wetten)
Perkins, Ms. Jean E.
   (Mrs. Leland E. Hutchinson)
Perry, Mrs. Charles L.
   (Sunday E. Principato)
Peters, Mrs. Ralph N.
   (Ingrid Ahrens)
Peterson, Mrs. James B.
   (Patricia Marie McKeogh)
Peterson, Miss Kristine E.

Peterson, Mrs. M. Roger
(Sally Ann Alder)
Peterson, Mrs. Roger M.
(Grace Gayle Younger)
Petry, Mrs. Lewis D.
(Shirley M. Mellor)
Petterson, Miss Sally Ann
Phelps, Mrs. Alva W.
(Genevieve Margaret Farls)
Phelps, Mrs. P. Michael
(Laura Pepe)
Philbrick, Mrs. Richard B.
(Ruth Andrew Rowe)
Phillips, Mrs. Marlene Welsh
Pierce, Mrs. Robert J.
(Cathy Williams)
Piette, Mrs. Philippe O.
(Lyssa June Mashek)
Pike, Mrs. Joan
(Joan Thompson)
Polizzotto, Mrs. Salvatore F.
(Eileen Ryan)
Pollock, Mrs. Charles A.
(Colette O'Malley)
Pollock, Mrs. G. Lee
(Jill Gosden)
Poole, Mrs. Christopher
(Linda Nelsen)
Powell, Mrs. Daniel Edmund
(Frances M. Lavezzorio)
Powell, Mrs. Jeffrey
(Kristen Patricia Moffat)
Powers, Mrs. Donald
(Margaret Benoit)
Prendergast, Miss Maureen
Quateman, Mrs. Eva Grafft
(Eva Margaret Malone)
Quazzo, Mrs. Stephen
(Deborah Tyler Hicks)
Radler, Mrs. Leontine
(Leontine Van Lent)
Ransom, Mrs. Woodbury
(Christiana Seeyle Lutz)
Rasmussen, Mrs. Barbara B.
(Barbara Ann Biesel)
Rassas, Mrs. George J.
(Frances Loretta McGuire)
Rassas, Mrs. Nicholas C.
(Theresa Dillon)
Read, III, Mrs. V. Ross
(Mary Ellen Boice)
Redmond, Miss Elizabeth
Reed, Mrs. Frank F.
(Jaquelin Silverthorne)
Rees, Mrs. James G.
(Lilli E. Fetsch-Wenzel)
Reese, Mrs. John D.
(Sandra Kay Arnold)
Reid, Mrs. James T.
(Karen Christina Campbell)
Reid, Mrs. John B.
(Ellen Tobin)
Reid, Mrs. M.V.
(Marian Moreland Vilas)
Reilly, Mrs. Brendan
(Janice Dickerson)
Rieckhoff, Mrs. Conrad
(Barbara Ann Stacy)
Riley, Miss Colleen Anne

Riley, Mrs. Daryl
(Daryl Jean Heitman)
Riley, Ms. Rebecca R.
(Mrs. David L. Carden)
Robb, Mrs. Richard P.
(Barbara L. Hunt)
Robertson, Mrs. James Y
(Sara Royall Stewart)
Robinson, Jr., Mrs. Paul
(Martha C. Bidwell)
Roe, Mrs. Frederick
(Florence Elizabeth McGuire)
Rogers, Mrs. Ward Cadwell
(Virginia Holben)
Rohlen, Miss Frances Ann
Roland, Mrs. Edwin
(Mary Beaney)
Rooney, Miss Patricia Ann
Rooney, Mrs. Philip
(Suzanne V. Perillo)
Rooney, Jr., Mrs. Philip B.
(Susan Ann Etten)
Rosa, Mrs. Nicholas
(Jamee Marie O'Donoghue)
Rossetter, Mrs. Thomas Bryan
(Roberta Burbank Whitaker)
Rowland, Ms. Pleasant T.
(Mrs. W. Jerome Frautschi)
Ruberry, Mrs. Edward F
(Karen A. Buy)
Rucker, Mrs. Rhodes S.
(Marianne Boswell)
Rusack, Mrs. Alison Wrigley
Russell, Mrs. B. Arthur
(Charlotte Emma Von Katz)
Ruzicka, Mrs. Jeffrey F.
(Pamela Lanier Barnard)
Ryan, Mrs. Ann Meeker
(Mrs. Steven Ryan)
Ryan, Mrs. James W.
(Donna Daly)
Ryan, Mrs. Matthew J.
(Heather Browne)
Ryan, Mrs. Patrick G.
(Shirley Ann Welsh)
Ryan, Mrs. Robert W.
(Marti McMahan)
Ryan, Miss Therese
Ryan, Mrs. William
(Mary A. Burke)
Sadler, Mrs. John
(Wendy Williams)
Sanders, Mrs. William David
(Louann Hoover Feuille)
Scazzero. Mrs. Verne
(Cynthia Hanna Moore)
Schaefer, Mrs. Robert W.
(Patricia Louise Schaefer)
Schink, Mrs. James H.
(April Townley)
Schlemmer, Mrs. Dennis
(Carla K. Kogan)
Schmidt, Mrs. Theodore J.
(Patricia J. Jaruckis)

Schmiege, Mrs. Robert
(Jane Marie Heavey)
Schmitt, Mrs. F. Eugene
(Barbara Marion Boesel)
Schmitz, Ms. Jenny Q.
(Jenny Quest)
Schnadig, Mrs. Richard H.
(Patricia Oakley)
Schreiber, Mrs. Marc
(Elise Atkinson)
Schuetz, Mrs. Homer A.
(Roberta Folonie)
Schultz, Mrs. Gerald Ernest
(Barbara Elaine Potocny)
Schulz, Mrs. George H. D.
(Deborah Ann Craft)
Schwalm, Mrs. Walter A.
(Ruth Elizabeth Johnson)
Schwartz, Ms. Lynne Mavon
(Mrs. Larry Jay Schwartz)
Scott, Miss Stephanie Ingersoll
Scott, Mrs. Stuart L.
(Anne Capp O'Laughlin)
Scoville, Mrs. James Benson
(Margaret Woodward)
Seagren, Mrs. David
(Sharon Scheibelhut)
Sealy, Mrs. George Paul
(Joan Marie Kemper)
Searcy, Jr., Mrs. W. Tunstall
(Marsha Ann Bent)
Segal, Mrs. Gordon
(Carole Diane Browe)
Segal, Miss Robin Lynn
Seidel, Mrs. Gerhard E.
(Lois Carol Wellman)
Selander, Mrs. Larry
(Mary Ladish)
Senior, Miss Alicia Morgan
Sennott, Mrs. W. Jay
(Janet G. Pigman)
Sethness, Jr., Mrs. Charles H.
(Mary G. Buckley)
Sewell, Mrs. Florence D.
(Florence L. Davis)
Sexton, Mrs. William M.
(Deborah Reid Long)
Shafer, Mrs. J. Bradley
(Cynthia Cozad)
Shaffer, Mrs. Evelyne
Sharp, Mrs. Charles Dee
(Judith Carol Gadness)
Shea, Mrs. Brian C.
(Fredericka Kostner)
Shea, Mrs. Timothy J.
(Megan Elizabeth Carroll)
Sheffield, Miss Grace Wacker
Sheffield, Jr., Mrs. Thomas C.
(Pamela Starry)
Shennan, Miss Melissa
Sheridan, Mrs. Frank
(Rita Tighe)
Shute, Mrs. David
(Gerri L. Hilt)
Sick, Mrs. William N.
(Stephanie Anne Williams)
Simanton, Mrs. Robert M.
(Lois Kay Willard)

Simmons, Mrs. Brian P.
(Julie Dowdall)
Simon, Mrs. Marion E.
(Dr. Theodore L. Gross)
Simonds, Mrs. Richard
(Bonnie Whiteside)
Simpson, Mrs. David W.
(Patricia Jacobsen)
Simpson, Mr. Harry E.
Skilling, Mrs. Raymond I.
(Alice Mae Welsh)
Skinner, Mrs. Honey Jacobs
(Mrs. Samuel Skinner)
Small, Mrs. Thomas Putnam
(Deborah Ann Loeser)
Smelcer, Miss Wilma Jean
Smith, Mrs. Michael M.
(Charlotte Jean Mitchell)
Smith, Mrs. Walter N.
(Susan Garman Rummel)
Sneed, Ms. Michael
Snyder, Mrs. James M.
(Julia Foster Corbett)
Sola, Mrs. George L.
(Sigrid Ritter)
Soler, Mrs. Antonio
(Marianela Garcia)
Solti, Lady
(Anne Valerie Pitts)
Spence, Mrs. William A.
(Lavern Dellora Gaynor)
Spencer, III, Mrs. George
(Cassie Paskevich)
Spieth, Mrs. Lawrence R.
(Ann C. Thirolf)
Spindell, Mrs. Robert F.
(Ethel Grimmer)
Spoto, Mrs. Angelo
(Virginia Hagney)
Sprowl, Mrs. Robert Allen
(Sarah Freeman Dyer)
Stack, Mrs. Christopher
(Adelia Ann Morris)
Staley, III, Mrs. A. E.
(Uta Helga Fengler)
Staley, Mrs. William D.
(Arlene Dorothy Silber)
Standen, Mrs. Charles R.
(Maxine Jeanette Lundgren)
Staples, Mrs. William L.
(Marjorie Anne Kimmel)
Star, Ms. Sara Crown
Stebbins, Mrs. John B.
(Lisa Carney)
Steel, Ms. Joan Elizabeth
Steele, Mrs. Eric H.
(Edith Talmage Mullen)
Steiner, Mrs. Wallace
(Robin Rapp)
Steingraber, Mrs. Frederick G.
(Veronika Wagner)
Steinhaus, Mrs. Orin
(Constance Evans)

Stepan, Mrs. John
(Bonnie Ware)
Stibolt, Mrs. Thomas B.
(Erminie Jeanne Hiney)
Stiffel, Mrs. Jules N.
(Lisbeth Cherniack)
Stoik, Mrs. Theodore M.
(Elizabeth Czamanske Marten)
Stone, Mrs. Steven M.
(Barbara Ann West)
Strandell, Mrs. Donald R.
(Julie Kay Strom)
Strohl, Mrs. Lee H.
(Karen S. Maatman)
Struthers, Mrs. Harvey
(Mary Payne Ray)
Stuckey, Mrs. Richard J.
(Lois Ilene Engel)
Stukel, Mrs. James
(Joan Helpling)
Sudler, Mrs. Laura F.
(Laura Fairbank)
Sullivan, Miss Mary Kay
Sullivan, Ms. Melinda Martin
(Mrs. Paul R. C. Sullivan)
Svendsen, Sr., Mrs. Robert William
(Valda M. Trammell)
Swanson, Mrs. Joseph A.
(Lucia Kristine Swanson)
Swanson, Mrs. Robert W.
(Miriam Elaine Brown)
Sweeney, Miss Sharon S.
Swenson, Mrs. Gregory R.
(Mary Ellen Marlas)
Swift, Mrs. Nathan B.
(Melinda Anne Sherman)
Tague, Mrs. Philip N.
(Francine Carolyne Topping)
Tait, Mrs. James
(Gail Prewitt)
Tampas, Ms. Jessica
Tausche, Mrs. Thomas J.
(Louise Gaylord Ingersoll)
Taylor, Miss Collette
Taylor, Jr., Mrs. Perry L.
(Karen J. Beardsley)
Tenney, Mrs. David Hill
(Mary Katherine Fite)
Terlato, Mrs. Anthony J.
(Josephine Paterno)
Terra, Mrs. Daniel J.
(Judith Farabee)
Tetzlaff, Mrs. Theodore R.
(Janna Dee Bounds)
Thiessen, Mrs. Willard
(Bonita Anne Bell)
Thilman, Mrs. E. Thomas
(Laura Huff)
Thoma, Mrs. Carl D.
(Marilynn Joyce Benbrook)
Thomas, Mrs. Lawrason D.
(Barbara Marie Barter)
Thornburg, Mrs. D. Robert
(Marie Dora Louise Wettlaufer)
Tobias, Mrs. Randall Lee
(Marianne Williams)
Topping, Mrs. David M.
(Alice Phillips)

Tower, Mrs. Raymond C.
(Shirley N. Barndt)
Tretheway, Mrs. Barton G.
(Jennifer Eileen Kamp)
Trigere, Miss Pauline
Trutter, II, Miss Edith English
Turner-Leonard, Mrs. Martha
(Martha Turner)
Turner, Mrs. Robert W.
(Gloria Belvel)
Uihlein, Mrs. Edgar J.
(Lucia Long Ellis)
Ullyot, Ms. Kathryn Lee
Vacin, Mrs. Donald E.
(Cynthia Ann Mauck)
Vaile, Mrs. Nan B.
(Nancy Ann Bolks)
Van Der Meulen, Ms. Anne
(Mrs. Davey Joe Cunningham)
Van Husen, Mrs. Frank
(Barbara Ann Herbster)
Van Mell, Mrs. Helen S.
(Helen Margaret Strotz)
Van Nice, Mrs. Peter Errett
(Jeanette Hunt)
Van Zelst, Mrs. T. David
(Cynthia Kampen)
Vance, Mrs. Herbert A.
(Dorothy Jane Jones)
Vaughan, Jr., Mrs. Howard A.
(Heidi Benz)
Velde, Mrs. Jane
(Jane Doolittle)
Vert, Ms. Linda
Vert, Ms. Nancy Patricia
Victor, Mrs. George E.
(Nancy Carolyn Obrecht)
Viti, Jr., Mrs. Blase J.
(Kristine Kaep)
Vititoe, Mrs. William P.
(Susan Alice Hoover)
Vogl, Mrs. Susan Starrett
Vogt Kugler, Mrs. Barbara
(Mrs. Michael J. Kugler)
Walgreen, III, Mrs. Charles R.
(Kathleen F. Bonsignore)
Walsh, Mrs. Robert Edward
(Lucy Scott Watkins)
Walter, Mrs. John R.
(Carol Ann Kost)
Walton, Mrs. Wesley S.
(Jurdis Dierauer)
Ware, Mrs. Gordon Keith
(Ethlyn Dulin)
Watkins, Mrs. M. Hubachek
(Marjorie Ann Hubachek)
Watrous, Mrs. Matthew G.
(Patrice L. Salisbury)
Watson, Mrs. Deloris
(Deloris Fitts)
Weaver, Mrs. Andrew M.
(Cricket Barlow)
Weaver, Mrs. William D.
(Virginia Laura Osborne)
Webb, Dr. Catherine Louise

Webster, Ms. Heather Anne
Marsland
Webster, Jr., Mrs. James R.
(Joan Eleanor Burchfield)
Webster, Mrs. Roderick S.
(Marjorie Kelly)
Weiss, Mrs. William L.
(Josephine Elizabeth Berry)
Weldon, Mrs. William G.
(Patricia Butler)
Wendnagel, Mrs. Charles E.
(Renny Ann Zirkle)
Wendt, Mrs. William H.
(Dalia Kristina Puzinauskas)
Wenner, Mrs. Hardy
(Stella Adamczyk)
Wharton, Mrs. Richard F.
(Betty Sue Wyatt, M.D.)
White, Jr., Mrs. Thomas S.
(Stathy Manos)
Wienke, Mrs. Robert O.
(Jane Elizabeth Asmuth)
Wilde, Jr., Mrs. Harold R.
(Benna Brecher)
Williams, Jr., Mrs. Thomas L.
(Marguerite Heard Neel)
Williamson, Mrs. Joel V.
(Cheryle B. McHargue)
Wilson, Mrs. Thomas
(Cheryl Kien)
Wolf, Mrs. George Dorr
(Margaret Winifred Hurlbutt)
Wood, Jr., Mrs. Arthur M.
(Peggy Pilas)
Wood, Mrs. J. Howard
(Barbara M. Johnston)
Woody, Miss Maxyne J.
Woulfe, Mrs. Donald P.
(Nancy May)
Wright, Miss Jocelyn O. F.
Wright, Mrs. John B.
(Caryl Brainard Moore)
Wright, Mrs. Robert W.
(Nancy Tucker)
Wrigley, Jr., Mrs. William
(Kandis Ann Hanson)
Wunderlich, Mrs. Rudy
(Susan Clay)
Yabunaka, Mrs. Mitoji
(Naomi Kitagawa)
Yarline, Mrs. Frank W.
(Jean Stuart Hanna)
Yelton, Mrs. Carey M.
(Carolyn Jean Spann)
Youker, Mrs. James E.
(Sally Dwyer)
Youssefi, Mrs. Hossein
(Mary Marsha Blomquist)
Zengeler, Mrs. Robert G.
(Terry Suzanne Foltz)
Zick, Mrs. John W.
(Mary Sutter)
Ziegler, Mrs. Hans P.
(Ann Kvaraceus)
Zimmer, Mrs. William W.
(Elizabeth Ann Johnson)
Zubrod, Mrs. Justin F.
(Deirdre Rassas)

PHOTO CREDITS

9. Photo by Raymond Trowbridge, printed by Hedrich-Blessing, Courtesy of Mrs. Robert A. Beatty; 13. (upper) The Newberry Library, (middle) Chicago Historical Society ICHi-28756, (lower) Chicago Historical Society ICHi-28773; 14. (upper) Courtesy of Mrs. Harlow Niles Higinbotham, (lower right) Chicago Historical Society DN-005482; 17. Chicago Historical Society ICHi-28755; 18. Chicago Historical Society ICHi-19130; 22. Chicago Public Library Special Collections and Preservation Division CCW 1.378; 24. (upper) Chicago Historical Society ICHi-29261, (middle) The Newberry Library, (lower) The Newberry Library; 29. (left) Chicago Historical Society ICHi-24012; 30. Photo by John Alderson; 32. Courtesy of Karen Zupko Stuart; 36. (left) Chicago Historical Society ICHi-26966; 39. (lower) Chicago Historical Society ICHi-28749; 40. (upper left) Courtesy of Mrs. Beverly W. Pattishall, (right) Courtesy of Mrs. Beverly W. Pattishall; 42. Chicago Historical Society ICHi-28762; 47. (right) Chicago Historical Society DN-070224; 49. Chicago Historical Society DN-070874; 50. Courtesy of Arthur L. Kelly; 53. Chicago Historical Society DN-93741; 54. (lower) Courtesy of Mrs. David C. Hilliard; 57. (lower) Courtesy of Marshall Field's; 58. (center) Courtesy of Mrs. Philip L. Cochran, (lower) Gift of Mrs. Edward R. Weed; 61. Chicago Historical Society ICHi-29253; 62. (lower) Courtesy of William O. Petersen; 66. From *Chicago's Accomplishments and Leaders*, 1932, Courtesy of the The Art Institute of Chicago; 70. Chicago Historical Society ICHi-20101; 75. (upper) Chicago Historical Society, (lower) John Alden Carpenter Papers, The Newberry Library; 80. Chicago Historical Society DN-76422; 83. (upper) Courtesy of William O. Petersen, (lower) Courtesy of Mrs. Robert A. Carr; 85. Courtesy of Rush-Presbyterian-St. Luke's Medical Center Woman's Board Archive; 87. Chicago Historical Society ICHi-28757; 88. (upper) Courtesy of Mrs. Christopher J. Chamales, (lower) Courtesy of Mrs. Dale Ashcraft; 91. Photo by Michael Tropea; 92.

(lower) Chicago Historical Society ICHi-28751: 97. Courtesy of Mrs. Richard Marra; 101. Photo by Michael Tropea; 104. (upper right) Courtesy of Mrs. Christopher J. Chamales; 106. Courtesy of the Chicago Tribune; 113. Photo by John Alderson, Courtesy of Charles C. Haffner III; 118. Chicago Historical Society; 125. Department of Special Collections, University of Chicago Library; 129. Courtesy of Donald R. Mowat; 131. Courtesy of the Art Institute of Chicago, Museum Archives; 134–35. Courtesy of the Chicago Tribune; 137. Courtesy of the Chicago Tribune; 138. Photo by Stuart-Rodgers Photography; 140. (right) Courtesy of Melinda Martin Sullivan; 143. (upper) Courtesy of Mrs. Jon N. Ekdahl, (lower) Courtesy of Sue Holinger; 145. Photo by Michael Tropea; 149. Courtesy of the Chicago Tribune; 152. Photo by Stuart-Rodgers Photography; 154. Courtesy of Mrs. Earnest E. Christensen; 157. Photo by Michal D, Miller; 158. Photo by Michal D. Miller; 160. Courtesy of Cynthia W. Rummel; 162. Courtesy of Mrs. John C. Kern; 163. Courtesy of Nena Ivon; 164. Photo by Stuart-Rodgers Photography; 166. (upper left) Photo by Stuart-Rodgers Photography, (center) Photo by Michal D. Miller; 167. (right) Photo by Stuart-Rodgers Photography, (left) Photo by Michal D. Miller; 168. Courtesy of Mrs. Henry C. Woods, Jr.; 170. Photo by Stuart-Rodgers Photography; 173. Photo by Stuart-Rodgers Photography; 174. (upper) Photo by Ewing Kranin, Courtesy of Mrs. James N. Bay, Jr.; 175. Photo by Michael Tropea; 176. Courtesy of Dr. Catherine L. Choy; 179. (right) Photo by Jessica Tampas, Courtesy of Mrs. Robert A. Beatty; 180. (lower right and left) Photo by Jessica Tampas; 183. Photo by Jessica Tampas; 184–85. Photo by Michael Tropea; 188–89. (far left) Photo by Stuart-Rodgers Photography, (upper left) Photo by Alan De Rolf, (center) Photo by Jessica Tampas, (upper right) Photo by Jessica Tampas, (lower right) Photo by Melanie Dunea; 190–91. Photo by Jessica Tampas; 192–93. (center) Photo by Jessica Tampas, (right upper, middle and lower) Photos by Jessica Tampas; 194–95. Photo by Jessica Tampas; 208. Photo by Michael Tropea.

1,500 copies printed
by Meridian Printing, East
Greenwich, RI

PRODUCED BY Kim Coventry
DESIGNED BY studio blue,
Chicago

BODY TYPE: Walbaum
DISPLAY TYPE:
Avalon and Bodoni
LEGEND TYPE: Franklin
Gothic and Trade Gothic
TEXT: Mead Signature
ENDPAPERS: Strathmore
Grandee

DUST JACKET FRONT:
The Woman's Athletic Club build-
ing at 626 North Michigan
Avenue in May 1930, one year
after completion. Chicago
Historical Society, Hedrich-
Blessing-00242.

ENDPIECE:
Chromium figure of a graceful
young athlete by Chicago
artist Walter Reid Williams,
mounted on a silvered
wooden base in the club's foyer.
Photo by Michael Tropea.

ENDPAPERS:
Detail of the original Chinese
wallpaper in the Silver Room,
installed circa 1937.
Photo by Michael Tropea.